Canadian Semantic Web

Weichang Du • Faezeh Ensan
Editors

Canadian Semantic Web

Technologies and Applications

 Springer

Editors
Weichang Du
Faculty of Computer Science
University of New Brunswick
E3B 5A3 Fredericton
Canada
wdu@unb.ca

Faezeh Ensan
Faculty of Computer Science
University of New Brunswick
E3B 5A3 Fredericton
Canada
faezeh_ensan@yahoo.com

ISBN 978-1-4899-9922-1   ISBN 978-1-4419-7335-1 (eBook)
DOI 10.1007/978-1-4419-7335-1
Springer New York Dordrecht Heidelberg London

Printed on acid-free paper

Springer is part of Springer Science+Business Media (www.springer.com)

Preface

The emergence of Web technologies for the distribution of an immense amount of data and knowledge has given rise to the need for supportive frameworks for knowledge management. Semantic Web technologies aim at providing shared semantic spaces for Web contents, such that people, applications and communities can use a common platform to share information.

Canadian Semantic Web: Technologies and Applications aims at contributing to the advancement of the Semantic Web by providing the most recent significant research on Semantic Web theory, techniques and applications in academia, industry and government in Canada and all over the world. It also enlightens possible Semantic Web research directions in future by reporting some works in-progress that present on-going research on principles and applications of the Semantic Web, while their implementation or deployment may have not been completed.

This book consists of ten chapters. The chapters are extended versions of a selected set of papers from the second Canadian Semantic Web Working Symposium (CSWWS 2009) and the twenty-first international Conference on Software Engineering and Knowledge Engineering (SEKE 2009). CSWWS 2009 was held in Kelowna, British Columbia in May 2009. Since many of the challenging aspects of the research problems tackled in the Semantic Web area fall in the realm of Artificial Intelligence or employ of AI techniques, CSWWS 2009 was organized in association with the 22nd Canadian Conference on Artificial Intelligence. SEKE 2009 was held in Boston, July 2009, aiming at bridging the two domains of Software Engineering and Knowledge Engineering together. Hence, the content of this book covers the theory and applications of Semantic Web techniques from both important perspectives of Artificial Intelligence and Software Engineering.

Canadian Semantic Web: Technologies and Applications covers a combination of theory-based and application-based topics. Three chapters: 'Incremental Query Rewriting with Resolution' by Alexandre Riazanov and Marcelo A. T. Aragão (Chapter 1), 'Knowledge Representation and Reasoning in Norm-Parameterized Fuzzy Description Logics' by Jidi Zhao and Harold Boley (Chapter 2) , and 'A Generic Evaluation Model for Semantic Web Services' by Omair Shafiq (Chapter 3) focus on theoretical aspects of the Semantic Web. Chapter 1 provides methods for computing *schematic* answers to deductive queries and transforming these schematic answers into standard SQL queries. Further, this chapter discusses the completeness and soundness of the presented techniques. Chapter 2 provides an extension to standard Description Logics in order to enrich them with capability of representing imprecise, uncertain and fuzzy knowledge. It also provides a procedure for reasoning over these extended Description Logics and proves its soundness, completeness, and termination. Chapter 3 discusses the requirement for evaluating Semantic Web Services and provides a generic evaluation model for this purpose.

The remaining seven chapters present implementation support for existing Semantic Web techniques or investigate applications of the Semantic Web in different domains. 'A Modular Approach to Scalable Ontology Development' by Faezeh Ensan and Weichang Du (Chapter 4) provides an extension to the OWL ontology language and also introduces an ontology editor and browser for creating modular ontologies. It also proposes a set of metrics for evaluating modular ontologies and investigates four developed modular ontologies with regards to these metrics. 'Corporate Semantic Web: Towards the Deployment of Semantic Technologies in Enterprises' by Adrian Paschke, et al. (Chapter 5) investigates the Corporate Semantic Web idea for applying semantic technologies in enterprises. It also discusses the main challenges and research areas with regards to this idea. 'Semantic Service Matchmaking in the ATM Domain Considering Infrastructure Capability Constraints' by Thomas Moser et al. (Chapter 6) analyzes the application of Semantic Web techniques in the Air Traffic Management (ATM) domain. It introduces a framework for semi-automatic semantic matchmaking for software services in this domain. These chapters (Chapters 1 to 6) present accomplished research in the area of the Semantic Web, while the following four chapters (Chapter 7 to 10) are the shorter ones, presenting on-going research.

'Developing Knowledge Representation in Emergency Medical Assistance by Using Semantic Web Techniques' by Heloise Manica, et al. (Chapter 7) introduces an architecture for utilizing ontologies in mobile emergency medical assistance systems. The authors discuss that the proposed architecture can improve query processing and reduce network traffic in mobile environments. 'Semantically Enriching the Search System of a Music Digital Library' by Paloma de Juan and Carlos Iglesias (Chapter 8) describes two search systems over digital music libraries: a traditional key-word search and a semantic-based search system, evaluates and compares them and concludes how a semantic-based representation of information can lead to more flexibility in search systems. Chapter 9, 'Application of an Intelligent System Framework and the Semantic Web for the CO_2 Capture Process' by Chuansan Luo, Qing Zhou, and Christine W. Chan, describes the application of Semantic Web techniques in the domain of carbon dioxide capture process. Finally, Chapter 10, 'Information Pre-Processing using Domain Meta-Ontology and Rule Learning System' by Girish R Ranganathan and Yevgen Biletskiy, provides a solution for semi-automatic population of meta-ontologies, when a meta-ontology conceptualizes a domain of interest from huge amounts of source documents.

Semantic Web is an emerging research topic in the Canadian research community. Several important universities have started large projects and have dedicated specific laboratories to the Semantic Web. Reasoning engines for different Description Logics and ontologies, application of Semantic Web in healthcare and bioinformatics, applying Semantic Web techniques in business domain and business document management and semantic interoperability are among current research directions on Semantic technologies in the Canadian community. Based on the current status, we would expect to see more comprehensive Semantic Web research in Canadian organizations and also in collaboration with the international research community.

Weichang Du

June 2010   *Faezeh Ensan*

Program Committee

Program Committee of The Second Canadian Semantic Web Working Symposium 2009

Abdolreza Abhari (Ryerson University, Canada)

Christopher Baker (University of New Brunswick, Canada)

Virendra C Bhavsar (University of New Brunswick, Canada)

Yevgen Biletskiy (University of New Brunswick, Canada)

Harold Boley (NRC Institute for Information Technology, Canada)

Greg Butler (Concordia University, Canada)

Stephen Downes (National Research Council of Canada, Canada)

Michel Dumontier (Carlton University, Canada)

Jinan Fiaidhi (Lakehead University, Canada)

Dragan Gasevic (Athabasca University, Canada)

Pankaj Kamthan (Concordia University, Canada)

Bernard Lefebvre (University of Quebec, Montreal, Canada)

Olga Marino (University of Quebec, Canada)

Sheila McIlraith (University of Toronto, Canada)

Alan Meech (CGI, Canada)

Sehl Mellouli (Laval University, Canada)

Sabah Mohammed (Lakehead University, Canada)

Vale H. Nasser (University of Calgary)

Roger Nkambou (University of Quebec, Montreal, Canada)

Fred Popowich (Simon Fraser University, Canada)

Arash Shaban-Nejad (Concordia University, Canada)

Weiming Shen (National Research Council of Canada, Canada)

Nematollaah Shiri (Concordia University, Canada)

Bruce Spencer (National Research Council of Canada, Canada)

Jose Leomar Todesco (Federal University of Santa Catarina)

Andre Trudel (Acadia University, Canada)

Ren Witte (Concordia University, Canada)

Contents

Chapter 1
Incremental Query Rewriting with Resolution

Alexandre Riazanov and Marcelo A. T. Aragão

Abstract We address the problem of semantic querying of relational databases
(RDB) modulo knowledge bases using *very expressive* knowledge representation
formalisms, such as full first-order logic or its various fragments. We propose to
use a *resolution*-based first-order logic (FOL) reasoner for computing *schematic
answers* to deductive queries, with the subsequent translation of these schematic answers to SQL queries which are evaluated using a conventional relational DBMS.
We call our method *incremental query rewriting*, because an original semantic query
is rewritten into a (potentially infinite) series of SQL queries. In this chapter, we
outline the main idea of our technique – using *abstractions* of databases and *constrained clauses* for deriving schematic answers, and provide completeness and
soundness proofs to justify the applicability of this technique to the case of resolution for FOL without equality. The proposed method can be directly used with
regular RDBs, including *legacy databases*. Moreover, we propose it as a potential
basis for an efficient Web-scale semantic search technology.

1.1 Introduction.

1.1.1 Settings and motivation.

Consider the following scenario. Suppose we have a relational database (RDB) and
some expressive knowledge bases (KB) for domains to which the data in the RDB
is related, e. g., rule bases in expressive sublanguages of RuleML [8, 2] and/or ontologies in OWL. We would like to work with *arbitrary* (reasonably well designed)

Alexandre Riazanov
RuleML, e-mail: alexandre.riazanov@gmail.com

Marcelo A. T. Aragão
The University of Manchester, e-mail: mat_aragao@yahoo.co.uk

W. Du and F. Ensan (eds.), *Canadian Semantic Web: Technologies and Applications*,
DOI 10.1007/978-1-4419-7335-1_1, © Springer Science+Business Media, LLC 2010

RDBs, and, consequently, the database relations are not assumed to directly correspond to concepts and relations described by the KBs. So, optionally, we may also have some mapping between the RDB schema and the logical language of the domains, i. e., a logical description of the relations in the RDB, to link them to the concepts and relations defined by the KBs. In these settings, we would like to be able to formulate queries logically, and answer them w. r. t. the KBs and the RDB treated virtually as a collection of ground atomic facts, e. g., by viewing each table row as a separate ground fact. *To make this process efficient, we would like to use the modern RDB technology as much as possible by delegating as much work as possible to the RDBMS hosting the database.*

We propose a novel method to implement this scenario, based on the use of *resolution for incremental transformation of semantic queries into sequences of SQL queries* that can be directly evaluated on the RDB, and whose results provide answers to the original queries.

We envisage three main applications for the proposed technology.

Enhancing the interface to conventional relational databases *Ad hoc self-service querying* of conventional RDBs by non-programmer users is very problematic because real-life enterprise databases often have complex designs. Writing correct queries requires good understanding of technical details of the DB schema, such as table and attribute names, foreign key relationships, nullable fields, etc., not to mention the knowledge of query languages like SQL. So most of RDB querying by non-programmer users is done with preprogrammed parameterised queries, usually represented as forms of various kinds.

Even when special methodologies are used, like Query-by-Example (see, e. g. [26]), that hide some of the complexities of SQL and database designs from the end users, one important inherent limitation remains in force. Whereas mapping some domain concepts to the RDB schema elements may be easy, many other concepts may be much more difficult to map. For example, it is easy to select instances of the concept "student" if there is a table explicitly storing all students, but if the user wants to extract a list of all members of a department in a university, he may have to *separately* query different tables storing information about students, faculty and support staff (assuming that there is no table specifically storing members of all these kinds), and then create a union of the results.

This example exposes well the root of the problem: mapping some domain concepts to the data is difficult because it requires *application of the domain knowledge*. In the example, the involved piece of domain knowledge is the fact that students, faculty and support staff are all department members, and the user has to apply it *manually* to obtain the required results.

Semantic querying is based on automatic application of domain knowledge written in the form of, e. g., rules and ontological axioms. In this approach, DB programmers "semantically document" their DB designs by providing an explicit mapping between the RDB schemas and domain terminologies, e. g., in the form of logical axioms. This alone allows an end user to formulate queries directly in the terminology of the domain, without even a slightest idea about how the underlying RDBs are structured[1]. However, the biggest advantage comes from the fact that reasoning w. r. t. additional, completely external KBs can be employed to generate and justify some answers, which makes querying not just *semantic*, as in [28], but also *deductive*. In our current example, the user can provide, as a part of the query, some KB that links the relations of being a department member, being a student in the department, etc. In some application contexts, it is important to be able to use rather expressive KBs for such purposes. Rule-based KBs and expressive DL ontologies are of a special interest, especially in combination.

Semantic Data Federation Data Integration (DI) in general means technologies for providing uniform query interfaces to autonomous distributed heterogeneous sources of information – mostly RDBs, but also Web services, spreadsheets and XML repositories. The problem of DI arises in several fields, such as Business Intelligence, Health care IT and Bioinformatics.

The currently dominating approach to DI - *datawarehousing* - essentially means gathering all the necessary data from various sources in one central DB. It has some drawbacks: it is generally *non-incremental* – adding a new data source may require changing the central DB schema, and *inflexible* – design commitments once made may be difficult to retract from later. A more agile alternative to datawarehousing is *data federation*. The essence of this approach is that a *virtual* (rather than physical) central DB is created by mapping different source DB schemas onto a global schema, so that queries to the virtual DB can be translated into queries to source DBs. A particularly agile flavour of data federation – called *local-as-view* – only requires that local DB schemas are described in terms of the central ("global") DB schema, although this can complicate the evaluation of queries over the global schema. This approach is completely incremental: new data sources can be added without any knowledge of how other sources are mapped.

Implementations of semantic querying modulo ontologies, that allow to cross-query several DBs, essentially implement local-as-view data federation, because the ontologies to which the DB schemas are mapped, play the role of the global schema. Given the practical importance of the data federation task, it's not surprising that many implementation of semantic querying make a special emphasis on this application rather than just enhanced interfaces to single RDBs. For example, SIMS [5] – the most cited early semantic querying project – already targeted specifically data federation. The technology proposed in this chapter also has this advantage of straightforward applicability to local-as-view data federation.

Web-scale semantic search The Semantic Web is accumulating a lot of data in the form of RDF and OWL assertions referring to various formalised vocabularies – ontologies. In some cases the expressivity of RDF(S) and OWL may not be enough[2]

---

[1] This does not alleviate the need for convenient query interfaces, but they are outside the scope of this chapter.

[2] For example, OWL cannot express the following simple rule
$hasUncle(X, Y) : - hasParent(X, Z), hasBrother(Z, Y)$ [3]. OWL also restricts the arity of predicates to 2 and does not directly support functions, thus limiting knowledge engineering possibilities. This toy example also illustrates a typical pattern of domain knowledge capture in

and knowledge in other formalisms, e. g., RuleML [8, 2], RIF [1] or SWRL [3], have to be used to capture more complex dependencies between domain concepts and relations, thus making the data descriptions sufficiently semantically rich.

The utility of the Semantic Web data will strongly depend on how easily and how efficiently users and agents can query it. Roughly speaking, we need to *query extremely large volumes of highly distributed data modulo expressive knowledge bases*, so that not only direct answers based on the stored data are returned, but also implied answers that can only be obtained by reasoning.

The approach proposed here may be a part of a solution to this problem: large sets of RDF triples and OWL data descriptions (coming from Semantic Web documents) can be loaded into an-RDB based triplestore or instance store, and then queried deductively modulo the relevant knowledge bases. Loading data descriptions into an RDB is essentially a linear operation, so it is unlikely to become a real performance bottleneck. Moreover, we can start producing answers even before the data is fully loaded. So the efficiency of such a scheme depends mostly on how efficiently the deductive querying on the RDB underlying the triplestore/instance store, can be done.

Just like text-based Web search engines do not indiscriminately scan all the accessible documents each time a new query is processed, semantic search systems cannot examine all accessible data descriptions in every retrieval attempt. Instead, some form of indexing is necessary that would allow to avoid downloading data that is irrelevant to a specific query, and would focus the processing on the sets of assertions that are likely to contribute to some answers to the query. We will show that the core feature of our approach to deductive querying of RDB – incremental query rewriting – suggests a natural way of semantically indexing large numbers distributed data sources.

1.1.2 Outline of the proposed method.

To implement the target scenario, we propose to use a first-order logic reasoner in combination with a conventional RDBMS, so that the reasoner does the "smart" part of the job, and the RDBMS is used for what it is best at – relatively simple processing of large volumes of relational data by computing table joins. Roughly, the reasoner works as a query preprocessor. It accepts a semantic query, the relevant knowledge bases and a semantic mapping for a DB as its input, and generates a (possibly infinite) number of expressions which we call *schematic answers*, that can be easily converted into SQL queries. These SQL queries are then evaluated on the DB with the help of the RDBMS. The union of the results for these SQL queries contains all answers to the original deductive query.

---

conceptual relational data models, viz., referential integrity constraints expressed as joins. These cannot be easily represented in OWL, in particular because many table predicates have arities greater than 2. Also, conjunctive queries and Datalog can be directly translated into FOL without resort to tricks or expensive knowledge reengineering.

This idea can be implemented with a relatively simple architecture as shown in Figure 1.1. The architecture introduces two main modules – a reasoner for finding schematic solutions and an SQL generator to turn these solutions into SQL queries. We also assume that some off-the-shelf RDBMS is used to answer the SQL queries. All three components (can) work in parallel, practically asynchronously: while the reasoner searches for more schematic answers, the SQL generator can process some previous schematic answers and the RDBMS can generate instances for some earlier schematic answers and communicate them to the user.

Optionally, the reasoner may try to prune the search space by checking certain constraints over the RDB (details will be provided in Section 1.4). These constraints are also converted into SQL queries and sent to the RDBMS for evaluation. The results of the evaluation ($'satisfiable'$ or $'unsatisfiable'$) are sent back to the reasoner which can use the absence of solutions for a constraint as a justification for suppressing certain inferences.

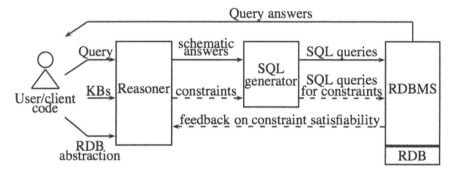

Fig. 1.1 Architecture for incremental query rewriting

In the rest of this chapter, we (i) introduce the method, first intuitively and then formally; (ii) prove soundness and completeness of some standard resolution-based calculi for rewriting semantic queries into sequences of schematic answers; (iii) describe some optimisations; (iv) describe a proof-of-concept implementation and experiments; (v) briefly discuss how semantic indexing can be done using data abstractions; and (vi) discuss related and future work.

1.2 Informal method description.

We *model* an RDB as a finite set of ground atomic formulas, so that RDB table names provide the predicates, and rows are conceptually treated as applications of the predicates to the row elements. In the example below, we have a table *takesCourse* from a University DB, keeping information about which student takes which course, whose rows are mapped to a set of facts.

takesCourse	student	course
	s1	c1
	s2	c2
	s3	c3
	...	...

$\longrightarrow$	takesCourse(s1,c1)
$\longrightarrow$	takesCourse(s2,c2)
$\longrightarrow$	takesCourse(s3,c3)
...	

Note that in all our examples in this chapter, the data is assumed to be a relational representation of some DL ABoxes. This is done not to clutter the presentation of the main ideas with RDB schema-related details. In particular, there is no need for a special RDB-to-KB mapping because the RDB tables directly correspond to concepts and properties. It bears repeating that this assumption is made *only to simplify the presentation* – our approach is applicable to any RDBs, including legacy ones, as long as their designs allow reasonable semantic mapping.

Suppose we are trying to answer a query over our RDB modulo some KB.

Naive approach as a starting point Hypothetically, we can explicitly *represent the DB as a collection of ground atomic facts* and use some resolution-based FOL reasoner supporting query answering, e.g., Vampire [27] or Gandalf [31].

Even if we have enough memory to load the facts, this approach is likely to be very inefficient for the following reason. If the RDB is large and the selectivity of the query is not very high, we can expect that *many answers will be obtained with structurally identical proofs*. For example, if our DB contains facts $graduateStudent(s_1), \dots, graduateStudent(s_{100})$ (representing some table $graduateStudent$ that simply keeps a list of all graduate students), the facts will give rise to 100 answers to the query $student(X)^3$, each having a refutational proof of the form shown in Figure 1.2 (where $grStud$, $takesC$, $pers$ and $stud$ abbreviate $graduateStudent$, $takesCourse$, $person$ and $student$, and $sk0$ is a Skolem function).

[0]	$\neg grCourse(X) \vee course(X)$	; input, $grCourse \sqsubseteq course$
[1]	$grStud(s_i)$	; input, DB row
[2]	$\neg grStud(X) \vee grCourse(sk0(X))$	; input, from $grStud \sqsubseteq \exists takesC.grCourse$
[3]	$grCourse(sk0(s_i))$	; from [1] and [2]
[4]	$course(sk0(s_i))$	; from [0] and [3]
[5]	$\neg grStud(X) \vee takesC(X, sk0(X))$	; input, from $grStud \sqsubseteq \exists takesC.grCourse$
[6]	$takesC(s_i, sk0(s_i))$	; from [1] and [5]
[7]	$\neg takesC(X,Y) \vee \neg course(Y) \vee$ $\neg pers(X) \vee stud(X)$	; input, from $stud \equiv pers \sqcap \exists takesC.course$
[8]	$\neg course(sk0(s_i)) \vee \neg pers(s_i) \vee stud(s_i)$	; from [6] and [7]
[9]	$\neg pers(s_i) \vee stud(s_i)$	; from [4] and [8]
[10]	$\neg grStud(X) \vee pers(X)$	; input, $grStud \sqsubseteq pers$
[11]	$pers(s_i)$	; from [1] and [10]
[12]	$stud(s_i)$	; from [9] and [11]
[13]	$\neg stud(X) \vee answer(X)$	; input, query $find\ X.stud(X)$
[14]	$answer(s_i)$	; from [12] and [13]

Fig. 1.2 Resoluton derivation of the answer $X := s_i$ for the query $stud(X)$.

---

[3] Query 6 from LUBM [17].

This example is intended to demonstrate how *wasteful reasoning on the per-answer basis* is. Roughly speaking, the required amount of reasoning is multiplied with the number of answers. Even if the selectivity of the query is very high, the reasoner is still likely to waste a lot of work in unsuccessful attempts represented by derivations not leading to any answers.

Note that these observations are not too specific to the choice of the reasoning method. For example, if we used Prolog or a tableaux-based DL reasoner, we would have a similar picture: the same rule applications performed for each answer s_i.

Main idea The main idea of our proposal is that *answers with similar proofs should be obtained in bulk*. More specifically, we propose to *use reasoning to find schematic answers* to queries, which can be later very efficiently *instantiated by querying the RDB via the standard highly optimised RDBMS mechanisms*. Technically, we propose to search for the schematic answers by *reasoning on an abstraction of the RDB in some resolution- and paramodulation-based calculus* (see [6, 21]). The abstraction and the reasoning on it should be organised in such a way that the obtained schematic answers can be turned into *regular RDBMS queries* (e.g., SQL queries).

Constrained clauses and table abstractions To illustrate our main idea, we apply it to the current example. The clause $grStud(X) \mid grStud(X)$ is the *abstraction* of the relevant part of the RDB, i.e., it represents (generalises) all the facts $grStud(s_1), \ldots, grStud(s_{100})$. This is a very important feature of our approach, so we emphasise that a potentially very large set of facts is compactly represented with just one clause. The part before "$\mid$" is the ordinary logical content of the clause. What comes after "$\mid$" is a special constraint. These constraints will be *inherited* in all inference rules, *instantiated* with the corresponding unifiers and *combined* when they come from different premises, just like, e. g., ordering or unifiability constraints in paramodulation-based theorem proving [21]. Although our constraints can be used as regular constraints – that is to identify redundant inferences by checking the satisfiability of the associated constraints w.r.t. the RDB (see Section 1.4) – *their main purpose is to record which RDB fact abstractions contribute to a schematic answer and what conditions on the variables of the abstractions have to be checked when the schematic answer is instantiated, so that the obtained concrete answers are sound.*

A derivation of a schematic answer for the query $student(X)$, covering all the concrete solutions $X := s_1, \ldots, X := s_{100}$, is shown in Figure 1.3. Note that the last inference simply merges three identical atomic constraints. Also note that we write the answer literals on the constraint sides of the clauses, because they are not intended for resolution.

SQL generation Semantically, the derived schematic answer $\square \mid \neg answer(X)$, $grStud(X)$ means that if some value x is in the table $graduateStudent$, then x is a legitimate concrete answer to the query. So, assuming that **id** is the (only) attribute in the RDB table representing the instances of $graduateStudent$, the derived schematic answer $\square \mid \neg answer(X), grStud(X)$ can be turned into the following simple SQL:

[0]	$\neg grCourse(X) \vee course(X)$	; input, KB
[1]	$grStud(X) \mid grStud(X)$	; DB table abstraction
[2]	$\neg grStud(X) \vee grCourse(sk0(X))$	; input, KB
[3]	$grCourse(sk0(X)) \mid grStud(X)$	; from [1] and [2]
[4]	$course(sk0(X)) \mid grStud(X)$	; from [0] and [3]
[5]	$\neg grStud(X) \vee takesC(X, sk0(X))$	; input, KB
[6]	$takesC(X, sk0(X)) \mid grStud(X)$	; from [1] and [5]
[7]	$\neg takesC(X, Y) \vee \neg course(Y) \vee \neg pers(X) \vee stud(X)$	; input, KB
[8]	$\neg course(sk0(X)) \vee \neg pers(X) \vee stud(X) \mid grStud(X)$	; from [6] and [7]
[9]	$\neg pers(X) \vee stud(X) \mid grStud(X), grStud(X)$	; from [4] and [8]
[10]	$\neg grStud(X) \vee pers(X)$	; input, KB
[11]	$pers(X) \mid grStud(X)$	; from [1] and [10]
[12]	$stud(X) \mid grStud(X), grStud(X), grStud(X)$	; from [9] and [11]
[13]	$\neg stud(X) \mid \neg answer(X)$	; query
[14]	$\square \mid \neg answer(X), grStud(X), grStud(X), grStud(X)$	; from [12] and [13]
[15]	$\square \mid \neg answer(X), grStud(X)$	; from [14]

Fig. 1.3 Resolution derivation of some schematic answer for $stud(X)$.

SELECT **id** AS X

FROM graduateStudent

Evaluating this query over the RDB will return all the answers $X := s_1, \ldots, X := s_{100}$.

Resolution reasoning on a DB abstraction may give rise to *more than one schematic answer*. For example, $\square \mid \neg answer(X), grStud(X)$ does not necessarily cover all possible solutions of the initial query – it only enumerates graduate students. If our KB also postulates that any person taking a course is a student, we want to select all such people as well. So, suppose that our DB also contains the facts $person(P_1), \ldots, person(P_{100}), takesCourse(P_1, C_1), \ldots,$ takesCourse(P_{100}, C_{100}) and $course(C_1), \ldots, course(C_{100})$ in the corresponding tables $person$, $takesCourse$ and $course$. These relations can be represented with the abstraction clauses
$person(X) \mid person(X), takesCourse(X, Y) \mid takesCourse(X, Y)$ and
$course(X) \mid course(X)$. Simple reasoning with these clauses modulo, say, a KB containing the rule $student(P) : - person(P), takesCourse(P, C), course(C)$ or the DL axiom $person \sqcap \exists takesC.course \sqsubseteq student$, produces the schematic answer $\square \mid \neg answer(X), person(X), takesCourse(X, Y), course(Y)$. Semantically it means that if table $takesCourse$ contains a record {**student** $= s$, **course** $= c$}, and tables $person$ and $course$ contain s and c correspondingly, then $X := s$ is a legitimate concrete answer. Thus, the schematic answer can be turned into this SQL query:

SELECT person.**id** AS X

FROM person, takesCourse, course

WHERE person.**id** = takesCourse.**student**

AND course.**id** = takesCourse.**course**

The join conditions $person.\textbf{id} = takesCourse.\textbf{student}$ and
$course.\textbf{id} = takesCourse.\textbf{course}$ reflect the fact that the corresponding arguments of the predicates in the constraint attached to the schematic answer are equal:
e.g., the only argument of $person$, corresponding to $person.\textbf{id}$, and the first argument of $takesCourse$, corresponding to $takesCourse.\textbf{student}$, are both the same variable X.

Incremental query rewriting In general, resolution over DB abstractions in the form of constrained clauses may produce many, even infinitely many, schematic answers and, consequently, SQL queries. They are produced one by one, and the union of their answers covers the whole set of concrete answers to the query. If there is only a finite number of concrete answers, e. g., if the query allows concrete answers to contain only plain data items from the database, then all concrete answers are covered after some finite number of steps. In a sense, the original semantic query is rewritten as a sequence of SQL queries, so we call our technique *incremental query rewriting*.

Benefits The main advantage of the proposed scheme is the *expressivity scalability*. For example, in applications not requiring termination, the expressivity of the knowledge representation formalisms is only limited by the expressivity of the full FOL[4], although specialised treatment of various FOL fragments is likely to be essential for good performance. The use of such a powerful logic as FOL as the common platform also allows easy practical simultaneous use of heterogeneous knowledge bases, at least for some data retrieval tasks. In particular, it means that users can freely mix all kinds of OWL and RDFS ontologies with all kinds of (first-order, monotonic) declarative rule sets, e. g., in RuleML, RIF or SWRL.

It is important that we don't pay too high a price in terms of performance, for the extra expressivity. The method has good data scalability: roughly, *the cost of reasoning is not multiplied by the volume of data*. Note also that we don't have to do any static conversion of the data into a different data model, e. g., RDF triples or OWL ABox – querying can be done on *live databases* via the hosting RDBMSs. All this makes our method potentially usable with very large DBs in real-life settings.

An additional advantage of our approach is that answers to semantic queries can be relatively easily given rigorous explanations. Roughly speaking, if we need to explain a concrete answer, we simply instantiate the derivation of the corresponding schematic answer by replacing DB table abstractions with concrete DB rows, and propagating this data through the derivation. Thus, we obtain a resolution proof of the answer, which can be relatively easily analysed or transformed into a more intuitive representation.

Since our method is essentially an incremental variant of query rewriting, there are no special obstacles to using it for data federation. Given a semantic query over a number of distributed autonomous data sources, we rewrite the query into a sequence of schematic answers just as if we were querying a single RDB. However, the obtained schematic answers can no longer be just converted to SQL, because a

---

[4] Complete methods for efficient schematic answer finding in FOL *with equality* are yet to be formulated and proved formally (see the brief discussion in Section 1.9).

schematic answer may use predicates defined in different data sources. In general, we have to create a *query schedule* – a special interpreted data structure that specifies subqueries to separate data sources, the order in which this queries are evaluated and the way their results are combined. More detailed discussion of distributed querying is outside the scope of this chapter.

1.3 Soundness and completeness of schematic answer computation.

So far we have only speculated that schematic answer search can be implemented based on resolution. In this section we are going to put it on a formal basis. We will show that in the context of FOL without equality some popular resolution-based methods can deliver the desired results. In particular, we will characterise a class of resolution-based calculi that are both sound and complete for query answering over database abstractions.

We assume familiarity of the reader with the standard notions of first-order logic, such as terms, formulas, literals and clauses, substitutions, etc., and some key results, such as the Herbrand's theorem. Bibliographic references are provided for more specialised concepts and facts.

Deductive queries In our settings, a *deductive query* is a triple $\langle DB, KB, \varphi \rangle$, where (i) the logical representation DB of some relational database is a set of ground atomic non-equality formulas, each representing a row in a table in the database, (ii) the *knowledge base KB* is a finite set of FOL axioms, corresponding to both the domain ontologies and semantic RDB schema mappings in our scenario, and (iii) the *goal φ* of the query is a construct of the form $\langle X_1, \ldots, X_k \rangle$ $\langle Y_1, \ldots, Y_m \rangle$ C, where C is a nonempty clause, $k, m \geq 0$, $\{X_1, \ldots, X_k, Y_1, \ldots, Y_m\} = vars(C)$, all X_i and Y_i are pairwise distinct. We call X_i *distinguished variables*, and Y_j *undistinguished variables* of the query. Intuitively, the deductive query represents a request to find all X_i, such that there exist some Y_j, such that $\varphi(\overline{X}, \overline{Y})$ is *inconsistent* with $DB \cup KB$. In other words, answers to the query refute φ rather than prove it[5]. This convention is made for technical convenience. Users of our technology can work in terms of positive queries.

Recording literals In our settings, a clause with *recording literals*[6] is a construct of the following form: $C \mid \gamma$, where C is a regular first-order clause, possibly empty, and γ is a finite multiset of literals, possibly empty. We will say that the literals of γ are *recording literals*.

Semantically, $C \mid \lambda_1, \ldots, \lambda_n$ is the same as the regular clause $C \vee \overline{\lambda_1} \vee \ldots \vee \overline{\lambda_n}$, which will be denoted as $Sem(C \mid \lambda_1, \ldots, \lambda_n)$. All semantic relations between

---

[5] Recall the part $\neg stud(X)$ of clause [13] from Fig. 1.2.

[6] We prefer this to the more general term "constrained clause" because we want to emphasise the nature and the role of our constraints, and to avoid confusion with other kinds of constraints used in automated reasoning and logic programming.

$Sem(C \mid \gamma)$ and other formulas are transferred to $C \mid \gamma$. For example, when we say that $C \mid \gamma$ is implied by something, it means that $Sem(C \mid \gamma)$ is implied, and vice versa.

Regular clauses will be often identified with clauses with empty recording parts, i.e., we will not distinguish C from $C \mid \emptyset$.

We say that a clause $C' \mid \gamma'$ subsumes the clause $C \mid \gamma$ if there is a substitution θ that makes $C'\theta$ a submultiset of C, and $\gamma'\theta$ a submultiset of γ'. In this case we will also say that $C' \mid \gamma'$ is a *generalisation* of $C \mid \gamma$.

Concrete and schematic answers We distinguish a special predicate symbol @[7]. A ground atomic formula $@(t_1, \ldots, t_k)$ is a *concrete* answer to the deductive query $\langle DB, KB, \langle X_1, \ldots, X_k \rangle \langle Y_1, \ldots, Y_m \rangle C \rangle$, if the clause $C[X_1/t_1, \ldots, X_k/t_k]$ is *inconsistent* with $DB \cup KB$ or, equivalently, the formula $\exists Y_1 \ldots Y_m \neg C[X_1/t_1, \ldots, X_k/t_k]$ is implied by $DB \cup KB$.

We say that a clause $\square \mid \gamma$ is a *schematic answer* to a deductive query $\langle DB, KB, \langle X_1, \ldots, X_k \rangle \langle Y_1, \ldots, Y_m \rangle C \rangle$, if every atomic ground formula of the form $@(t_1, \ldots, t_k)$ implied by $DB \cup \{\square \mid \gamma\}$, is a concrete answer to the query. Every such concrete answer will be called an *instance* of the schematic answer. For example, $@(s_1), \ldots, @(s_{100})$ are instances of the schematic answer $\square \mid \neg@(X)$, $grStud(X)$ in the main example in Section 1.2.

Database abstractions In our settings, a finite set DB' of clauses of the form $p(t_1, \ldots, t_k) \mid p(t_1, \ldots, t_k)$ is an *abstraction* of the logical representation DB of a database if for every atomic formula $\rho \in DB$, there is a clause $\rho' \mid \rho' \in DB'$ and a substitution θ, such that $\rho'\theta = \rho$. Note that *semantically* all clauses in DB' are tautologies, because $Sem(p(t_1, \ldots, t_k) \mid p(t_1, \ldots, t_k)) = p(t_1, \ldots, t_k) \vee \neg p(t_1, \ldots, t_k)$.

The simplest kind of an abstraction for an RDB is the set of all clauses $p(X_1, \ldots, X_k) \mid p(X_1, \ldots, X_k)$, where all X_i are pairwise distinct variables, and each p corresponds to a table in the RDB (see, e. g., clause [1] in Fig. 1.2). Dealing with such an abstraction can be viewed as reasoning on the schema of the RDB. However, in principle, we can have more specific abstractions. For example, if we know that the first column of our RDB table p contains only values a and b, we may choose to have two abstraction clauses: $p(a, X_2, \ldots, X_k) \mid p(a, X_2, \ldots, X_k)$ and $p(b, X_2, \ldots, X_k) \mid p(b, X_2, \ldots, X_k)$[8].

Calculi Here we only deal with calculi that are sound and complete variants of resolution[9] (see, e. g., [6]). All inference rules in these calculi are of the form

---

[7] Corresponds to the predicate $answer$ used in our previous examples.

[8] Moreover, we can have just one abstraction clause, e. g., $p(X_1, \ldots, X_k) \mid p(X_1, \ldots, X_k)$, $X_1 \in \{a, b\}$ with the additional *ad hoc constraint* $X_1 \in \{a, b\}$, but this kind of optimisations is outside the scope of this chapter.

[9] Paramodulation is also briefly discussed as a future research opportunity in Section 1.9.

$$\frac{C_1 \quad C_2 \quad \dots \quad C_n}{D}$$

where C_i and D are ordinary clauses, and $n \geq 1$. Most such rules have a substitution θ associated with them, which is required to unify some subexpressions in C_i, usually atoms of complementary literals. Rules in the calculi that are of interest to us can be easily extended to clauses with recording literals as shown in Figure 1.4(a). So, for example, the binary resolution rule extended to clauses with recording literals is shown in Figure 1.4(b). If a calculus R' is obtained by extending the rules of a

$$\frac{C_1 \mid \gamma_1 \quad C_2 \mid \gamma_2 \quad \dots \quad C_n \mid \gamma_n}{D \mid \gamma_1\theta, \gamma_2\theta, \dots, \gamma_n\theta} \ (a) \qquad \frac{C_1' \lor A \mid \gamma_1 \quad C_2' \lor \neg B \mid \gamma_2}{C_1'\theta \lor C_2'\theta \mid \gamma_1\theta, \gamma_2\theta} \ (b)$$

$$\text{where } \theta = mgu(A, B)$$

Fig. 1.4 Inferences on clauses with recording literals: (a) general form, (b) binary resolution

calculus R to clauses with recording literals, we will simply say that R' is a *calculus with recording literals* and R is its *projection to regular clauses*.

Apart from nonredundant inferences, resolution calculi used in practice usually include some *admissible* redundant inferences. Implementers have the freedom of performing or not performing such inferences without affecting the completeness of the reasoning process. However, for the purposes of this chapter it is convenient to assume that calculi being considered only contain nonredundant inferences. This assumption does not affect generality.

A calculus with recording literals is *sound* if Sem of the conclusion of every derivation is logically implied by the Sem images of the clauses in the leaves. It is obvious that a calculus with recording literals is sound if its projection to regular clauses is sound because recording literals are fully inherited. A calculus with recording literals is *refutationally complete* if its projection to regular clauses is refutationally complete, i.e., an empty clause can be derived from any unsatisfiable set of clauses.

In this chapter we will mention *fully specified calculi* to distinguish them from generic (parameterised) calculi. For example, the ordered binary resolution in general is not fully specified – it is a generic calculus *parameterised* by an order on literals. If we fix this parameter by specifying a concrete order, we obtain a fully specified calculus. We view a fully specified calculus as the set of all its elementary inferences.

We say that a fully specified calculus R with recording literals is *generalisation-tolerant* if every inference in R is generalisation-tolerant. An elementary inference

$$\frac{C_1 \mid \gamma_1 \quad C_2 \mid \gamma_2 \quad \dots \quad C_n \mid \gamma_n}{D \mid \delta}$$

from the calculus R is generalisation-tolerant if for every generalisation $C_i' \mid \gamma_i'$ of a premise $C_i \mid \gamma_i$, the calculus R also contains an elementary inference of some generalisation $D' \mid \delta'$ of $D \mid \delta$, where the premises are a submultiset of
$$\{C_1 \mid \gamma_1, \ldots, C_{i-1} \mid \gamma_{i-1}, \quad C_i' \mid \gamma_i', \quad C_{i+1} \mid \gamma_{i+1}, \ldots, C_n \mid \gamma_n\}.$$

Unordered binary resolution and hyperresolution provide simple examples of generalisation-tolerant calculi. Their ordered versions using admissible orderings (see, e. g., [6]) also cause no problems because application of generalisation to a clause cannot make a maximal literal nonmaximal, because of the *substitution property* of admissible orderings: $L_1 > L_2$ implies $L_1\theta > L_2\theta$. Adding (negative) literal selection (see, e. g., [6]) requires some care. In general, if a literal is selected in a clause, its image, if it exists, in any generalisation should be selected too. Such selection functions are still possible. For example, we can select *all* negative literals that are maximal w. r. t. some ordering satisfying the substitution property. In this case, however, we can no longer restrict ourselves to selecting a single literal in a clause, because the ordering can only be partial.

Note that such calculi are the main working horses in several efficient FOL reasoners, e. g., Vampire.

Theorem 1.1 (soundness). *Suppose R is a sound fully specified calculus with recording literals. Consider a deductive query $Q = \langle DB, KB, \langle X_1, \ldots, X_k \rangle \langle Y_1, \ldots, Y_m \rangle C \rangle$. Suppose DB' is an abstraction of DB. Suppose we can derive in R a clause $\square \mid \gamma$ from $DB' \cup KB \cup \{C \mid \neg@(X_1, \ldots, X_k)\}$. Then $\square \mid \gamma$ is a schematic answer to Q.*

Proof. Suppose $DB \cup \{\square \mid \gamma\}$ implies a ground formula $@(t_1, \ldots, t_k)$. We have to show that $@(t_1, \ldots, t_k)$ is a concrete answer to Q, i.e., $DB \cup KB \cup \{C[X_1/t_1, \ldots, X_k/t_k]\}$ is unsatisfiable.

Since R is sound, $\square \mid \gamma$ is derived from $DB' \cup KB \cup \{C \mid \neg@(X_1, \ldots, X_k)\}$ and DB' contains only clauses that are semantically tautologies, the clause $\square \mid \gamma$ is implied by $KB \cup \{C \mid \neg@(X_1, \ldots, X_k)\}$. Under our assumption, this means that $DB \cup KB \cup \{C \mid \neg@(X_1, \ldots, X_k)\}$ implies $@(t_1, \ldots, t_k)$. Note that the predicate @ does not occur in DB, KB or C and, therefore, $DB \cup KB \cup \{C[X_1/t_1, \ldots, X_k/t_k]\}$ is unsatisfiable. □

Theorem 1.2 (completeness). *Suppose R is a refutationally complete and generalisation-tolerant fully specified calculus with recording literals. Consider a deductive query $Q = \langle DB, KB, \langle X_1, \ldots, X_k \rangle \langle Y_1, \ldots, Y_m \rangle C \rangle$. Suppose DB' is an abstraction of DB. Then, for every concrete answer $@(t_1, \ldots, t_k)$ to Q one can derive in R from $DB' \cup KB \cup \{C \mid \neg@(X_1, \ldots, X_k)\}$ a clause $\square \mid \gamma$, such that $@(t_1, \ldots, t_k)$ is an instance of the schematic answer $\square \mid \gamma$.*

Proof. The refutational completeness of R means that we can construct a refutation Δ of $DB \cup KB \cup C[X_1/t_1, \ldots, X_k/t_k]$. The main idea of this proof is that in a generalisation-tolerant calculus finding an answer to a query is not much more difficult than just proving the answer. Technically, we will convert Δ into a derivation of a schematic answer covering the concrete answer $@(t_1, \ldots, t_k)$.

Assume that ρ_i, $i \in [1 \ldots p]$, are all the facts from DB that contribute to Δ (as leaves of the refutation). We can convert Δ into a derivation Δ' of a clause of the form $\Box \mid \rho_1, \ldots, \rho_p, \neg A_1, \ldots, \neg A_n$, where $p, n \geq 0$ and all atoms $A_i = @(t_1, \ldots, t_k)$, from the clauses $\rho_1 \mid \rho_1$, $\ldots$, $\rho_p \mid \rho_m$, $C[X_1/t_1, \ldots, X_k/t_k] \mid \neg @(t_1, \ldots, t_k)$ and some clauses from KB. To this end, we simply add the recording literals in the corresponding leaves of Δ and propagate them all the way to the root. Obviously, $DB \cup \{\Box \mid \rho_1, \ldots, \rho_m, \neg A_1, \ldots, \neg A_n\}$ implies $@(t_1, \ldots, t_k)$.

To complete the proof, we will show that Δ' can be converted into a derivation of a generalisation $\Box \mid \gamma$ for the clause $\Box \mid \rho_1, \ldots, \rho_m, \neg A_1, \ldots, \neg A_n$ from $DB' \cup KB \cup \{C \mid \neg @(X_1, \ldots, X_k)\}$. This is a corollary of a more general statement: if we can derive some clause D from clauses $C_1, \ldots, C_q$ in R, and $C'_1, \ldots, C'_q$ are some generalisations of those clauses, then there is a derivation from some of $C'_1, \ldots, C'_q$ in R of some generalisation D' of D. This can be easily proved by induction on the complexity of the derivation. Indeed, if the derivation contains some inferences, we apply the inductive hypothesis to the derivations of the premises of the last inference (resulting in D), deriving some generalisations of the premises. The induction step simply applies the generalisation-tolerance of R, possibly several times, to derive a generalisation of D from some of the new premises.

Finally, note that $\Box \mid \gamma$ implies $\Box \mid \rho_1, \ldots, \rho_m, \neg A_1, \ldots, \neg A_n$, and therefore $DB \cup \{\Box \mid \gamma\}$ implies $@(t_1, \ldots, t_k)$. $\quad\Box$

1.4 Recording literals as search space pruning constraints.

Let us make an important observation: *some schematic answers to deductive queries cover no concrete answers*. These schematic answers are useless and the work spent on their generation is wasted. We can address this problem by trying to block search directions that can only lead to such useless schematic answers.

Suppose we are searching for schematic answers to $\langle DB, KB, \langle X_1, \ldots, X_k \rangle \langle Y_1, \ldots, Y_m \rangle C \rangle$ by deriving consequences of $DB' \cup KB \cup \{C \mid \neg @(X_1, \ldots, X_k)\}$ in an appropriate calculus, where DB' is an abstraction of DB.

Database abstraction literals Suppose we have derived a clause $E = D \mid \rho'_1, \ldots, \rho'_p, \neg A_1, \ldots, \neg A_n$ where $p > 0, n \geq 0$, all the atoms A_i are of the form $@(t_1^i, \ldots, t_k^i)$ and all the literals ρ'_j are inherited from the recording literals of clauses from DB'. We can treat $\rho'_1, \ldots, \rho'_p$ as follows: if we can somehow establish that the constraint $\rho'_1, \ldots, \rho'_p$ *has no solutions* w. r. t. DB, we can remove the clause E from the search space. A *solution* of $\rho'_1, \ldots, \rho'_p$ w. r. t. DB is a substitution θ, such that all $\rho'_i \theta \in DB$.

Such a treatment can be justified with the following argument. It is obvious that if $\rho'_1, \ldots, \rho'_p$ has no solutions w. r. t. DB, then any more specific constraint $\rho'_1 \sigma, \ldots, \rho'_p \sigma$, where σ is some substitution, also has no solutions. Since all recording literals are fully inherited in the calculi we are dealing with, any clause derived from E and any other clauses, will have the same property. Therefore, any schematic answer $\square \mid \gamma$ whose derivation contains the clause, will contain in γ a nonempty subconstraint without @, having no solutions w. r. t. DB. Thus, $\square \mid \gamma$ cannot cover any concrete answers because the non-@ part of the constraint γ cannot be satisfied.

To summarise, we can discard clauses like E without sacrificing the completeness w. r. t. concrete answers. Practically, this can be done by converting $\rho'_1, \ldots, \rho'_p$ into an SQL query (similar to how it is done in Section 1.5 for schematic answers) and evaluating the query on the database – empty result set indicates absence of solutions w. r. t. DB. For efficiency, we can remember the constraints that are not satisfied: if $\rho'_1, \ldots, \rho'_p$ is not satisfied by our DB, then no constraint containing $\rho'_1 \theta, \ldots, \rho'_p \theta$ in the constraint part, for some substitution θ, can be satisfied with the DB and, thus, a clause with such a constraint can be discarded.

In the following important special case we don't even need to perform subsumption tests on constraints. A *p-chain* of length n is a finite set of literals of the form $p(X_1, X_2), p(X_2, X_3), \ldots, p(X_n, X_{n+1})$ where the variables X_i are pairwise distinct. If a p-chain is not satisfied by our DB, any longer p-chain is subsumed and thus cannot be satisfied either. For a given binary database abstraction predicate p, we can find the maximal length of p-chains that are satisfied by our DB before we run the reasoner to search for schematic answers. When the reasoner runs, it can discard clauses containing longer p-chains in the constraints, which is a relatively cheap test. This optimisation is practically relevant (see Section 1.6) because increasingly long chains often appear if our KBs contain transitive predicates.

Answer literals Suppose we have derived a schematic answer $\square \mid D, \neg A_1, \ldots, \neg A_n$ where D only contains database abstraction literals or is empty, and $n > 0$. For the schematic answer to have instances, the answer literals $\neg A_i$ must be simultaneously unifiable. Indeed, suppose $@(t_1, \ldots, t_k)$ is an instance of the schematic answer. By Herbrand's theorem, $DB \cup \{\neg @(t_1, \ldots, t_k)\}$ is inconsistent with a finite set of ground clauses of the form $\square \mid D\theta, \neg A_1 \theta, \ldots, \neg A_n \theta$. We assume that the set is minimal. It cannot be empty because @ does not occur in DB and DB itself is trivially consistent. Consider any clause $\square \mid D\theta, \neg A_1 \theta, \ldots, \neg A_n \theta$ from the set. All the atoms $A_i \theta$ from this clause are equal to $@(t_1, \ldots, t_k)$ because otherwise the set would not be minimal – any model of the set without this clause could be extended to make this clause true by making an appropriate $A_i \theta$ true. Thus, all A_i are simultaneously unifiable.

The fact proved above can be used to prune the search space as follows: if we derive an intermediate clause with some @-literals that are not simultaneously unifiable, we can discard the clause because any schematic answer derived from it will have no instances. Moreover, we can use the most general unifier for @-literals to strengthen the test on database abstraction literals by applying the unifier to them before solving them on the database.

1.5 SQL generation.

Suppose that we have found a schematic answer $\Box \mid \rho_1, \ldots, \rho_p, \neg A_1, \ldots, \neg A_n$ to a query $\langle DB, KB, \langle X_1, \ldots, X_k \rangle \langle Y_1, \ldots, Y_m \rangle C \rangle$. Now our task is to enumerate all instances of the schematic answer by querying the relational database modelled by the fact set DB, with an SQL query.

We have four cases to consider. (1) If $p = n = 0$, then we simply have a refutation of KB. Formally, this means that any ground $@(t_1, \ldots, t_k)$ is a correct answer, but for practical purposes this is useless. Instead, we should simply inform the user about the inconsistency. (2) If $p = 0$ but $n \neq 0$, we have to try to unify all the literals A_i. If $\theta = mgu(A_1, \ldots, A_n)$, then the set of instances of the schematic answer coincides with the set of ground instances of $A_1 \theta$. (3) If $p \neq 0$ but $n = 0$, there is a possibility that $DB \cup KB$ is inconsistent. We may want to check this possibility by checking if $\rho_1, \ldots, \rho_p$ has solutions over DB – if it does, DB is inconsistent with KB. The check itself can be done by converting $\rho_1, \ldots, \rho_p$ into an SQL query as in the next case, and checking if an answer to the SQL query exists. (4) In the rest of this section we will be considering the most interesting case when $p \neq 0$ and $n \neq 0$.

Using the considerations about answer literals from Section 1.4, we can prove that we only need to consider the case when $n = 1$. We can make another simplifying assumption: we only have to deal with schematic answers of the form $\Box \mid D, \neg @(X_1, \ldots, X_k)$, where X_i are pairwise distinct variables, each X_i occurs in D, and D contains only database abstraction literals. Enumeration of instances of more complex answer literals is reduced to this case.

Recall that all facts in DB are of the form $r_i(a_1^i, \ldots)$, where the predicates r_i correspond to tables in a relational database and all a_j^i are constants. Recalling Section 1.4, we can assume that literals from D do not contain compound terms.

Under these assumptions, it is straightforward to represent the schematic answer with a *semantically equivalent* clause of the form $E_a \vee E_c \vee E_d \vee D_x \vee A$, where (i) $A = @(X_1, \ldots, X_k)$ and all *answer variables* X_i are pairwise distinct; (ii) $D_x = \neg r_1(Y_1^1, \ldots, Y_{k(1)}^1) \vee \ldots \vee \neg r_p(Y_1^p, \ldots, Y_{k(p)}^p)$ and all variables Y_j^i are pairwise distinct; (iii) E_a consists of k negative equality literals $\alpha_i \not\simeq X_i$, $i = 1 \ldots k$, where $\alpha_i \in \{Y_1^1, \ldots, Y_{k(p)}^p\}$; (iv) E_c consists of zero or more negative equality literals of the form $\alpha \not\simeq \beta$, where $\alpha \in \{Y_1^1, \ldots, Y_{k(p)}^p\}$ and β is a constant; (v) E_d consists of zero or more negative equality literals of the form $\alpha \not\simeq \beta$, where $\alpha, \beta \in \{Y_1^1, \ldots, Y_{k(p)}^p\}$.

The transformed schematic answer $E_a \vee E_c \vee E_d \vee D_x \vee A$ can be translated into an SQL query of the form

$$SELECT \ \langle columns \rangle \ FROM \ \langle tables \rangle \ WHERE \ \langle join \ conditions \rangle.$$

The expression $\langle columns \rangle$ is a comma-separated list of answer column declarations of the form $R_i.\#_j \ AS \ X_e$ for each $Y_j^i \not\simeq X_e \in E_a$. Here R_i is a fresh table alias corresponding to the literal $r_i(Y_1^i, \ldots, Y_{k(i)}^i)$ and $\#_j$ denotes the j-th attribute name in the table r_i from our RDB schema. The expression $\langle tables \rangle$ is a comma-separated list of table aliases of the form $r_i \ AS \ R_i$, $i = 1 \ldots p$. We have to use aliases because, in general, some r_i may coincide. The expression $\langle join\ conditions \rangle$ is a conjunction of elementary join condition of two kinds: (i) $R_i.\#_j = \beta$ for each $Y_j^i \not\simeq \beta \in E_c$, and (ii) $R_i.\#_j = R_u.\#_v$ for each $Y_j^i \not\simeq Y_v^u \in E_d$.

1.6 Implementation and experiments.

To illustrate the incremental query rewriting method, and to facilitate further research on it, we created a simple proof-of-concept prototype. It has two main components.

Firstly, we modified a version of the Vampire prover [27] to enable reasoning with database abstractions and derivation of schematic answers. To this end, the reasoner simply allows to identify some literals in clauses as constraint literals, thus protecting these literals from resolution. Another necessary change was to modify some literal selection functions in order to make them generalisation tolerant, as described in Section 1.3. Generated schematic answers are output in a simple XML format. All in all, the reasoner part of the implementation was very easy – only a few dozen lines of code had to be added or replaced. However, the full optimisation based on checking constraints over the DB (see Section 1.4) would complicate the architecture, so we chose to implement only the chain length restriction in the current prototype.

Secondly, we wrote an SQL generator in Java that almost literally implements the procedure described in Section 1.5. The difference is that in the implementation the DB abstraction predicates need not directly correspond to DB tables. For greater flexibility, we allow to define the DB abstraction predicates with any relation-valued SQL expressions, including SELECT and UNION queries. The SQL generator reads the schematic answers in XML, and outputs SQL queries corresponding to them. Optionally, it can directly submit the SQL queries to a specified MySQL or Derby DB for evaluation, and output the results.

The implementation components are glued together with a simple shell script.

Since Vampire's input format is TPTP [30], we have also written converters from OWL 2, SWRL and RIF BLD [1] to the TPTP format.

Regular RDB experiment To be able to demonstrate our technology, and to have a source of use cases for future research, we created a toy benchmark RDB, called MyUniversityDB[10], inspired by LUBM [17]. The benchmark models a database of a university, that contains information about departments, courses, students, faculty members, publications, etc. The content is generated randomly, with realistic distributions. To model only minimal assumptions that can affect performance, indexes are created only for primary and foreign keys. Like LUBM, the benchmark is scalable – the user can set the number of departments.

The schema of MyUniversityDB is semantically mapped to concepts and relations of the OWL ontology from LUBM, describing the university domain. This is

---

[10] We are planning to publish the benchmark under an Open Source license when it matures.

done with a small number of simple axioms in TPTP. For example, consider the following axiom:

```
fof(attribute_graduate_identifies_course_level, axiom,
  ! [Id,Dept,Name,Grad] :
     ((db_courses(Id,Dept,Name,Grad) & (Grad = 1))
      =>
      p_GraduateCourse(courseEntity(Id))))).
```

The DB abstraction predicate db_courses directly corresponds to a table that keeps the information about various courses, including a boolean flag that indicates if the course is a graduate course. The axiom above maps the records of the table containing the value 1 ("true") in the flag attribute, to instances of the concept http://www.lehigh.edu/~zhp2/2004/0401/univ-bench.owl#GraduateCourse[11] from the LUBM ontology.

For the initial experiments with MyUniversityDB, we wrote 14 queries that closely resemble the 14 LUBM queries (see [17]) – the only difference is that our queries report various retrieved entities using their names rather than URIs identifying the entities, which we don't have in the DB. All queries were computed by our system, which demonstrates the viability of our approach. The reasoner generated all schematic answers to all queries almost instantaneously, and all the generated SQL queries were evaluated in real time.

Sesame triplestore experiment To explore the possibility of using our method for expressive querying of third-party RDB-based *semantic databases*, such as triplestores and instance stores, we conducted an experiment with the popular triplestore Sesame [9]. This experiment seems important, in particular, because of the possibility of using our approach as a part of a Web-scale semantic search technology, as was outlined in the introduction.

We implemented a utility that analyses the DB schema of a MySQL-based Sesame repository keeping some RDF models, and creates a mapping of property URIs into SQL queries over this schema, *which is just a special case of a semantic mapping* that can be given to our SQL generator. Let us briefly describe how this mapping is extracted. The MySQL Sesame back-end uses the following scheme for representing RDF triples. First, instead of keeping URIs as strings, the MySQL back-end replaces them with integer surrogate keys: this saves memory and also allows faster joins. The correspondence between the URIs and their surrogate keys is kept in a special binary relation URI_VALUES(pk *id*: INTEGER, *value*: VARCHAR(255)). Similarly, string literals are replaced with surrogate keys with the help of a special relation LABEL_VALUES(pk *id*: INTEGER, *value*: VARCHAR(255)).

Predicate URIs, i. e., URIs playing the role of predicates in triples, are mapped to separate tables. For example, there are tables *emailAddress_25* and *type_3*.

---

[11] Conversion from OWL to TPTP does not preserve predicate names, because using URIs would make TPTP axioms unreadable, so http://www.lehigh.edu/~zhp2/2004/0401/univ-bench.owl#GraduateCourse is mapped to p_GraduateCourse, etc.

The numeric indexes in the table names are the surrogate key values corresponding to the URIs, so, by finding 25 and 3 in URI_VALUES, we retrieve the URIs
http://www.lehigh.edu/~zhp2/2004/0401/univ-bench.owl#emailAddress and
http://www.lehigh.edu/~zhp2/2004/0401/univ-bench.owl#type correspondingly, thus
connecting the contents of the tables to the corresponding predicates.

Taking into account the URI-to-surrogate-key mapping, our schema analyser
could map the DB abstraction predicate ub:emailAddress into the following SQL
query:

```
SELECT subj_uri.value AS subject,
       obj_val.value AS object
FROM emailAddress_25 rel,
     URI_VALUES subj_uri,
     LABEL_VALUES obj_val
WHERE rel.subj = subj_uri.id
  AND rel.obj = obj_val.id
```

However, this is not complete. The MySQL back-end has additional tables –
LONG_URI_VALUES and LONG_LABEL_VALUES – for mapping too long URIs
and string literals to surrogate keys. So, the real query generated by our schema
analyser considers all combinations of short and long URIs and string literals, and
builds a union of the corresponding subqueries.

Unary predicates corresponding to the classes of OWL ontologies are treated
slightly differently. For example, ub:GraduateCourse is mapped to the query

```
SELECT instance_uri.value as instance
  FROM type_3 rel,
       URI_VALUES instance_uri,
       URI_VALUES class_uri
 WHERE instance_uri.id = rel.subj
   AND class_uri.id = rel.obj
   AND class_uri.value =
          'http://www.lehigh.edu/ ... #GraduateCourse'
```

The schema analyser also extracts a list of the DB abstraction predicate URIs that
can be submitted to the reasoner for answer generation. Together with the semantic mapping, this is enough to *enable the use of our implementation for answering
queries over the Sesame repository modulo practically any KBs that can be translated to FOL.*

To test our implementation, we generated an instance of LUBM for 5 universities and loaded it into a MySQL-based Sesame repository. This is a relatively large
ABox: there are about 100,000 instance assertions and 500,000 property assertions.
Naturally, we query it via the LUBM ontology which is expressive enough to provide an interesting initial test – it uses a number of DL constructs outside RDFS,
such as inverse and transitive properties. We also use the 14 LUBM queries for the
test.

The first experiments revealed that the transitivity axiom for the predicate
ub:subOrganizationOf causes nontermination when the reasoner searches for

schematic answers. Moreover, the derivation of some schematic answers takes several minutes. This motivated us to look for ways of reducing search space and led to the discovery of the chain length-based technique described in Section 1.4. With this optimisation, the reasoner computes all schematic answers instantaneously.

The first tests with the generated SQL queries also exposed some performance problems. Initially, the evaluation of some of the queries was taking hours. Our investigation revealed that MySQL (v5.2) does not really inline so-called *table subqueries*, which are also known as *inline views*. Practically, this means that if a query selects from a relation which is itself a SELECT, than the subquery is computed separately as a temporary table, rather than be embedded into the larger query. This significantly restricts the MySQL query optimiser in the choice of the join order. This affects our implementation because table subqueries occur from the mapping of database abstraction predicates to SELECTs rather than just tables. Fortunately, MySQL does the inlining when the selection is done from a named view. We solved this problem by creating views for semantic mappings specified as complex queries.

A similar problem was caused by UNIONs in the semantic mappings – UNIONs are also computed as temporary tables. To overcome this, when a union has to be embedded into a larger query corresponding to a schematic answer, our SQL generator splits the larger query into several ones by distributing over the members of the union. This leads to several SQL queries instead of one, but the smaller queries do not contain UNIONs and can be optimised more effectively.

Finally, one Sesame-specific optimisation was necessary: indexes had to be added on the *value* attribute in URL_VALUES and similar tables.

After these changes, all the queries were evaluated in a practically acceptable time. Only two queries – 6 and 8 – took more than a few seconds: 9 and 15 minutes.

1.7 A note on indexing Semantic Web documents with data abstractions.

In the context of Semantic Web (SW), it is important to be able to index distributed semantic data description sets (SW documents, for simplicity), so that, given a semantic query modulo some knowledge bases, we can load only the SW documents that are potentially relevant to the query. In this section we briefly sketch a possible indexing scheme compatible with our approach to deductive querying.

Conventional search engines index regular Web documents by words appearing in them. We cannot simply follow this example by indexing SW documents by the names of objects, concepts and relations occurring in them. This is so because retrieval in general may require reasoning, and thus the relevant documents may use no common symbols with the query. For example, a query may request to find animals of bright colours. If some SW document describes, e. g., pink elephants, it is relevant, but lexically there is no overlap with the query. Only reasoning reveals the relation between "http://zooontology.org/concept#elephant" and "http://zooontology.org/concept#animal", and between

"http://www.colors.org/concept#pink" and
"http://www.colors.org/concept#bright_colour".

Note that conceptually there is hardly any difference between RDBs and, say, OWL data description sets based on the Web: an RDB can be *modelled* as a set of ground atomic logical assertions, and, practically, an SW document *is* such a set. So, just like we use abstractions to represent relational data compactly in reasoning, we can use abstractions to represent SW documents. For example, a potentially large SW document introducing many pink elephants can be compactly represented by its abstraction $zoo{:}elephant(X) \mid zoo{:}elephant(X)$, $colors{:}hasColour(X, Y) \mid colors{:}hasColour(X, Y)$ and $colors{:}pink(X) \mid colors{:}pink(X)$.

It seems natural to use such abstraction clauses as indexes to the corresponding SW documents in a semantic search engine. Then, the query answering process can be organised as follows. As in the case of reasoning over RDB abstractions, a reasoner is used to derive schematic answers to a given query, based on all available abstractions of indexed SW documents. Each schematic answer to the query depends on some abstraction clauses. The documents associated with these clauses are potentially relevant to our query, so we download them, and only them, into our local RDB for further processing.

Of course, the indexing scheme presented here is just a conceptual one. The developers have the flexibility to chose a concrete representation – for example, they may just index by the URIs of concepts and relations, and only create the corresponding abstraction clauses when the reasoner is ready to inject them in the search space. There is also a possibility of adjusting the degree of generality of abstraction clauses by adding some ad hoc constraints. For example, the first of the abstraction clauses from the example above can be replaced with the more specific $zoo{:}elephant(X) \mid zoo{:}elephant(X), \ pref(X," http : // www.elephants.com/")$. The ad hoc constraint $pref(X," http : //www. elephants.com/")$ requires the prefix of the URI X to be "http://www.elephants.com/". The constraint is incompatible with, e.g., $pref(X," http : // www.rhinos.com/")$, so if our reasoner derives a clause with these two constraints, it can safely discard it, thus improving the precision of indexing.

1.8 Related work.

We are not aware of any work that uses resolution-based reasoning in a way similar to the one proposed in this chapter, i. e., for incremental query rewriting based on the use of complete query answering over database abstractions, implemented with constraints over the concrete data.

In general, semantic access to relational databases is not a new concept. Some of the work on this topic is limited to semantic access to, or semantic interpretation of relational data in terms of Description Logic-based ontologies or RDF (see, e. g., [5, 25, 11, 7, 4]), or non-logical semantic schemas (see [28]). There is also a large number of projects and publications on the use of RDBs to implement *semantic databases*, i. e., for storing and querying large RDF and OWL datasets: see, e. g., [24, 18, 12, 13, 14], to mention just a few. We cannot give a comprehensive overview of such work. Instead, we will concentrate on the research that tries to go beyond the expressivity of DL and, at the same time, is applicable to legacy relational databases.

The work presented here was originally inspired by the XSTONE project [32]. In XSTONE, a resolution-based theorem prover (a reimplementation of Gandalf, which is, in particular, optimised for taxonomic reasoning) is integrated with an RDBMS by loading rows from a database as ground facts into the reasoner and using them to answer queries with resolution. The system is highly scalable in terms of expressiveness: it accepts full FOL with some useful extensions, and also has parsers for RDF, RDFS and OWL. We believe that our approach has better data scalability and can cope with very large databases which are beyond the reach of XSTONE, mostly because our approach obtains answers in bulk, and also due to the way we use highly-optimised RDBMS.

Papers [23] and [22] describe, albeit rather superficially, a set of tools for mapping relational databases into OWL and semantic querying of the RDB. Importantly, the queries are formulated as SWRL [3] rule bases. Although SWRL only allows Horn rules built with OWL concepts, properties and equality, its expressivity is already sufficient for many applications. Given a semantic query in the form of a SWRL rule base, the software generates SQL queries in order to extract some relevant data in the form of OWL assertions and runs a rule engine on this data to generate final answers. So the reasoning is, at least partially, sensitive to the amount of data. This gives us hope that our approach can scale up better because the reasoning part of the process is completely independent of the concrete data.

Another project, OntoGrate [15], uses an approach to deductive query answering, which is based on the same ideas as ours: their FOL reasoner, OntoEngine [16], can be used to rewrite original queries formulated in terms of some ontology, into a finite set of conjunctive queries in terms of the DB schema, which is then converted to SQL. For this task, the reasoner uses *backward chaining with Generalised Modus Ponens* [29], which corresponds to negative hyperresolution on Horn clauses in the more common terminology. A somewhat ad hoc form of term rewriting [21] is used to deal with equality. Termination is implemented by setting some limits on chaining, which allows them to avoid incremental processing. We hope to go much further, mainly, but not only, by putting our work on a *solid theoretical foundation*. In particular, we are paying attention to completeness. Since our approach is based on well-studied calculi, we hope to exploit the large amount of previous research on completeness and termination, which seems very difficult to do with the approach taken by OntoEngine. Although we are very likely to make various concessions to pragmatics, we would like to do this in a controllable and reproducible manner.

On the more theoretical side, it is necessary to mention two other connections. The idea of using constraints to represent schematic answers is borrowed from Constraint Logic Programming [19] and Constrained Resolution [10]. Also, the general idea of using reasoning for preprocessing expressive queries into a database-related formalism, was borrowed from [20], where a resolution- and paramodulation-based calculus is used to translate expressive DL ontologies into Disjunctive Datalog. This work also shares a starting point with ours – the observation that reasoning methods that treat individuals/data values separately can not scale up sufficiently.

Semantic querying of RDBs can be considered a flavour of the *deductive database* technology, if the latter term is understood very broadly. However, we prefer not to refer to deductive databases to avoid confusion with the Datalog- and Prolog-related technologies. The differences between the semantic querying technologies, including ours, and deductive databases in the narrow sense, are quite strong. First, semantic querying is not seen as a replacement for RDBs, but rather an enhancement of the RDB technology. Second, there is a crucial technical difference: semantic querying works with completely declarative KBs, whereas Datalog and Prolog queries are often real programs.

1.9 Summary and future work.

The main contributions of the work reported here are (i) an adaptation of resolution to compute *schematic answers* to deductive queries, (ii) development of a method to translate these schematic answers into standard SQL queries, (iii) completeness and soundness proofs to justify the applicability of the proposed technique, and (iv) an exploration of the proposed approach as a potential basis for an efficient Web-scale semantic search technology.

We make a strong emphasis on the high expressivity of the KBs and query languages that can be used with our approach. The application scenarios discussed in the introduction can benefit from the *gain in expressiveness* without *unnecessary performance overhead* and, more importantly, *without any major re-engineering effort*. Note that our technique is designed to combine the power of a FOL reasoner with the speed and scalabitiy of standard RDBMS. Also note that this technique supports querying over existing RDF or OWL stores as well as existing relational databases and, thus, it can be deployed without major changes in the existing knowledge and data legacies.

Our future work will be mostly concentrated in the following directions:

Implementation and case studies In Section 1.6 we described a proof-of-concept implementation and two preliminary experiments. This exploratory work provides a basis for a more comprehensive implementation effort, including the implementation of a front-end for all first-order monotonic sublanguages of Derivation RuleML [2], an implementation of a client-server Java API that will support data federation, back-ends for querying data sources other than RDBs, e.g., Web services, spreadsheets and XML files, and tuning the reasoner for the task of schematic answer derivation over RDB abstractions. Later on, the implementation work will be guided by realistic scale case studies with health care databases and Business Intelligence benchmarks.

Equality treatment If the equality predicate is present in our knowledge bases (e. g., in the form of OWL number restrictions), we can extend the standard superposition calculus (see [21]) to clauses with recording literals as we did with resolution. However, the completeness proof does not fully transfer to such use of superposition: an obvious obstacle to generalisation-tolerance is the absence of paramodulations into variables in the standard paramodulation-based calculi (for details, see, e. g., [21]). Therefore, one of our main priorities now is to look for adjustments of the superposition calculus that would be provably complete w. r. t. schematic answers, without being too inefficient due to, e.g., unrestricted paramodulations into variables.

We are trying to exploit the specificity of reasoning over DB abstractions. Intuitively, we only need to allow paramodulations into variables ranging over data values from the DB (see the proof of Theorem 1.2). By adjusting the term ordering in our superposition calculus so that all (constants representing) data values are smaller than any other terms, we restrict the choice of positive equality literals suitable for paramodulation into variables, to equalities of the form $t_1 \simeq t_2$, where each t_i is either a data value or a variable ranging over data values. Finally, assuming that syntactically distinct data values a and b are also distinct semantically, i. e., the disequality $a \not\simeq b$ has to be assumed, we can replace every paramodulation from $t_1 \simeq t_2$ into a variable, with an inference that just resolves the literal $t_1 \simeq t_2$, thus completely eliminating the need for paramodulations into variables ranging over such datatypes. For datatypes that do not allow the distinctness assumption, such as URIs, the ordering adjustment still leads to a dramatic reduction in the search space. We are going to elaborate these ideas in a forthcoming publication.

Completeness with redundancy deletion Static completeness, proven in Section 1.3, is enough to guarantee that we will find all necessary answers only if our search procedure generates absolutely all possible derivations in the given calculus. In practice, such approach is almost always inefficient. Typically, some criteria are applied to detect redundant clauses and remove them from the current clause set.

It seems relatively easy to prove completeness of schematic answer derivation process in presence of the most important redundancy deletion technique: roughly, a clause subsumed by another clause can be deleted from the current clause set. The main idea for such a proof is as follows: if subsumption removes an answer derivation from the search space, the search space will still contain a structurally simpler derivation of the same answer or a more general answer. Note that this is a property of generalisation-tolerant calculi. However, if we want to use other important search space reduction techniques, e. g., *demodulation* [21], we have to demonstrate compatibility of our approach with the *standard redundancy criterion* (see, e. g., [6, 21]).

Termination Very often it is desirable that a query answering implementation terminates on a given query having exhausted all solutions, e. g., for counting and aggregation of other kinds, and negation as failure. We are interested in identifying combinations of practically relevant fragments of FOL with reasoning methods and strategies, that guarantee termination.

Acknowledgements Many thanks to RuleML for supporting this publication, and to Harold Boley for numerous productive discussions on the subject, especially for drawing the attention of the first author to modern rule languages.

References

1. RIF Basic Logic Dialect. http://www.w3.org/TR/rif-bld/
2. The Rule Markup Initiative Web Site. http://www.ruleml.org/
3. W3C SWRL Submission:. http://www.w3.org/Submission/SWRL/
4. A.Ranganathan, Liu, Z.: Information Retrieval from Relational Databases using Semantic Queries. In: Proc. ACM CIKM, pp. 820–821 (2006)
5. Arens, Y., Chee, C.Y., Hsu, C.N., Knoblock, C.A.: Retrieving and Integrating Data from Multiple Information Sources. International Journal on Intelligent and Cooperative Information Systems **2**(2), 127–158 (1993)
6. Bachmair, L., Ganzinger, H.: Resolution Theorem Proving. In: Handbook of Automated Reasoning, vol. I (2001)
7. Bizer, C.: D2RQ – Treating Non-RDF Databases as Virtual RDF Graphs. In: ISWC 2004
8. Boley, H.: The RuleML Family of Web Rule Languages. In: PPSWR06 (2006)
9. Broekstra, J., Kampman, A., van Harmelen, F.: Sesame: A Generic Architecture for Storing and Querying RDF and RDF Schema. In: ISWC, pp. 54–68 (2002)
10. Bürckert, H.J., Nutt, W.: On Abduction and Answer Generation through Constrained Resolution. Tech. Rep. DFKI RR-92-51 (1992)
11. Calvanese, D., Giacomo, G.D., Lembo, D., Lenzerini, M., Poggi, A., Rosati, R.: MASTRO-I: Efficient Integration of Relational Data through DL Ontologies. In: DL-07 (2007)
12. Calvanese, D., Giacomo, G.D., Lembo, D., Lenzerini, M., Rosati, R.: DL-Lite: Tractable Description Logics for Ontologies. In: AAAI'05, pp. 602–607 (2005)
13. Chen, C.M., Haarslev, V., Wang, J.Y.: LAS: Extending Racer by a Large Abox Store. In: DL-2005
14. Dolby, J., Fokoue, A., Kalyanpur, A., Ma, L., Patel, C., Schonberg, E., Srinivas, K., Sun, X.: Efficient reasoning on large SHIN Aboxes in relational databases (2007). (unpublished)
15. Dou, D., LePendu, P., Kim, S., Qi, P.: Integrating Databases into the Semantic Web through an Ontology-based Framework. In: International Workshop on Semantic Web and Databases at ICDE 2006 (2006)
16. Dou, D., McDermott, D., Qi, P.: Ontology Translation on the Semantic Web. Journal of Data Semantics **2**, 35–37 (2005)
17. Guo, Y., Heflin, J., Pan, Z.: An Evaluation of Knowledge Base Systems for Large OWL Datasets. In: ISWC 2004, pp. 613–627 (2004)
18. Horrocks, I., Li, L., Turi, D., Bechhofer, S.: The Instance Store: Description Logic Reasoning with Large Numbers of Individuals. In: DL'04 (2004)
19. Jaffar, J., Maher, M.J.: Constraint Logic Programming: a Survey. Journal of Logic Programming **19**(20), 503–581 (1994)
20. Motik, B.: Reasoning in Description Logics using Resolution and Deductive Databases. PhD Thesis (2006)
21. Nieuwenhuis, R., Rubio, A.: Paramodulation-Based Theorem Proving. In: A. Robinson, A. Voronkov (eds.) Handbook of Automated Reasoning, vol. I (2001)
22. O'Connor, M., Shankar, R., Tu, S., Nyulas, C., Das, A., Musen, M.: Efficiently Querying Relational Databases Using OWL and SWRL. In: RR 2007 (2007)
23. O'Connor, M., Shankar, R., Tu, S., Nyulas, C., Parrish, D., Musen, M., Das, A.: Using Semantic Web Technologies for Knowledge-Driven Querying of Biomedical Data. In: AIME 07 (2007)
24. Pan, Z., Heflin, J.: DLDB: Extending Relational Databases to Support Semantic Web Queries. In: Workshop on Practical and Scaleable Semantic Web Systems, ISWC 2003 (2003)

25. Paton, N.W., Stevens, R., Baker, P., Goble, C.A., Bechhofer, S., Brass, A.: Query Processing in the TAMBIS Bioinformatics Source Integration System. In: SSDBM (1999)
26. Ramakrishnan, R., Gehrke, J.: Database Management Systems. McGraw-Hill (2003)
27. Riazanov, A., Voronkov, A.: The Design and Implementation of Vampire. AI Communications **15**(2-3), 91–110 (2002)
28. Rishe, N.: SemanticSQL: A Semantic Wrapper for Relational Databases. `http://n1.cs.fiu.edu/semantic.wrapper.pdf` (2004). (white paper)
29. Russel, S., Norvig, P.: Artificial Intelligence: A Modern Approach. Prentice-Hall (2003)
30. Sutcliffe, G., Suttner, C.: The TPTP Problem Library. TPTP v. 2.4.1. Tech. rep., University of Miami (2001)
31. Tammet, T.: Gandalf. Journal of Automated Reasoning **18**(2), 199–204 (1997)
32. Tammet, T., Kadarpik, V., Haav, H.M., Kaaramees, M.: A Rule-based Approach to Web-based (Database) Application Development. In: 7th International Baltic Conference on Databases and Information Systems, pp. 202–208 (2006)

Chapter 2
Knowledge Representation and Reasoning in Norm-Parameterized Fuzzy Description Logics

Jidi Zhao, Harold Boley

Abstract The Semantic Web is an evolving extension of the World Wide Web in which the semantics of the available information are formally described, making it more machine-interpretable. The current W3C standard for Semantic Web ontology languages, OWL, is based on the knowledge representation formalism of Description Logics (DLs). Although standard DLs provide considerable expressive power, they cannot express various kinds of imprecise or vague knowledge and thus cannot deal with uncertainty, an intrinsic feature of the real world and our knowledge. To overcome this deficiency, this chapter extends a standard Description Logic to a family of norm-parameterized Fuzzy Description Logics. The syntax to represent uncertain knowledge and the semantics to interpret fuzzy concept descriptions and knowledge bases are addressed in detail. The chapter then focuses on a procedure for reasoning with knowledge bases in the proposed Fuzzy Description Logics. Finally, we prove the soundness, completeness, and termination of the reasoning procedure.

2.1 Introduction

The Semantic Web is an evolving extension of the World Wide Web in which the semantics of the available information are formally described by logic-based standards and technologies, making it possible for machines to understand the information on the Web [3].

Uncertainty is an intrinsic feature of real-world knowledge, which is also reflected in the World Wide Web and the Semantic Web. Many concepts needed in

Jidi Zhao
Faculty of Computer Science, University of New Brunswick, Fredericton, NB, E3B 5A3 Canada,
e-mail: Judy.Zhao[AT]unb.ca

Harold Boley
Institute for Information Technology, National Research Council of Canada, Fredericton, NB, E3B
9W4 Canada, e-mail: Harold.Boley[AT]nrc.gc.ca

W. Du and F. Ensan (eds.), *Canadian Semantic Web: Technologies and Applications*,
DOI 10.1007/978-1-4419-7335-1_2, © Springer Science+Business Media, LLC 2010

knowledge modeling lack well-defined boundaries or, precisely defined criteria. Examples are the concepts of young, tall, and cold. The Uncertainty Reasoning for the World Wide Web (URW3) Incubator Group defined the challenge of representing and reasoning with uncertain information on the Web. According to the latest URW3 draft report, uncertainty is a term intended to encompass different forms of uncertain knowledge, including incompleteness, inconclusiveness, vagueness, ambiguity, and others [18]. The need to model and reason with uncertainty has been found in many different Semantic Web contexts, such as matchmaking in Web services [20], classification of genes in bioinformatics [28], multimedia annotation [27], and ontology learning [6]. Therefore, a key research direction in the Semantic Web is to handle uncertainty.

The current W3C standard for Semantic Web ontology languages, OWL Web Ontology Language, is designed for use by applications that need to process the content of information instead of just presenting information to humans [21, 23]. It facilitates greater machine interpretability of Web content than that supported by other Web languages such as XML, RDF, and RDF Schema (RDFS). This ability of OWL is enabled by its underlying knowledge representation formalism Description Logics (DLs). Description Logics (DLs) [2][1][12] are a family of logic-based knowledge representation formalisms designed to represent and reason about the conceptual knowledge of arbitrary domains. Elementary descriptions of DL are atomic concepts (classes) and atomic roles (properties or relations). Complex concept descriptions and role descriptions can be built from elementary descriptions according to construction rules. Different Description Logics are distinguished by the kinds of concept and role constructors allowed in the Description Logic and the kinds of axioms allowed in the terminology box (TBox). The basic propositionally closed DL is $\mathcal{ALC}$ in which the letters $\mathcal{AL}$ stand for attributive language and the letter $\mathcal{C}$ for complement (negation of arbitrary concepts). Besides $\mathcal{ALC}$, other letters are used to indicate various DL extensions. More pecisely, $\mathcal{S}$ is often used for $\mathcal{ALC}$ extended with transitive roles (R^+), $\mathcal{H}$ for role hierarchies, $\mathcal{O}$ for nominals, $\mathcal{I}$ for inverse roles, $\mathcal{N}$ for number restrictions, $\mathcal{Q}$ for qualified number restrictions, and $\mathcal{F}$ for functional properties. OWL[1] has three increasingly expressive sublanguages: OWL Lite, OWL DL, and OWL Full. If we omit the annotation properties of OWL, the OWL-Lite sublanguage is a syntactic variant of the Description Logic $\mathcal{SHIF}(\mathcal{D})$ where $(\mathcal{D})$ means data values or data types, while OWL-DL is almost equivalent to the $\mathcal{SHOIN}(\mathcal{D})$ DL [13]. OWL-Full is the union of OWL syntax and RDF, and known to be undecidable mainly because it does not impose restrictions on the use of transitive properties. Accordingly, an OWL-Lite ontology corresponds to a $\mathcal{SHIF}(\mathcal{D})$ knowledge base, and an OWL-DL ontology corresponds to a $\mathcal{SHOIN}(\mathcal{D})$ knowledge base.

Although standard DLs provide considerable expressive power, they are limited to dealing with crisp, well-defined concepts and roles, and cannot express vague or uncertain knowledge. To overcome this deficiency, considerable work has been carried out in integrating uncertain knowledge into DLs in the last decade. One im-

---

[1] In the following, OWL refers to OWL 1. Similar sublanguages exist for OWL 2.

portant theory for such integration is Fuzzy Sets and Fuzzy Logic. Yen [33] is the first who combines fuzzy logic with term subsumption languages and proposes a fuzzy extension to a very restricted DL, called $\mathcal{FTSL}^-$. The corresponding standard DL $\mathcal{FL}^-$, as defined in [5], is actually a sublanguage of $\mathcal{ALC}$, and only allows primitive concepts, primitive roles, defined concepts formed from concept intersection, value restriction and existential quantification. Semantically, the min function is used to interpret the intersection between two $\mathcal{FTSL}^-$ concepts. The knowledge base in $\mathcal{FTSL}^-$ includes only fuzzy terminological knowledge in the form of $C \sqsubseteq D$, where C and D are two fuzzy concepts. The inference problem Yen is interested in is testing subsumption relationships between fuzzy concepts. A concept D subsumes a concept C if and only if D is a fuzzy superset of C, i.e., given two concepts C, D defined in the fuzzy DL, $C \sqsubseteq D$ is viewed as $\forall x.C(x) \leq D(x)$. Thus, the subsumption relationship itself is a crisp Yes/No test. A structural subsumption algorithm is given in his work. Tresp and Molitor [32] consider a more general extension of $\mathcal{ALC}$ to many-valued logics, called $\mathcal{ALC}_{\mathcal{FM}}$. The language $\mathcal{ALC}_{\mathcal{FM}}$ allows constructors including conjunction, disjunction, manipulator, value restriction, and existential qualification in the definition of complex concepts. They define the semantics of a value restriction differently from Yen's work. This work also starts addressing the issue of a fuzzy semantics of modifiers M, such as *mostly*, *more or less*, and *very*, which are unary operators that can be applied to concepts. An example is *(very)TallPerson(John)*, which means that "John is a very tall person". In both of the work by [33] and [32], knowledge bases include only fuzzy terminological knowledge. But different from Yen's work, Tresp and Molitor are interested in determining fuzzy subsumption between fuzzy concepts, i.e., given concepts C, D, they want to know to which degree C is a subset of D. Such a problem is reduced to the problem of determining an adequate evaluation for an extended ABox which corresponds to a solution for a system of inequations. The degree of subsumption between concepts is then determined as the minimum of all values obtained for some specific variable. [32] presents a sound and complete reasoning algorithm for $\mathcal{ALC}_{\mathcal{FM}}$ which basically is an extension of each completion rule in the classical tableau algorithm for standard ALC. Another fuzzy extension of $\mathcal{ALC}$ is due to [30]. In this work, the interpretation of the Boolean operators and the quantifiers is based on the min and max functions, and the knowledge base includes both fuzzy terminological and fuzzy assertional knowledge. That is, the ABox assertions are equipped with a degree from [0,1]. Thus in this context, one may also want to find out to which degree other assertions follow from the ABox, which is called a *fuzzy entailment problem*. A decision algorithm for such fuzzy entailment problems in this fuzzy extension of $\mathcal{ALC}$ is presented. Similar to Yen, [30] is interested in crisp subsumption of fuzzy concepts, with the result being a crisp Yes or No, instead of a fuzzy subsumption relationship. Although [31] addresses the syntax and semantics for more expressive fuzzy DLs, no reasoning algorithm for the fuzzy subsumption between fuzzy concepts is given in his work. [25] consider modifiers in a fuzzy extension of the Description Logic $\mathcal{ALCQ}$, but the knowledge base in their work only consists of the TBox. They also present an algorithm which calculates the satisfiability interval for a fuzzy concept in fuzzy $\mathcal{ALCQ}$. The recent work in [29] presents an expressive fuzzy DL language with the underlying standard DL $\mathcal{SHIN}$. As we will explain in the following section, Fuzzy Logic is in fact a family of multi-valued logics derived from Fuzzy Set Theory. Identified by the specific fuzzy operations applied in the logic, the Fuzzy Logic family consists of Zadeh Logic, Product Logic, Gödel Logic, and more. Generally speaking, all existing work uses the basic fuzzy logic known as Zadeh Logic. Surprisingly enough, little work uses other logics with the exception of [4], which considers concrete domains and provide an algorithm for fuzzy $\mathcal{ALC}(\mathcal{D})$ under product semantics, and the work by Hájek [8, 9], which considers a fuzzy DL under arbitrary t-norms with $\mathcal{ALC}$ as the underlying DL language.

In this chapter, in order to extend standard DLs with Fuzzy Logic in a broad sense, we propose a generalized form of norm-parameterized Fuzzy Description Logics. The main contributions of this chapter can be explained as follows. First, unlike other approaches except [31], which only deal with crisp subsumption of fuzzy concepts, our Fuzzy Description Logic deals with fuzzy subsumption of fuzzy concepts and addresses its semantics. We argue that fuzzy subsumption of fuzzy concepts permits more adequate modeling of the uncertain knowledge existing in real world applications. Second, almost all of the existing work employs a single set of fuzzy operations, which limits their applicability in various real-world system and knowledge requirements. We propose a set of t-norms and s-norms in the semantics of our norm-parameterized Fuzzy Description Logics, so that the interpretation of complex concept descriptions can cover different logics in the Fuzzy Logic family, such as Zadeh Logic, Lukasiewicz Logic, Product Logic, Gödel Logic, and Yager Logic. Most importantly, Product Logic interprets fuzzy intersection as the inner product of the truth degrees between fuzzy concepts and fuzzy union as the product-sum operation. It thus broadens Fuzzy Logic and sets up a connection between Fuzzy Logic in the narrow sense and Probability Theory [22]. Third, the notion of fuzzy subsumption was first proposed in [31] and used in the forms $\geq n$ and $\leq n$, where $n \in [0,1]$, but it was left unsolved how to do reasoning on fuzzy knowledge bases. In this chapter, we define a Fuzzy Description Logic with a unified uncertainty intervals of the form $[l, u]$, where $l, u \in [0,1]$ and $l \leq u$, and present its reasoning procedure.

Besides the work based on Fuzzy Sets and Fuzzy Logic, there is also some work based on other approaches. Probabilistic Description Logics [16][17][19] are built on Probability Theory; [11, 27] follows Possibility Theory; and [15] proposes a framework called $\mathcal{ALCu}$, which extends the standard DL $\mathcal{ALC}$ with a combination of different uncertainties. Due to space limitation, we point readers to our work in [35] for an in-depth review of various uncertainty extensions to Description Logics.

The current chapter presents the whole methodology of our proposed Fuzzy Description Logic, including the underlying Fuzzy Logics, the syntax, the semantics, the knowledge bases, the reasoning procedure, and its decidability. The rest of the chapter is organized as follows. Section 2.2 briefly introduces the syntax and semantics of the standard Description Logic $\mathcal{ALCN}$. Section 2.3 reviews Fuzzy Logic and Fuzzy Set Theory. Section 2.4 presents the syntax and semantics of the expressive Fuzzy Description Logic $f\mathcal{ALCN}$, as well as the components of knowledge bases using this knowledge representation formalism. Section 2.5 explains different reasoning tasks on the knowledge base. Section 2.6 addresses General Concept Inclusion (GCI) axioms, the $f\mathcal{ALCN}$ concept Negation Normal Form (NNF), and the ABox augmentation. In Section 2.7, we put forward the reasoning procedure for the consistency checking problem of an $f\mathcal{ALCN}$ knowledge base and illustrate fuzzy completion rules. Section 2.8 proves the decidability of the reasoning procedure by addressing its soundness, completeness, and termination. Finally, in the last section, we summarize our main results and give an outlook on future research .

2.2 Preliminaries

We briefly introduce Description Logics (DLs) in the current section. Their syntax and semantics in terms of classical First Order Logic are also presented. As a notational convention, we will use a, b, x for individuals, A for an atomic concept, C and D for concept descriptions, R for atomic roles.

Concept descriptions in $\mathcal{ALCN}$ are of the form:

$C \rightarrow \top|\bot|A|\neg A|\neg C|C \sqcap D|C \sqcup D|\exists R.C|\forall R.C| \geq nR| \leq nR$

The special concept names $\top$ (*top*) and $\bot$ (*bottom*) represent the most general and least general concepts, respectively.

Table 2.1 Syntax and Semantics of $\mathcal{ALCN}$ constructors

DL Constructor	DL Syntax	Semantics
top concept	$\top$	$\triangle^I$
bottom concept	$\bot$	$\emptyset$
atomic concept	A	$A^I \subseteq \triangle^I$
concept	C	$C^I \subseteq \triangle^I$
atomic negation	$\neg A$	$\triangle^I \setminus A^I$
concept negation	$\neg C$	$\triangle^I \setminus C^I$
concept conjunction	$C \sqcap D$	$C^I \cap D^I$
concept disjunction	$C \sqcup D$	$C^I \cup D^I$
exists restriction	$\exists R.C$	$\{x \in \triangle^I \mid \exists y. <x, y> \in R^I \wedge y \in C^I\}$
value restriction	$\forall R.C$	$\{x \in \triangle^I \mid \forall y. <x, y> \in R^I \rightarrow y \in C^I\}$
at-most restriction	$\leq nR$	$\{x \in \triangle^I \mid \sharp\{y \in \triangle^I \mid R^I(x, y)\} \leq n\}$
at-least restriction	$\geq nR$	$\{x \in \triangle^I \mid \sharp\{y \in \triangle^I \mid R^I(x, y)\} \geq n\}$

DLs have a model theoretic semantics, which is defined by interpreting concepts as sets of individuals and roles as sets of pairs of individuals. An interpretation I is a pair $I = (\triangle^I, \cdot^I)$ consisting of a domain $\triangle^I$ which is a non-empty set and an interpretation function $\cdot^I$ which maps each individual x into an element of $\triangle^I$ ($x^I \in \triangle^I$), each concept C into a subset of $\triangle^I$ ($C^I \subseteq \triangle^I$) and each atomic role R into a subset of $\triangle^I \times \triangle^I$ ($R^I \subseteq \triangle^I \times \triangle^I$). The semantic interpretations of complex concept descriptions are shown in Table 2.1. In the at-most restriction and the at-least restriction, $\sharp\{\cdot\}$ denotes the cardinality of a set.

A knowledge base in DLs consists of two parts: the terminological box (TBox $\mathcal{T}$) and the assertional box (ABox $\mathcal{A}$). There are two kinds of assertions in the ABox of a DL knowledge bas: concept individual and role individual. A concept individual assertion has the form $C(a)$ while a role individual assertion is $R(a,b)$. The semantics of assertions is interpreted as the assertion $C(a)$ (resp. $R(a,b)$) is satisfied by I iff $a \in C^I$ (resp. $(a,b) \in R^I$).

The TBox of a DL knowledge base has several kinds of axioms. A concept inclusion axiom is an expression of subsumption of the form $C \sqsubseteq D$. The semantics of a concept inclusion axiom is interpreted as the axiom is satisfied by I iff $\forall x \in \Delta^I, x \in C^I \rightarrow x \in D^I$. A concept equivalence axiom is an expression of the form $C \equiv D$. Its semantics is that the axiom is satisfied by I iff $\forall x \in \Delta^I, x \in C^I \rightarrow x \in D^I$ and $x \in D^I \rightarrow x \in C^I$.

2.3 Fuzzy Set Theory and Fuzzy Logic

Fuzzy Set Theory was first introduced by Zadeh [34] as an extension to the classical notion of a set to capture the inherent vagueness (the lack of crisp boundaries of sets). Fuzzy Logic is a form of multi-valued logic derived from Fuzzy Set Theory to deal with reasoning that is approximate rather than precise. Just as in Fuzzy Set Theory the set membership values can range between 0 and 1, in Fuzzy Logic the degree of truth of a statement can range between 0 and 1 and is not constrained to the two truth values $\{false, true\}$ as in classical predicate logic [24]. Formally, a fuzzy set X is characterized by a membership function $\mu(x)$ which assigns a value in the real unit interval [0,1] to each element $x \in X$, mathematically notated as $\mu : X \rightarrow [0,1]$. $\mu(x)$ gives us a degree of an element x belonging to a set X. Such degrees can be computed based on some specific membership functions which can be linear or non-linear. Figure 2.1 shows the most general form of linear membership functions, also known as a trapezoidal membership function. Formally, we define it as *trapezoidal(a,b,c,d)* with the range of the membership function being $[k_1, k_2]$. Other linear membership functions can be regarded as its special forms. Specifically, if *a=b* and *c=d*, it defines a crisp membership function, *crisp(a,c)*. If *a=b=0*, it defines a left-shoulder membership function *leftshoulder(c,d)*. Similarly, it defines a right-shoulder membership function *rightshoulder(a,b)* when *c=d=∞*. It defines a triangular membership function *triangular(a,b,d)* if *b=c*.

For example, as shown in Figure 2.2, the fuzzy set *Young* is defined by a left_shoulder membership function *leftshoulder(30,50)*, while the fuzzy set *Old* is defined by a right_shoulder membership function *rightshoulder(40,70)*. Assume we know, John is 45 years old. Therefore, we have $Young(John) = 0.25$ which means the statement "John is young" has a truth value of 0.25. We also have $Old(John) = 0.17$ which means the statement "John is old" has a truth value of 0.17. But more often, we want to make vaguer statements, saying that "John is old" has a truth value of

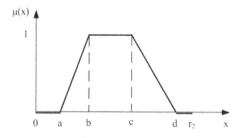

Trapezoidal Membership Function

Fig. 2.1 Fuzzy Membership Function

greater than or equal to 0.17. Such a statement can be written as $Old(John) \geq 0.17$. Another kind of often-used statement is less than or equal to, e.g., the truth degree for "John is young" is less than or equal to 0.25 ($Young(John) \leq 0.25$). In order to describe all of the above statements in a uniform form, we employ an interval syntax $[l, u]$ with $0 \leq l \leq u \leq 1$. Then $Young(John) = 0.25$ can be written as $Young(John)$ $[0, 0.25]$, $Young(John) \leq 0.25$ as $Young(John)$ $(0, 0.25]$, $Old(John) \geq 0.17$ as $Old(John)$ $[0.17, 1]$.

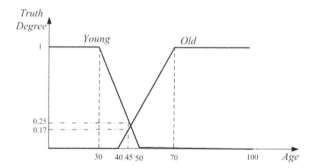

Fig. 2.2 A membership function for the concept Young

A fuzzy relation R over two fuzzy sets X_1 and X_2 is defined by a function $R : X_1 \times X_2 \to [0, 1]$. For example, the statement that "John drives 150" has a truth value of greater than or equal to 0.6 can be defined as $drives(John, 150)$ $[0.6, 1]$.

In the context of fuzzy sets and fuzzy relations, Fuzzy Logic extends the Boolean operations complement, union, and intersection defined on crisp sets and relations. The fuzzy operations in Fuzzy Logic are interpreted as mathematical functions over the unit interval [0,1]. The mathematical functions for fuzzy intersection are usually called t-norms ($t(x, y)$) and those for fuzzy union are called s-norms ($s(x, y)$). All mathematical functions satisfying certain mathematical properties can serve as t-norms and s-norms. For example, in particular, a binary operation t(x,y) on the interval [0,1] is a t-norm if it is commutative, associative, non-decreasing and 1 is its unit element. The most well-known fuzzy operations for t-norms and s-norms include Zadeh Logic, Lukasiewicz Logic, Product Logic, Gödel Logic, and Yager Logic, as summarized in Table 2.2[2].

Table 2.2 Fuzzy Operations

	Zadeh Logic	Lukasiewicz Logic	Product Logic	Gödel Logic	Yager Logic
t-norm $(t(x,y))$	$\min(x,y)$	$\max(x+y-1,0)$	$x \cdot y$	$\min(x,y)$	$min(1,(x^w+y^w)^{\frac{1}{w}})$
s-norm $(s(x,y))$	$\max(x,y)$	$\min(x+y,1)$	$x+y-x\cdot y$	$\max(x,y)$	$1-min(1,((1-x)^w+(1-y)^w)^{\frac{1}{w}})$

Mathematical functions for fuzzy negation ($\neg x$) have to be non-increasing, and assign 0 to 1 and vice versa. There are at least two fuzzy complement operations satisfying the requirements. One is Lukasiewicz negation ($\neg x = 1 - x$) and the other is Gödel negation ($\neg x = \begin{cases} 1 & if\ x = 0 \\ 0 & else \end{cases}$).

Fuzzy implication (x⇒y) is also of fundamental importance for Fuzzy Logic but is sometimes disregarded, as we can use a straightforward way to define implication from fuzzy union and fuzzy negation using the corresponding tautology of classical logic; such implications are called S-implications (also known as the Kleene-Dienes implication). That is, denoting the s-norm as s(x,y) and the negation as $\neg x$, we have $x \Rightarrow y \equiv s(\neg x, y)$.

Another way to define implication is R-implications [10]: an R-implication is defined as a residuum of a t-norm; denoting the t-norm t(x,y) and the residuum ⇒, we have $x \Rightarrow y \equiv \max\{z | t(x,z) \leq y\}$. This is well-defined only if the t-norm is left-continuous.

2.4 Fuzzy Description Logic

In this section, we present the syntax and semantics of $f\mathcal{ALCN}$, as well as $f\mathcal{ALCN}$ knowledge bases.

---

[2] w satisfies $0 < w < \infty$, $w = 2$ is mostly used.

2.4.1 Syntax of fALCN

Definition 1 *Let* $\mathbf{N_C}$ *be a set of concept names. Let* $\mathbf{R}$ *be a set of role names. The set of fALCN roles only consists of atomic roles. The set of fALCN concepts is the smallest set such that*

1. *every concept name is a concept and*
2. *if* C *and* D *are fALCN concepts and* R *is a fALCN role, then* $(\neg C)$, $(C \sqcap D)$, $(C \sqcup D)$, $(\exists R.C)$, $(\forall R.C)$, $(\geq R)$, *and* $(\leq R)$ *are concepts.*

We can see that the syntax of this Fuzzy Description Logic is identical to that of the standard Description Logic $\mathcal{ALCN}$. But in $f\mathcal{ALCN}$, the concepts and roles are defined as fuzzy concepts (i.e. fuzzy sets) and fuzzy roles (i.e. fuzzy relations), respectively. A fuzzy concept here can be either a *primitive concept* defined by a membership function, or a *defined concept* constructed using the above fuzzy concept constructors.

2.4.2 Semantics of fALCN

Similar to standard DL, the semantics of $f\mathcal{ALCN}$ is based on the notion of interpretation. Classical interpretations are extended to the notion of fuzzy interpretations by using membership functions that range over the interval [0,1].

Definition 2 *A fuzzy interpretation* I *is a pair* $I = (\Delta^I, \cdot^I)$ *consisting of a domain* Δ^I, *which is a non-empty set, and a fuzzy interpretation function* $\cdot^I$, *which maps each individual* x *into an element of* Δ^I *(*$x \in \Delta^I$*), each concept* C *into a membership function* $C^I : \Delta^I \to [0, 1]$, *and each atomic role* R *into a membership function* $R^I : \Delta^I \times \Delta^I \to [0, 1]$.

Next we define the semantics of $f\mathcal{ALCN}$ constructors, including the top concept ($\top$), the bottom concept ($\bot$), concept negation ($\neg$), concept conjunction ($\sqcap$), concept disjunction ($\sqcup$), exists restriction ($\exists$), value restriction ($\forall$), and number restrictions ($\leq, \geq$). We explain how to apply the Fuzzy Logic operations of Table 2.2 to $f\mathcal{ALCN}$ with some examples.

The semantics of the top concept $\top$ is the greatest element in the domain Δ^I, that is, $\top^I = 1$. Note that, in standard DL, the top concept $\top \equiv A \sqcup \neg A$, while in $f\mathcal{ALCN}$, such an equivalence is not always true. After applying the s-norms $s(x, \neg x)$ of different logics in Table 2.2 on $A \sqcup \neg A$, only the result in Lukasiewicz Logic is still equal to 1. Thus, in $f\mathcal{ALCN}$, we have to explicitly define the top concept, stating that the truth degree of x in $\top$ is 1. Similarly, the bottom concept $\bot$ is the least element in the domain, defined as $\bot^I = 0$.

Concept negation (also known as concept complement) $\neg C$ is interpreted with a mathematical function which satisfies

1. $\neg \top^I(x) = 0, \neg \bot^I(x) = 1$.

2. self-inverse, i.e., $(\neg\neg C)^I(x) = C^I(x)$.

As we have discussed in Section 2.3, both Lukasiewicz negation and Gödel negation satisfy these properties. In our approach, we adopt Lukasiewicz negation ($\neg x = 1 - x$) as it reflects human being's intuitively understanding of the meaning of concept negation. For example, if we have that the statement "John is young" has a truth value of greater than or equal to 0.8 ($Young(John)$ $[0.8, 1]$), and after applying Lukasiewicz negation operator to the statement "John is not young", we have $\neg Young(John) = \neg[0.8, 1] = [0, 0.2]$.

The interpretation of concept conjunction (also called concept intersection) is defined by a t-norm as $(C \sqcap D)^I(x) = t(C^I(x), D^I(x))$ $(\forall x \in \Delta^I)$, that is, under the fuzzy interpretation I, the truth degree of x being an element of the concept $(C \sqcap D)$ is equal to the result of applying a t-norm function on the truth degree of x being an element of the concept C and the truth degree of x being an element of the concept D. For example, if we have $Young(John)$ $[0.8, 1]$ and $Tall(John)$ $[0.7, 1]$, and assume the minimum function in Zadeh Logic or Gödel Logic is chosen as the t-norm, then the truth degree that John is both young and tall is

$(Young \sqcap Tall)(John) = t_Z([0.8, 1], [0.7, 1]) = [0.7, 1]$.

If the multiplication function in Product Logic is chosen as the t-norm, then the degree of truth that John is both young and tall is

$(Young \sqcap Tall)(John) = t_P([0.8, 1], [0.7, 1]) = [0.56, 1]$.

Under Lukasiewicz Logic, the truth degree is $t_L([0.8, 1], [0.7, 1]) = [0.5, 1]$, while under Yager Logic with $w = 2$, the truth degree is $t_Y([0.8, 1], [0.7, 1]) = [1, 1]$ as $\min((0.8^2 + 0.7^2)^{1/2}, 1) = 1$ and $\min((1^2 + 1^2)^1/2, 1) = 1$.

The interpretation of concept disjunction (union) is defined by a s-norm as $(C \sqcup D)^I(x) = s(C^I(x), D^I(x))$ $(\forall x \in \Delta^I)$, that is, under the fuzzy interpretation I, the truth degree of x being an element of the concept $(C \sqcup D)$ is equal to the result of applying an s-norm function on the truth degree of x being an element of the concept C and the truth degree of x being an element of the concept D.

For example, if we have $Young(John)$ $[0.8, 1]$ and $Tall(John)$ $[0.7, 1]$, then under Zadeh Logic, the degree of truth that John is young or tall is $(Young \sqcup Tall)(John) = s_Z([0.8, 1], [0.7, 1]) = [0.8, 1]$. Under Product Logic, it is $(Young \sqcup Tall)(John) = s_P([0.8, 1], [0.7, 1]) = [0.94, 1]$. Under Lukasiewicz Logic, the truth degree is $S_L([0.8, 1], [0.7, 1]) = [1, 1]$, while under Yager Logic with $w = 2$, the truth degree is $s_Y([0.8, 1], [0.7, 1]) = [0.64, 1]$.

The semantics of exists restriction $\exists R.C$ is the result of viewing $\exists R.C$ as the open first order formula $\exists y.R(x, y) \wedge C(y)$ and the existential quantifier $\exists$ is viewed as a disjunction over the elements of the domain, defined as sup (supremum or least upper bound). Therefore, we define

$(\exists R.C)^I(x) = \sup_{y \in \Delta^I}\{t(R^I(x, y), C^I(y))\}$

Suppose in an ABox A_1, we have

$hasDisease(P001, Cancer)$ $[0.2, 1]$, $VitalDisease(Cancer)$ $[0.5, 1]$,

$hasDisease(P001, Cold)$ $[0.6, 1]$, $VitalDisease(Cold)$ $[0.1, 1]$.

Further we assume the minimum function in Zadeh Logic is chosen as the t-norm, then

$(\exists R.C)^I(x) = \sup\{t_Z(hasDisease(P001, Cancer), VitalDisease(Cancer)),$
$\qquad t_Z(hasDisease(P001, Cold), VitalDisease(Cold))\}$
$= \sup\{t_Z([0.2, 1], [0.5, 1]), t_Z([0.6, 1], [0.1, 1])\}$
$= \sup\{[0.2, 1], [0.1, 1]\} = [0.1, 1]$

That is, the truth degree for the complex concept assertion ($\exists$ *hasDisease. VitalDisease*) (*P001*) is greater than or equal to 0.1. Similarly, we can get the results under other logics.

A value restriction $\forall R.C$ is viewed as an implication of the form $\forall y \in \Delta^I$, $R^I(x, y) \rightarrow C^I(x)$. As explained in Section 2.3, both Kleene-Dienes implication and R-implication can be applied in the context of fuzzy logic. Following the semantics proposed by Hajek [7], we interpret $\forall$ as inf (infimum or greatest lower bound). Furthermore, in classical logic, $a \rightarrow b$ is a shorthand for $\neg a \lor b$; we can thus interpret $\rightarrow$ as the Kleene-Dienes implication and finally get its semantics as $(\forall R.C)^I(x) = \inf_{y \in \Delta^I}\{s(\neg R^I(x, y), C^I(y))\}$.

For example, with the ABox A_1 and Product Logic, we have
$(\forall R.C)^I(x) = \inf\{s_P(\neg hasDisease(P001, Cancer), VitalDisease(Cancer)),$
$\qquad s_P(\neg hasDisease(P001, Cold), VitalDisease(Cold))\}$
$= \inf\{s_P([0, 0.8], [0.5, 1]), s_P([0, 0.4], [0.1, 1])\}$
$= \inf\{[0.5, 1], [0.1, 1]\} = [0.5, 1]$

Similarly, we can get the results under other logics.

A fuzzy at-least restriction is of the form $\geq nR$, whose semantics
$(\geq nR)^I(x) = \sup_{y_1,\ldots,y_n \in \Delta^I, y_i \neq y_j, 1 \leq i < j \leq n} t_{i=1}^n\{R^I(x, y_i)\}$
is derived from its first order reformulation
$\exists y_1, \ldots, y_n. \bigwedge_{i=1}^n R(x, y_i) \bigwedge \bigwedge_{1 \leq i < j \leq n} y_i \neq y_j.$
The semantics states that there are at least n distinct individuals $(y_1, \ldots, y_n)$ all of which satisfy $R_I(x, y_i)$ to some given degree.

Furthermore, we define the semantics of a fuzzy at-most restriction as
$(\leq nR)^I(x) = \neg(\geq (n+1)R)^I(x)$
$= \neg \sup_{y_1,\ldots,y_{n+1} \in \Delta^I, y_i \neq y_j, 1 \leq i < j \leq n+1} t_{i=1}^{n+1}\{R^I(x, y_i)\}$
$= \inf_{y_1,\ldots,y_{n+1} \in \Delta^I, y_i \neq y_j, 1 \leq i < j \leq n+1} s_{i=1}^{n+1}\{\neg R^I(x, y_i)\}$
The semantics states that for $n + 1$ role assertions $R_I(x, y_i)$ $(1 \leq i \leq n+1)$ that can be formed, at least one satisfies $\neg R_I(x, y_i)$ to some given degree.

Note that, the semantics of fuzzy at-least restriction (respectively, fuzzy at-most restriction) in [31] and [29] is a special case of our fuzzy at-least restriction (respectively, fuzzy at-most restriction).

An alternative view of the semantics of a fuzzy at-most number restriction is that there are at most n unique individuals $(y_1, \ldots, y_n)$ that satisfy $R_I(x, y_i)$ to some given degree. For example, $\leq 2R$ [0.8,1] means that there are at most two role instance assertions about any individual a: $R(a, b_1)$ and $R(a, b_2)$. Moreover, assuming $x_{R(a,b_1)}$ is the truth degree of $R(a, b_1)$ and $x_{R(a,b_2)}$ is the truth degree of $R(a, b_2)$, both $x_{R(a,b_1)}=[0.8,1]$ and $x_{R(a,b_2)}=[0.8,1]$ hold, but $b_1 \neq b_2$ does not necessarily hold. Furthermore, for $\leq nR$ $[l, u]$, if we find there are $n + 1$ assertions satisfying the truth degree constraints, we have to find some individuals that can be merged, similar to the case in standard DL [1]. If we find there are more than n different individuals after merging, we say the concept $\leq 2R$ [0.8,1] is unsatisfiable.

It is easy to see that these fuzzy semantics generalize the crisp case of standard DL where the truth degree of all assertions is [1,1].

The semantics of the complex concept descriptions axioms for $f\mathcal{ALCN}$ are summarized in Table 2.3.

Table 2.3 Syntax and Semantics of $f\mathcal{ALCN}$ constructors

Constructor	Syntax	Semantics
top concept	$\top$	$\top^I = 1$
bottom concept	$\bot$	$\bot^I = 0$
atomic negation	$\neg A$	$(\neg A)^I(x) = \neg A^I(x)$
atomic negation	$\neg C$	$(\neg C)^I(x) = \neg C^I(x)$
concept conjunction	$C \sqcap D$	$(C \sqcap D)^I = t(C^I(x), D^I(x))$
concept disjunction	$C \sqcup D$	$(C \sqcup D)^I = s(C^I(x), D^I(x))$
exists restriction disjunction	$\exists R.C$	$(\exists R.C)^I(x) = \sup_{y \in \Delta^I}\{t(R^I(x,y), C^I(y))\}$
value restriction	$\forall R.C$	$(\forall R.C)^I(x) = \inf_{y \in \Delta^I}\{s(\neg R^I(x,y), C^I(y))\}$
at-least restriction	$\geq nR$	$(\geq nR)^I(x) = \sup_{y_1,\ldots,y_n \in \Delta^I, y_i \neq y_j, 1 \leq i < j \leq n} t_{i=1}^n\{R^I(x,y_i)\}$
at-most restriction	$\leq nR$	$(\leq nR)^I x \equiv \neg(\geq (n+1)R)^I(x)$

2.4.3 Knowledge Bases in $f\mathcal{ALCN}$

A fuzzy knowledge base in $f\mathcal{ALCN}$ consists of two parts: the fuzzy terminological box (TBox $\mathcal{T}$) and the fuzzy assertional box (ABox $\mathcal{A}$). The TBox contains several kinds of axioms. A fuzzy concept inclusion axiom has the form of $C \sqsubseteq D \ [l, u]$ with $0 \leq l \leq u \leq 1$, which describes that the subsumption degree of truth between concepts C and D is from l to u.

For example, the axiom

$Professor \sqsubseteq (\exists publishes. Journalpaper \sqcap \exists teaches.Graduatecourse) \ [0.8, 1]$

states that the concept *professor* is subsumed by entities that *publish* journal papers and *teach* graduate courses with a truth degree of at least 0.8.

In order to simplify the reasoning task of subsumption checking, some work on DL restricts a terminological box to introduction axioms of the form $A \sqsubseteq C$ where A is an atomic concept and C is a concept description. In this research, we permit general concept inclusion axioms (GCIs). The FOL translation of a general concept inclusion axiom $C \sqsubseteq D$ has the form $\forall x.C(x) \rightarrow D(x)$; therefore, its semantics is defined as

$$(C \sqsubseteq D)^I(x) = \inf_{x \in \Delta^I} C^I(x) \rightarrow D^I(x) = \inf_{x \in \Delta^I}\{s(\neg C^I(x), D^I(x))\}.$$

That is, for a fuzzy interpretation I, I satisfies $C \sqsubseteq D \; [l, u]$ iff $\forall x \in \Delta^I, l \leq \inf_{x \in \Delta^I} \{s(\neg C^I(x), D^I(x))\} \leq u$. For the above example, it means under every fuzzy interpretation I of the knowledge base, we have

$$0.8 \leq s(x_{\neg Professor}, x_{(\exists publishes.Journalpaper \sqcap \exists teaches.Graduatecourse)}) \leq 1.$$

We also permit a fuzzy concept equivalence axioms of the form $C \equiv D$ with the semantics $C^I = D^I$.

There are three kinds of assertions in the ABox: concept individual, role individual, and individual inequality. A fuzzy concept assertion and a fuzzy role assertion are of the form $C(a) \; [l, u]$ and $R(a, b) \; [l, u]$, respectively. An individual inequality in the $f\mathcal{ALCN}$ ABox is identical to standard DLs and has the form $a \neq b$ for a pair of individuals a and b. Given a fuzzy Interpretation I, I satisfies $C(a) \; [l, u]$ iff $l \leq C^I(a) \leq u$, I satisfies $R(a, b) \; [l, u]$ iff $l \leq R^I(a, b) \leq u$, and I satisfies $a \neq b$ iff $a \neq b$ under I.

2.5 Reasoning Tasks

We are interested in several reasoning tasks for an $f\mathcal{ALCN}$ knowledge base. First, **consistency checking** refers to the reasoning task of determining whether the knowledge base is consistent.

In order to define what it means for a knowledge base to be consistent, we first explain the general idea of how the $f\mathcal{ALCN}$ reasoning procedure works and then give several formal definitions. The reasoning procedure derives new assertions through applying completion rules (cf. Table 2.4) in an arbitrary order, adds derived assertions to an extended ABox A_i^ε, and at the same time adds corresponding constraints that incorporate the semantics of the assertions to a constraint set $\mathcal{C}_j$ in the form of (linear or non-linear) inequations. The reasoning procedure stops when either A_i^ε contains a clash or no further rule can be applied to A_i^ε.

Definition 3 *Let A_i^ε be an extended ABox obtained by applications of the completion rules. Let $\mathcal{C}_i$ be a constraint set obtained by applications of the completion rules. An extended ABox A_i^ε is called **complete** if no more completion rule can be applied to A_i^ε.*

Definition 4 *For a constraint set $\mathcal{C}_i$ with respect to a complete ABox A_i^ε, let $Var(\mathcal{C}_i)$ be the set of variables occurring in $\mathcal{C}_i$. If the system of inequations in $\mathcal{C}_i$ is solvable, the result of the constraint set, i.e., the mapping $\Phi : Var(\mathcal{C}) \to [0, 1]$, is called a **solution**.*

Definition 5 *We say there is a **clash** in the extended ABox A_i^ε iff one of the following situations occurs:*

1. $\{\bot(a) \; [l, u]\} \subseteq A_i^\varepsilon$ *and* $0 < l \leq u$
2. $\{\top(a) \; [l, u]\} \subseteq A_i^\varepsilon$ *and* $l \leq u < 1$
3. $\{A(a) \; [l_1, u_1], A(a) \; [l_2, u_2]\} \subseteq A_i^\varepsilon$ *and* $(u_1 < l_2$ *or* $u_2 < l_1)$

4. $\{(\leq nR)(a)\ [l, u]\} \cup \{R(a, b_i)\ [l_i, u_i]|1 \leq i \leq n + 1\} \cup \{b_i \neq b_j|1 \leq i < j \leq n + 1\} \subseteq A_i^{\varepsilon}$ and $\{[l_i, u_i] \subseteq [l, u]|1 \leq i \leq n + 1\}$

For example, if a knowledge base contains both assertions *Tall(John)* [0,0.2] and *Tall(John)* [0.7,1], since 0.2<0.7, the third clash will be triggered.

Note that we do not make the unique names assumption for individuals in the ABox. Since number restrictions may lead to the identification of different individual names, we therefore define explicit inequality assertions of the form: $b_i \neq b_j$ for two individuals b_i and b_j, as in clash 4.

The following is our definition of a model of an $f\mathcal{ALCN}$ knowledge base.

Definition 6 *Let A_i^{ε} be the extended ABox obtained by applications of the completion rules. Let $I = (\Delta^I, \cdot^I)$ be a fuzzy interpretation, $\Phi : Var(\mathcal{C}) \rightarrow [0,1]$ be a solution, x_{α} be the variable representing the truth degree of assertion α. For each concept assertion $C(a)$, $C^I(a) = \Phi(x_{C(a)})$. For each role assertion $R(a, b)$, $R^I(a, b) = \Phi(x_{R(a,b)})$. The pair $< I, \Phi >$ is a **model** of the extended ABox A_i^{ε} if the following properties hold:*
   $\forall a, b \in \Delta^I$,

1. *if $\{(\neg C)(a)\} \in A_i^{\varepsilon}$, then $\Phi(x_{(\neg C)(a)}) = 1 - \Phi(x_{C(a)})$,*
2. *if $\{(C \sqcap D)(a)\} \in A_i^{\varepsilon}$, then $\Phi(x_{(C \sqcap D)(a)}) = t(\Phi(x_{C(a)}), \Phi(x_{D(a)}))$,*
3. *if $\{(C \sqcup D)(a)\} \in A_i^{\varepsilon}$, then $\Phi(x_{(C \sqcup D)(a)}) = s(\Phi(x_{C(a)}), \Phi(x_{D(a)}))$,*
4. *if $\{(\exists R.C)(a)\} \in A_i^{\varepsilon}$, then $\Phi(x_{(\exists R.C)(a)}) = \sup_{b \in \Delta^I}\{t(\Phi(x_{R(a,b)}), \Phi(x_{C(a)}))\}$,*
5. *if $\{(\forall R.C)(a)\} \in A_i^{\varepsilon}$, then $\Phi(x_{(\forall R.C)(a)}) = \inf_{b \in \Delta^I}\{s(1 - \Phi(x_{R(a,b)}), \Phi(x_{C(a)}))\}$,*
6. *if $\{(\geq nR)(a)\} \in A_i^{\varepsilon}$, then there are at least n distinct individuals $(y_1, \ldots, y_n)$ all of which satisfy $\Phi(x_{R_I(x,y_i)})$, and*
7. *if $\{(\leq nR)(a)\} \in A_i^{\varepsilon}$, then there are at most n distinct individuals $(y_1, \ldots, y_n)$ all of which satisfy $\Phi(x_{R_I(x,y_i)})$.*

Definition 7 *Let $KB = < T, A >$ be a $f\mathcal{ALCN}$ knowledge base where T is the fuzzy TBox and A is the fuzzy ABox. Let $I = (\Delta^I, \cdot^I)$ be a fuzzy interpretation, and $\Phi : Var(\mathcal{C}) \rightarrow [0, 1]$ be a solution. If there exists a model $< I, \Phi >$ for the extended ABox resulting from $KB = < T, A >$, we say the knowledge base $KB = < T, A >$ is **consistent**. If there is no such model, we call the knowledge base inconsistent.*

The second reasoning task is **instance checking**, which determines the degree to which an assertion is true. That is, let α be an assertion $C(a)$. We want to check whether $KB \models \alpha$ and to what degree the entailment is true. Such a problem can be reduced to the consistency problem. We first check whether $KB \cup \{\neg C(a)\ (0, 1]\}$ is consistent, and then solve the corresponding constraint set.

The third reasoning task is **subsumption checking**, which determines the subsumption degree between concepts C and D. That is, let α be an assertion $C \sqsubseteq D$. We want to check whether $KB \models \alpha$ and its truth degree. Such a problem can also be reduced to the consistency problem. We first check whether $KB \cup \{C \sqcap \neg D\ (0, 1]\}$ is consistent, and then solve the corresponding constraint set.

Another interesting reasoning task is the classification of $f\mathcal{ALCN}$ knowledge base, i.e. computing all fuzzy subsumptions between concepts in a given knowledge base. An intuitive way is to choose each pair of concepts and check their subsumption. Classification problem can thus be further reduced to consistency checking. There are some ways to optimize such a reasoning procedure for classification, but we do not consider this issue in this chapter.

2.6 GCI, NNF, and ABox Augmentation

For the following note that, since GCI is the general form of concept subsumption, and concept equation is the general form of concept definition, we only use the general forms here. Let C and D be concept descriptions, R be roles, a and b be individuals. In this section we discuss how to deal with General Concept Inclusion (GCI) axioms, get the $f\mathcal{ALCN}$ concept Negation Normal Form (NNF), and augment the Extended ABox step by step.

First, every GCI axiom in the TBox is transformed into its normal form. That is, replace each axiom of the form $C \sqsubseteq D$ [l,u] with $\top \sqsubseteq \neg C \sqcup D$ [l,u]. As mentioned in the previous section, we consider GCIs in knowledge bases. In standard DL, we have the identity $C \sqsubseteq D \iff \bot \equiv C \sqcap \neg D$ [12]. Negating both sides of this equality gives $\top \equiv \neg C \sqcup D$. Accordingly, in fuzzy DL, we have $C \sqsubseteq D\,[l,u] \iff \top \sqsubseteq \neg C \sqcup D\,[l,u]$.

Second, transform every concept description (in the TBox and the ABox) into its Negation Normal Form (NNF). The NNF of a concept can be obtained by applying the following equivalence rules:

$\forall a, b \in \Delta^I,$

$$\neg\neg C\,[l, u] \equiv C\,[l, u]\,, \tag{2.1}$$

$$\neg(C \sqcup D)\,[l, u] \equiv \neg C \sqcap \neg D\,[l, u]\,, \tag{2.2}$$

$$\neg(C \sqcap D)\,[l, u] \equiv \neg C \sqcup \neg D\,[l, u]\,, \tag{2.3}$$

$$\neg\exists R.C\,[l, u] \equiv \forall R.\neg C\,[l, u]\,, \tag{2.4}$$

$$\neg\forall R.C\,[l, u] \equiv \exists R.\neg C\,[l, u]\,, \tag{2.5}$$

$$\neg(\leq nR)\,[l, u] \equiv\, \geq (n+1)R\,[l, u]\,, \tag{2.6}$$

$$\neg(\geq nR)\,[l, u] \equiv \begin{cases} \leq (n-1)R\,[l, u] & n > 1 \\ \bot & n = 1 \end{cases}, \tag{2.7}$$

Note that all of the above equivalence rules can be proved for the different logics in Table 2.2 as a consequence of choosing Lukasiewicz negation and Kleene-Dienes implication in explaining the semantics of $f\mathcal{ALCN}$ concepts. If we use R-implication and/or Gödel negation, such equivalence rules do not necessarily hold. Here we only show the equivalence of rule 10.2.

Proof: Besides applying Lukasiewicz negation, by applying the min t-norm and the max s-norm in Zadeh Logic, we have that the left side of rule 10.2 is equal to $1 - max(x, y)$ where x is the truth degree of $C(a)$ and y is the truth degree of $D(a)$, and the right side of rule 10.2 is equal to $min(1 - x, 1 - y)$. Since $1 - max(x, y) = min(1 - x, 1 - y)$, rule 10.2 holds under Zadeh Logic.

By applying the t-norm and the s-norm in Lukasiewicz Logic, we have that the left side of rule 10.2 is equal to $1 - min(x + y, 1)$ and the right side of rule 10.2 is equal to $max(1 - x - y, 0)$. Since $1 - min(x + y, 1) = max(1 - x - y, 0)$, rule 10.2 holds under Lukasiewicz Logic.

By applying the t-norm and the s-norm in Product Logic, we have that the left side of rule 10.2 is equal to $1 - (x + y - xy)$ and the right side of rule 10.2 is equal to $(1 - x)(1 - y)$. Since $1 - (x + y - xy) = (1 - x)(1 - y)$, rule 10.2 holds under Product Logic.

By applying the t-norm and the s-norm in Yager Logic with $w = 2$, we have that the left side of rule 10.2 is equal to $min(1, ((1 - x)^2 + (1 - y)^2)^{1/2})$ and the right side of rule 10.2 is also equal to $min(1, ((1 - x)^2 + (1 - y)^2)^{1/2})$. So rule 10.2 holds under Yager Logic.

When applying Lukasiewicz negation as the fuzzy complement operation, Zadeh Logic and Gödel Logic have the same t-norm and s-norm. So rule 10.2 holds under Gödel Logic.

Therefore, rule 10.2 holds under the different logics in Table 2.2.

$\square$

Third, augment the ABox $\mathcal{A}$ with respect to the TBox $\mathcal{T}$. This step is also called eliminating the TBox. That is, for each individual a in $\mathcal{A}$ and each axiom $\top \sqsubseteq \neg C \sqcup D$ [l,u] in $\mathcal{T}$, add $(\neg C \sqcup D)(a)$ [l,u] to $\mathcal{A}$. The resulting ABox after finishing this step is called the initial extended ABox, denoted by A_0^ε.

Now for a $f\mathcal{ALCN}$ $KB = < \mathcal{T}, \mathcal{A} >$, by following the above steps, we eliminate the TBox by augmenting the ABox and get an extended ABox $\mathcal{A}$ in which all concepts occurring are in NNF. Next, we initialize the set of constraints $\mathcal{C}_0$ and get ready for apply the reasoning procedure for the consistency checking problems. $\mathcal{C}_0$ is initialized as follows: For each concept assertion $\{C(a)\ [l, u]\} \in A_0^\varepsilon$, add $\{l \leq x_{C(a)} \leq u\}$ into $\mathcal{C}_0$; for each role assertion $\{R(a, b)\ [l, u]\} \in A_0^\varepsilon$, add $\{l \leq x_{R(a,b)} \leq u\}$ into $\mathcal{C}_0$.

Finally, the reasoning procedure continues to check whether A_i^ε contains a clash. If it detects clashes in all of the or-branches, it returns the result that the knowledge base is inconsistent. If the complete ABox does not contain an obvious clash, the reasoning procedure continues to solve the inequations in the constraint set $\mathcal{C}_j$. If the system of these inequations is unsolvable, the knowledge base is inconsistent, and consistent otherwise.

As for the other reasoning problems, including instance checking and subsumption checking, the values returned from the system of inequations, if solvable, serve as the truth degrees of these entailment problems.

2.7 Reasoning Procedure

The main component of the $f\mathcal{ALCN}$ reasoning procedure consists of a set of completion rules. Like standard DL tableau algorithms, the reasoning procedure for $f\mathcal{ALCN}$ consistency checking problem tries to prove the consistency of an extended ABox $\mathcal{A}$ by constructing a model of $\mathcal{A}$, which, in the context of Fuzzy Description Logic, is a fuzzy interpretation $I = (\triangle^I, \cdot^I)$ with respect to a solution Φ. Such a model has the shape of a forest, a collection of trees with nodes corresponding to individuals, root nodes corresponding to named individuals, and edges corresponding to roles between individuals. Each node is associated with a node label, $\mathcal{L}$(individual). But unlike in standard DL where a node is labeled only with concepts, each node in $f\mathcal{ALCN}$ is associated with a label that consists of a pair of elements $\langle concept, constraint \rangle$, to show the concept assertions for this individual and its corresponding constraints. Furthermore, each edge is associated with an edge label, $\mathcal{L}$(individual$_1$, individual$_2$) which consists of a pair of elements $\langle role, constraint \rangle$, instead of simply being labeled with roles as in standard DL.

Let λ be the constraint attached to an assertion α. The variable x_α denotes the truth degree of an assertion α. After getting the initial extended ABox A_0^ε and the initial set of constraints C_0, the reasoning procedure expands the ABox and the constraint set by repeatedly applying the completion rules defined in Table 2.4. Such an expansion in the reasoning procedure is completed when (1) A_i^ε contains a clash or (2) none of the completion rules is applicable.

Here we give some examples to explain some of the completion rules. Examples for explaining the reasoning procedure in detail are omitted here for space reasons. Interested readers can refer to [37].

For example, if the extended ABox A_i^ε contains $\neg Young(John)$ $[0.8, 1]$. The reasoning procedure adds $Young(John)$ $[0, 0.2]$ into A_i^ε and $x_{\neg Young(John)} = [0.8, 1]$ and $x_{Young(John)} = [0, 0.2]$ into the constraint set.

Assume the user specifies Zadeh Logic. If the extended ABox A_i^ε contains $(Young \sqcap Tall)(John)$ $[0.8, 1]$, by applying the concept conjunction rule, the reasoning procedure adds $Young(John)$ $x_{Young(John)}$ and $Tall(John)$ $x_{Tall(John)}$ into A_i^ε, and adds $min(x_{Young(John)}, x_{Tall(John)}) = [0.8, 1]$ into the constraint set. If the user specifies Product Logic, then the reasoning procedure instead adds the constraint $x_{Young(John)} * x_{Tall(John)} = [0.8, 1]$ into the constraint set.

If the extended ABox A_i^ε contains $(Young \sqcup Tall)(John)$ $[0.8, 1]$, by applying the concept disjunction rule, the reasoning procedure adds $Young(John)$ $x_{Young(John)}$ and $Tall(John)$ $x_{Tall(John)}$ into A_i^ε, and adds $max(x_{Young(John)}, x_{Tall(John)}) = [0.8, 1]$ into the constraint set if Zadeh Logic is chosen. If the user specifies Product Logic, then the reasoning procedure adds the constraint $x_{Young(John)} + x_{Tall(John)} - x_{Young(John)} * x_{Tall(John)} = [0.8, 1]$ into the constraint set instead.

Assume the user specifies Zadeh Logic. If the extended ABox A_i^ε contains $(\forall hasDisease.Disease)(P001)$ $[0.8, 1]$ and $hasDisease(P001, Cancer)$ $[0, 0.6]$, by applying the value restriction rule, the reasoning procedure adds $Disease$ $(Cancer)$ $x_{Disease(Cancer)}$ into A_i^ε, and adds $max(x_{\neg hasDisease(P001, Cancer)}$

Table 2.4 Completion Rules of the Tableau Procedure

The concept negation rule
Condition: $\mathcal{A}_i^\varepsilon$ contains $\neg A(a)\ \lambda$, but does not contain $A(a)\ \neg\lambda$.
Action: If λ is not the variable $x_{\neg A(a)}$, $C_{j+1} = C_j \cup \{x_{\neg A(a)} = [l,u]\} \cup \{x_{A(a)} = [1-u,1-l]\}$, $\mathcal{A}_{i+1}^\varepsilon = \mathcal{A}_i^\varepsilon \cup \{A(a)\ [1-u,1-l]\}$. Otherwise, $C_{j+1} = C_j \cup \{x_{\neg A(a)} = 1 - x_{A(a)}\}$, $\mathcal{A}_{i+1}^\varepsilon = \mathcal{A}_i^\varepsilon \cup \{A(a)\ x_{A(a)}\}$
The concept conjunction rule
Condition: $\mathcal{A}_i^\varepsilon$ contains $(C \sqcap D)(a)\ \lambda$, but C_j does not contain $t(x_{C(a)}, x_{D(a)}) = \lambda$.
Action: $C_{j+1} = C_j \cup \{t(x_{C(a)}, x_{D(a)}) = \lambda\}$. If λ is not the variable $x_{(C \sqcap D)(a)}$, $C_{j+1} = C_{j+1} \cup \{x_{(C \sqcap D)(a)} = \lambda\}$. If $\mathcal{A}_i$ does not contain $C(a)\ x_{C(a)}$, $\mathcal{A}_{i+1}^\varepsilon = \mathcal{A}_i^\varepsilon \cup \{C(a)\ x_{C(a)}\}$. If $\mathcal{A}_i$ does not contain $D(a)\ x_{D(a)}$, $\mathcal{A}_{i+1}^\varepsilon = \mathcal{A}_i^\varepsilon \cup \{D(a)\ x_{D(a)}\}$.
The concept disjunction rule
Condition: $\mathcal{A}_i^\varepsilon$ contains $(C \sqcup D)(a)\ \lambda$, but C_j does not contain $s(x_{C(a)}, x_{D(a)}) = \lambda$.
Action: $C_{j+1} = C_j \cup \{s(x_{C(a)}, x_{D(a)}) = \lambda\}$. If λ is not the variable $x_{(C \sqcup D)(a)}$, $C_{j+1} = C_{j+1} \cup \{x_{(C \sqcup D)(a)} = \lambda\}$. If $\mathcal{A}_i$ does not contain $C(a)\ x_{C(a)}$, $\mathcal{A}_{i+1}^\varepsilon = \mathcal{A}_i^\varepsilon \cup \{C(a)\ x_{C(a)}\}$. If $\mathcal{A}_i$ does not contain $D(a)\ x_{D(a)}$, $\mathcal{A}_{i+1}^\varepsilon = \mathcal{A}_i^\varepsilon \cup \{D(a)\ x_{D(a)}\}$.
The exists restriction rule
Condition: $\mathcal{A}_i^\varepsilon$ contains $(\exists R.C)(a)\ \lambda$, and a is not blocked.
Action: If there is no individual name b such that C_j contains $t(x_{C(b)}, x_{R(a,b)}) = x_{(\exists R.C)(a)}$, then $C_{j+1} = C_j \cup \{t(x_{C(b)}, x_{R(a,b)}) = \lambda\}$. If $\mathcal{A}_i$ does not contain $C(b)\ x_{C(b)}$, $\mathcal{A}_{i+1}^\varepsilon = \mathcal{A}_i^\varepsilon \cup \{C(b)\ x_{C(b)}\}$. If $\mathcal{A}_i$ does not contain $R(a,b)\ x_{R(a,b)}$, $\mathcal{A}_{i+1}^\varepsilon = \mathcal{A}_i^\varepsilon \cup \{R(a,b)\ x_{R(a,b)}\}$. For each axiom $\top \sqsubseteq \neg C \sqcup D\ [l,u]$ in the TBox, add $\mathcal{A}_{i+1}^\varepsilon = \mathcal{A}_{i+1}^\varepsilon \cup \{(\neg C \sqcup D)(b)\ [l,u]\}$. If λ is not the variable $x_{(\exists R.C)(a)}$, then if there exists $x_{(\exists R.C)(a)} = \lambda'$ in C_j, then $C_{j+1} = C_{j+1} \setminus \{x_{(\exists R.C)(a)} = \lambda'\} \cup \{x_{(\exists R.C)(a)} = sup(\lambda, \lambda')\}$, else add $C_{j+1} = C_{j+1} \cup \{x_{(\exists R.C)(a)} = \lambda\}$.
The value restriction rule
Condition: A_i^ε contains $(\forall R.C)(a)\ \lambda$ and $R(a,b)\ \lambda'$.
Action: $\mathcal{A}_{i+1}^\varepsilon = \mathcal{A}_i^\varepsilon \cup \{C(b)\ x_{C(b)}\}$, $C_{j+1} = C_j \cup \{s(x_{C(b)}, x_{\neg R(a,b)}) = x_{(\forall R.C)(a)}\}$. If λ is not the variable $x_{(\forall R.C)(a)}$, then if there exists $x_{(\forall R.C)(a)} = \lambda''$ in C_j, add $C_{j+1} = C_{j+1} \setminus \{x_{(\forall R.C)(a)} = \lambda''\} \cup \{x_{(\forall R.C)(a)} = inf(\lambda, \lambda'')\}$, otherwise, add $C_{j+1} = C_{j+1} \cup \{x_{(\forall R.C)(a)} = \lambda\}$.
The at-least rule
Condition: $\mathcal{A}_i^\varepsilon$ contains $(\geq nR)(a)\ \lambda$, a is not blocked, and there are no individual names $b_1, \ldots, b_n$ such that $R(a, b_i)\ \lambda_i\ (1 \leq i \leq n)$ are contained in $\mathcal{A}_i^\varepsilon$.
Action: $\mathcal{A}_{i+1}^\varepsilon = \mathcal{A}_i^\varepsilon \cup \{R(a, b_i)\ \lambda | 1 \leq i \leq n\} \cup \{b_i \neq b_j | 1 \leq i \leq n\}$, $C_{j+1} = C_j \cup \{t(x_{R(a,b_1)}, \ldots, x_{R(a,b_n)}) = \lambda\}$.
The at-most rule
Condition: $\mathcal{A}_i^\varepsilon$ contains $n+1$ distinguished individual names $b_1, \ldots, b_{n+1}$ such that $(\leq nR)(a)\ \lambda$, $R(a, b_i)\ \lambda_i\ (1 \leq i \leq n+1)$ are contained in $\mathcal{A}_i^\varepsilon$ and $b_i \neq b_j$ is not in $\mathcal{A}_i^\varepsilon$ for some $i \neq j$, and if λ is not the variable $x_{\leq nR(a)}$ and for any $i\ (1 \leq i \leq n+1)$, λ_i is not the variable $x_{R(a,b_i)}$, $\lambda_i \subseteq \lambda$ holds.
Action: For each pair b_i, b_j such that $j > i$ and $b_i \neq b_j$ is not in $\mathcal{A}_i^\varepsilon$, the ABox $\mathcal{A}_{i+1}^\varepsilon$ is obtained from $\mathcal{A}_i^\varepsilon$ and the constraint set C_{j+1} is obtained from C_j by replacing each occurrence of b_j by b_i, and if λ_i is the variable $x_{R(a,b_i)}$, $C_{j+1} = C_{j+1} \cup \{x_{R(a,b_i)} = \lambda\}$.

, $x_{Disease(Cancer)}) = x_{(\forall has Disease.Disease)(P001)}$ and $x_{(\forall has Disease.Disease)(P001)}$ $= [0.8, 1]$ into the constraint set. Now assume the extended ABox A_i^ε contains another assertion $(\forall has Disease.Disease)(P001)\ [0.7, 1]$; the reasoning procedure will replace $x_{(\forall hasDisease.Disease)(P001)} = [0.8, 1]$ in the constraint set with $x_{(\forall hasDisease.Disease)(P001)} = [0.7, 1]$.

If the extended ABox A_i^ε contains $(\leq 2hasDisease)(P001)$ $[0.6, 1]$, $hasDisease(P001, Disease1)$ $[0.6, 1]$, $hasDisease$ *(P001,Disease2)* $[0.6, 1]$, *has-Disease (P001,Disease3)* $[0.7, 1]$, *Disease1* $\neq$ *Disease2* and *Disease1* $\neq$ *Disease3*, by applying the at-most number restriction rule, the reasoning procedure replaces $hasDisease(P001, Disease3)$ $[0.7, 1]$ with $hasDisease(P001, Disease2)$ $[0.7, 1]$, *Disease1* $\neq$ *Disease3* with *Disease1* $\neq$ *Disease2* in the extended ABox A_i^ε, and replaces replace $x_{hasDisease(P001,Disease3)} = [0.7, 1]$ in the constraint set with $x_{hasDisease(P001,Disease2)} = [0.7, 1]$.

The completion rules in Table 2.4 are a set of consistency-preserving transformation rules. Each time the reasoning procedure applies a completion rule, it either detects a clash or derives one or more assertions and constraints. In the reasoning procedure, the application of some completion rules, including the role existential restrictions and at-least number restrictions, may lead to nontermination. Therefore, we have to find some blocking strategy to ensure the termination of the reasoning procedure.

Definition 8 *Let a, b be anonymous individuals in the extended ABox A_i^ε; let $A_i^\varepsilon(a)$ (respectively, $A_i^\varepsilon(b)$) be all the assertions in A_i^ε that are related to the individual a (respectively, b); let $C_j(a)$ (respectively, $C_j(b)$) be all the constraints in C_j that are related to a (respectively, b), $\mathcal{L}(a) = \{A_i^\varepsilon(a), C_j(a)\}$ and $\mathcal{L}(b) = \{A_i^\varepsilon(b), C_j(b)\}$ be the node labels for a and b. An individual b is said to be **blocked** by a if $\mathcal{L}(b) \subseteq \mathcal{L}(a)$.*

2.8 Soundness, Completeness, and Termination of the Reasoning Procedure for $f\mathcal{ALCN}$

Extending results for standard DL [2][1], the following lemmas show that the reasoning procedure for $f\mathcal{ALCN}$ is sound and complete. Together with the proof of termination, it is shown that the consistency of an $f\mathcal{ALCN}$ knowledge base is decidable. Note that our proof can be viewed as a norm-parameterized version of the soundness, completeness, and termination of the algorithm presented in [30] for $f\mathcal{ALC}$ as well as the $f\mathcal{ALCN}$ counterpart in [29].

Lemma 1 *Soundness Assume that $\mathcal{A}_{i+1}^\varepsilon$ is obtained from the extended $f\mathcal{ALCN}$ ABox $\mathcal{A}_i^\varepsilon$ by application of a completion rule, then $\mathcal{A}_{i+1}^\varepsilon$ is consistent iff $\mathcal{A}_i^\varepsilon$ is consistent.*

Proof:
$\implies$ This is straightforward. Let C_i and C_{i+1} be the constraint set associated with the extended ABox $\mathcal{A}_i^\varepsilon$ and $\mathcal{A}_{i+1}^\varepsilon$, respectively. Let $I = (\Delta^I, \cdot^I)$ be a fuzzy interpretation, and $\Phi : Var(\mathcal{C}) \to [0, 1]$ be a solution. From the definition of consistency, we know if $\mathcal{A}_{i+1}^\varepsilon$ is consistent, there should exist a model $< I, \Phi >$. Since $\mathcal{A}_i^\varepsilon \subseteq \mathcal{A}_{i+1}^\varepsilon$ and $C_i \subseteq C_{i+1}$, $< I, \Phi >$ is also a model of $\mathcal{A}_i^\varepsilon$, therefore, $\mathcal{A}_i^\varepsilon$ is consistent.

$\Longleftarrow$ This is a consequence of the definition of the completion rules. Let C and D be concept descriptions, a and b be individual names, and R be an atomic role. Let $< I, \Phi >$ be a model of $\mathcal{A}_i^\varepsilon$. Now we show the interpretation I also satisfies the new assertions when any of the completion rules is triggered. Hereafter, let λ denote a variable for a truth degree.

Case: When $\mathcal{A}_i^\varepsilon$ contains $(\neg C)(a)\ \lambda$, we apply the conjunction rule and obtain the extended ABox $\mathcal{A}_{i+1}^\varepsilon = \mathcal{A}_i^\varepsilon \cup \{C(a)\ x_{C(a)}\}$ and the constraint set $\mathcal{C}_{i+1} = \mathcal{C}_i \cup \{1 - x_{C(a)} = x_{\neg C(a)} = \lambda\}$. As $< I, \Phi >$ is a model of $\mathcal{A}_i^\varepsilon$, I satisfies $\{(\neg C)(a)\ \lambda\}$, that is, $\{(\neg C)^I(a) = \lambda\}$. Based on the semantics of concept negation, we know that $(C)^I(a) = 1 - (\neg C)^I(a)$. Therefore, $(C)^I(a)) = 1 - \lambda$ holds under the interpretation I. Let v_1 be a value in $1 - \lambda$, we have $C^I(a) = v_1$. Hence, I also satisfies $\{C(a)\ v_1\}$.

Case: When $\mathcal{A}_i^\varepsilon$ contains $(C \sqcap D)(a)\ \lambda$, we apply the conjunction rule and obtain the extended ABox $\mathcal{A}_{i+1}^\varepsilon = \mathcal{A}_i^\varepsilon \cup \{C(a)\ x_{C(a)}, D(a)\ x_{D(a)}\}$ and the constraint set $\mathcal{C}_{i+1} = \mathcal{C}_i \cup \{t(x_{C(a)}, x_{D(a)}) = \lambda\}$. As $< I, \Phi >$ is a model of $\mathcal{A}_i^\varepsilon$, I satisfies $\{(C \sqcap D)(a)\ \lambda\}$, that is, $\{(C \sqcap D)^I(a) = \lambda\}$. Based on the semantics of concept conjunction, we know that $(C \sqcap D)^I(a) = t(C^I(a), D^I(a))$. Therefore, $t(C^I(a), D^I(a)) = \lambda$ holds under the interpretation I. It is easily verified that there are values v_1, v_2 ($v_1, v_2 \in [0,1]$) which satisfy $t(v_1, v_2) = \lambda$ [3]. Therefore, we have $C^I(a) = v_1$ and $D^I(a) = v_2$. Hence, I also satisfies both $\{C(a)\ v_1\}$ and $\{D(a)\ v_2\}$.

Case: When $\mathcal{A}_i^\varepsilon$ contains $(C \sqcup D)(a)\ \lambda$, the disjunction rule is applied and we obtain either the extended ABox $\mathcal{A}_{i+1}^\varepsilon = \mathcal{A}_i^\varepsilon \cup \{C(a)\ x_{C(a)}, D(a)\ x_{D(a)}\}$ in the cases of Product Logic and Yager Logic, or, two extended ABoxes: $\mathcal{A}_{i+1}^\varepsilon = \mathcal{A}_i^\varepsilon \cup \{C(a)\ x_{C(a)}\}$ and $\mathcal{A}_{i+1}^{\varepsilon'} = \mathcal{A}_i^\varepsilon \cup \{D(a)\ x_{D(a)}\}$ in the cases of other logics in Table 2.2. We also obtain the constraint set $\mathcal{C}_{i+1} = \mathcal{C}_i \cup \{s(x_{C(a)}, x_{D(a)}) = \lambda\}$. As $< I, \Phi >$ is a model of $\mathcal{A}_i^\varepsilon$, I satisfies $\{(C \sqcup D)(a)\ \lambda\}$, that is, $\{(C \sqcup D)^I(a) = \lambda\}$. Based on the semantics of concept conjunction, we know that $(C \sqcup D)^I(a) = s(C^I(a), D^I(a))$. Therefore, $s(C^I(a), D^I(a)) = \lambda$ holds under the interpretation I. It is easily verified that there are values v_1, v_2 ($v_1, v_2 \in [0,1]$) which satisfy $s(v_1, v_2) = \lambda$ [4]. Therefore, we have $C^I(a) = v_1$ or $D^I(a) = v_2$. Hence, I also satisfies either $\{C(a)\ v_1\}$ or $\{D(a)\ v_2\}$, or both.

Case: When $\mathcal{A}_i^\varepsilon$ contains $(\exists R.C)(a)\ \lambda$, the role exists restriction rule is applied. There are two possible augmentations.

(1) If there exists an individual name b such that $C(b)\ x_{C(b)}$ and $R(a, b)\ x_{R(a,b)}$ are in $\mathcal{A}_i^\varepsilon$, but $\mathcal{C}_i$ does not contain $t(x_{C(b)}, x_{R(a,b)}) = x_{(\exists R.C)(a)}$, then $\mathcal{C}_{i+1} = \mathcal{C}_i \cup \{t(x_{C(b)}, x_{R(a,b)}) = x_{(\exists R.C)(a)}\}$; If λ is not the variable $x_{((\exists R.C)(a)}$, then if there exists $x_{((\exists R.C)(a)} = \lambda'$ in $\mathcal{C}_i$, then $\mathcal{C}_{i+1} = \mathcal{C}_{i+1} \backslash \{x_{((\exists R.C)(a)} = \lambda'\} \cup \{x_{((\exists R.C)(a)} = sup(\lambda, \lambda')\}$, else add $\mathcal{C}_{i+1} = \mathcal{C}_{i+1} \cup \{x_{(\exists R.C)(a)} = \lambda\}$. There is

---

[3] For different t-norms in Fuzzy Logic (the minimum function, the maximum function, the product function, and the Yager-and function), it is easy to show that we can always find such a pair of values.

[4] For different s-norms in Fuzzy Logic (the minimum function, the maximum function, the product-sum function, and the yager-or function), it is again easy to show that we can always find such a pair of values.

no new assertion, thus it is straightforward that if $\mathcal{A}_{i+1}^{\varepsilon}$ is consistent, then $\mathcal{A}_i^{\varepsilon}$ is consistent.

(2) If there is no individual name b such that $C(b)$ $x_{C(b)}$ and $R(a,b)$ $x_{R(a,b)}$ are in $\mathcal{A}_i^{\varepsilon}$, and $\mathcal{C}_j$ does not contain $t(x_{C(b)}, x_{R(a,b)}) = x_{(\exists R.C)(a)}$, then we obtain the extended ABox $\mathcal{A}_{i+1}^{\varepsilon} = \mathcal{A}_i^{\varepsilon} \cup \{C(b)\ x_{C(b)}, R(a,b)\ x_{R(a,b)}\}$ and the constraint set $\mathcal{C}_{i+1} = \mathcal{C}_i \cup \{t(x_{C(b)}, x_{R(a,b)}) = x_{(\exists R.C)(a)}\}$. In this case, we want to show I also satisfies both $R(a,b)$ to some degree and $C(b)$ to some degree. As $< I, \Phi >$ is a model of $\mathcal{A}_i^{\varepsilon}$, I satisfies $(\exists R.C)(a)$ λ, that is, $(\exists R.C)^I(a)$ λ. Based on the semantics of role exists restriction, we know that $(\exists R.C)^I(a,b) = \sup_{b \in \Delta^I} \{t(R^I(a,b), C^I(b))\}$. Therefore, $\sup_{b \in \Delta^I} \{t(R^I(a,b), C^I(b))\} = \lambda$ holds under the interpretation I. It is easily verified that there are an individual b and values v_1, v_2 ($v_1, v_2 \in [0,1]$) which satisfy $t(R^I(a,b), C^I(b))$. Therefore, we have $R^I(a,b) = v_1$ and $C^I(b) = v_2$. Hence, I also satisfies $\{R(a,b)\ v_1\}$ and $\{C(b)\ v_2\}$.

Case: When $\mathcal{A}_i^{\varepsilon}$ contains $(\forall R.C)(a)$ λ, the role value restriction rule is applied. Then, for every individual b that is an R-successor of individual a, we obtain $\mathcal{A}_{i+1}^{\varepsilon} = \mathcal{A}_i^{\varepsilon} \cup \{C(b)\ x_{C(b)}\}$, $\mathcal{C}_{i+1} = \mathcal{C}_i \cup \{s(x_{C(b)}, x_{\neg R(a,b)}) = x_{(\forall R.C)(a)}\}$. If λ is not the variable $x_{((\forall R.C)(a)}$, then if there exists $x_{((\forall R.C)(a)} = \lambda'$ in $\mathcal{C}_i$, add $\mathcal{C}_{i+1} = \mathcal{C}_{i+1} \backslash \{x_{((\forall R.C)(a)} = \lambda'\} \cup \{x_{((\forall R.C)(a)} = inf(\lambda, \lambda')\}$, otherwise, add $\mathcal{C}_{i+1} = \mathcal{C}_{i+1} \cup \{x_{(\forall R.C)(a)} = \lambda\}$.

As $< I, \Phi >$ is a model of $\mathcal{A}_i^{\varepsilon}$, I satisfies $(\forall R.C)(a)$ λ, that is, $(\forall R.C)^I(a) = \lambda$. For every individual b that is an R-successor of a, I satisfies $R(a,b)$ λ', that is, $R^I(a,b) = \lambda'$. Based on the semantics of role value restriction, we know that, $(\forall R.C)^I(a) = \inf_{b \in \Delta^I} \{s(\neg R^I(a,b), C^I(b))\}$. Therefore, $\inf_{b \in \Delta^I} \{s(\neg R^I(a,b), C^I(b))\} = \lambda$. Therefore, for every individual b that is an R-successor of a, $s(\neg \lambda', C^I(b)) = \lambda$ holds under the interpretation I. Hence, for each of these individuals b, we can find a value v_1 ($v_1 \in [0,1]$) which satisfies $s(\neg \lambda', C^I(b)) = \lambda$. Therefore, we have $C^I(b) = v_1$. Hence, I also satisfies $\{C(b)\ v_1\}$.

Case: When $\mathcal{A}_i^{\varepsilon}$ contains $(\geq nR)(a)$ λ, the at-least number restriction rule is applied. We obtain $\mathcal{A}_{i+1}^{\varepsilon} = \mathcal{A}_i^{\varepsilon} \cup \{R(a,b_i)\ \lambda | 1 \leq i \leq n\} \cup \{b_i \neq b_j | 1 \leq i < j \leq n)\}$ and $\mathcal{C}_{i+1} = \mathcal{C}_i \cup \{x_{R(a,b_i)} = \lambda | 1 \leq i \leq n)\}$. Based on the semantics of at-least number restriction, we know that $(\geq nR)^I(x) = \sup_{y_1,\ldots,y_n \in \Delta^I, y_i \neq y_j, 1 \leq i < j \leq n} t_{i=1}^n \{R^I(x, y_i)\}$. Since it is easy to see from the application of the at-least number restriction rule, we can form at least n pairs (a, b_i) for which $R(a, b_i)^I = \lambda_i$ and $\sup_{y_1,\ldots,y_n \in \Delta^I, y_i \neq y_j, 1 \leq i < j \leq n} t_{i=1}^n \{\lambda_i\} = \lambda$. Hence, $(\geq nR)^I(a) = \lambda$ and I satisfies $(\geq nR)(a)$ λ.

Case: When $n + 1$ distinguished individual names $b_1, \ldots, b_{n+1}$ such that $(\leq nR)(a)$ λ and $R(a, b_i)$ λ_i ($1 \leq i \leq n+1$) are contained in $\mathcal{A}_i^{\varepsilon}$, $b_i \neq b_j$ is not in $\mathcal{A}_i^{\varepsilon}$ for some $i \neq j$, the at-most number restriction rule is applied. For each pair b_i, b_j such that $j > i$ and $b_i \neq b_j$ is not in $\mathcal{A}_i^{\varepsilon}$, the ABox $\mathcal{A}_{i+1}^{\varepsilon}$ is obtained from $\mathcal{A}_i^{\varepsilon}$ and the constraint set $\mathcal{C}_{i+1}$ is obtained from $\mathcal{C}_i$ by replacing each occurrence of b_j by b_i, and if λ_i is the variable $x_{R(a,b_i)}$, $\mathcal{C}_{i+1} = \mathcal{C}_{i+1} \cup \{x_{R(a,b_i)} = \lambda\}$.

As $< I, \Phi >$ is a model of $\mathcal{A}_i^{\varepsilon}$, I satisfies $(\leq nR)(a)$ λ, that is $(\leq nR)^I(a) = \lambda$. Based on the semantics of at-most number restriction, we know that if there are $n+1$ R-role assertions $R(a, b_i)$ ($i \in \{1, 2, ldots, n + 1\}$) that can be formed from $\mathcal{A}_{i+1}^{\varepsilon}$, for which $R(a, b_i)^I = \lambda_i$, there would be at least one pair (a, b_k) for which $\lambda_k = \neg\lambda$ holds. Applying negation on both side of the equation, we thus have $\neg R(a, b_i)^I = \neg\neg\lambda = \lambda$ holds. This is equal to $\inf_{y_1,\dots,y_{n+1}\in\Delta^I, y_i\neq y_j, 1\leq i<j\leq n+1} s_{i=1}^{n+1}\{\neg R^I(x, y)\}$ $= \lambda$. Therefore, we finally have that $(\leq nR)^I(x) = \lambda$, and I also satisfies $(\leq nR)(a)\ \lambda$.

$\square$

Lemma 2 Completeness *Any complete and clash-free fALCN ABox $\mathcal{A}$ with a solvable constraints set $\mathcal{C}$ has a model.*

Proof:

Let $\mathcal{A}$ be a complete and clash-free ABox and $\mathcal{C}$ be the constraint set associated with $\mathcal{A}$. Since $\mathcal{A}$ is clash-free and complete, and the constraint set $\mathcal{C}$ is solvable, there exists a solution $\Phi : Var(\mathcal{C}) \to [0, 1]$ to the constraint set $\mathcal{C}$.

Let's define the fuzzy interpretation I of the ABox $\mathcal{A}$ as follows:

(1) the domain $\triangle^I$ consists of all the individual names occurring in $\mathcal{A}$;

(2) for all atomic concepts A, we define $A^I(a) = \Phi(x_{A(a)})$ where a is an individual name in $\mathcal{A}$ and $\Phi(x_{A(a)})$ denotes the truth degree of the variable $x_{A(a)}$.

(3) for all atomic roles R_0 we define $R_0^I(a, b) = \Phi(x_{R_0(a,b)})$ where a and b are individual names in $\mathcal{A}$ and $\Phi(x_{R(a,b)})$ denotes the truth degree of the variable $x_{R(a,b)}$.

To show that the pair $< I, \Phi >$ is a model of $\mathcal{A}$, we need to prove all the concept and role assertions in $\mathcal{A}$ can be interpreted by I, using induction techniques on the structure of an fALCN concept C.

If C is an atomic concept, then we have C^I according to its definition.

If C is of the form $C = \neg A$, $\mathcal{A}$ contains $\{\neg A(a)\ \lambda\}$. Since $\mathcal{A}$ is complete, we know the concept negation rule has been applied, thus $\mathcal{A}$ contains $\{A(a)\ \neg\lambda\}$ and $\mathcal{C}$ contains $x_{A(a)} = \neg\lambda$ and $x_{\neg A(a)} = \lambda$. By the induction hypothesis we know that I can interpret $A(a)\ \neg\lambda$, that is, $A^I(a) = \neg\lambda$. Based on the semantics of concept negation, we have $(\neg A)^I(a) = \neg A^I(a)$. Therefore, we obtain $(\neg A)^I(a) = \neg(\neg\lambda) = \lambda$; thus concept assertions of the form $\{\neg A(a)\ \lambda\}$ are correctly interpreted by I.

If C is of the form $C \sqcap D$, $\mathcal{A}$ contains $\{(C \sqcap D)(a)\ \lambda\}$. Since $\mathcal{A}$ is complete, we know the concept conjunction rule has been applied, thus $\mathcal{A}$ contains $\{C(a)\ x_{C(a)}\}$ and $\{D(a)\ x_{D(a)}\}$ and $\mathcal{C}$ contains $t(x_{C(a)}, x_{D(a)}) = \lambda$. By the induction hypothesis we know that I can interpret $C(a)\ x_{C(a)}$ and $D(a)\ x_{D(a)}$, that is, $C^I(a) = \Phi(x_{C(a)})$ and $D^I(a) = \Phi(x_{D(a)})$ where $\Phi(x_{C(a)})$ and $\Phi(x_{D(a)})$ denote the truth degrees of the variables $x_{C(a)}$ and $x_{D(a)}$, respectively. As Φ is a solution to the constraint set $\mathcal{C}$, $t(\Phi(x_{C(a)}), \Phi(x_{D(a)})) = \lambda$ holds. Therefore, $t(C^I(a), D^I(a)) = \lambda$. On the other hand, based on the semantics of concept conjunction, we have $(C \sqcap D)^I(a) = t(C^I(a), D^I(a))$. Therefore, we obtain $(C \sqcap D)^I(a) = \lambda$; thus concept assertions of the form $(C \sqcap D)(a)\ \lambda$ are correctly interpreted by I.

If C is of the form $C \sqcup D$, $\mathcal{A}$ contains $\{(C \sqcup D)(a)\ \lambda\}$. Since $\mathcal{A}$ is complete, we know the concept disjunction rule has been applied; thus $\mathcal{A}$ contains $\{C(a)\ x_{C(a)}\}$ or $\{D(a)\ x_{D(a)}\}$ and $\mathcal{C}$ contains $s(x_{C(a)}, x_{D(a)}) = \lambda$. By the induction hypothesis we know that I can interpret $C(a)$ $x_{(a)}$ and $D(a)$ $x_{D(a)}$, that is, $C^I(a) = \Phi(x_{C(a)})$ and $D^I(a) = \Phi(x_{D(a)})$ where $\Phi(x_{C(a)})$ and $\Phi(x_{D(a)})$ denote the truth degrees of the variables $x_{C(a)}$ and $x_{D(a)}$, respectively. Note that for a concept assertion $C(a)$, $C^I(a) = \Phi(x_{C(a)}) = 0$ still means I can interpret $C(a)$. As Φ is a solution to the constraint set $\mathcal{C}$, $s(\Phi(x_{C(a)}), \Phi(x_{D(a)})) = \lambda$ holds. Therefore, $s(C^I(a), D^I(a)) = \lambda$. On the other hand, based on the semantics of concept conjunction, we have $(C \sqcup D)^I(a) = s(C^I(a), D^I(a))$. Therefore, we obtain $(C \sqcup D)^I(a) = \lambda$; thus concept assertions of the form $(C \sqcup D)(a)$ λ are correctly interpreted by I.

If R is an atomic role, then we have R^I according to its definition.

If C is of the form $\exists R.C$, $\mathcal{A}$ contains $\{(\exists R.C)(a) \lambda\}$. Since $\mathcal{A}$ is complete, we know the role exists restriction rule has been applied. There could be three cases when applying the role exists restriction rule. (1) A new individual b was generated. $\mathcal{A}$ contains $\{R(a, b) \ x_{R(a,b)}\}$ and $\{C(b) \ x_{C(b)}\}$, $\mathcal{C}$ contains $t(x_{R(a,b)}, x_{C(b)}) = \lambda$; (2) An individual b and $R(a, b)$ λ' already exist in $\mathcal{A}$. Then we have $\mathcal{A}$ contains $\{C(b) \ x_{C(b)}\}$ and $\mathcal{C}$ contains $t(x_{R(a,b)}, x_{C(b)}) = \lambda$ as well as $x_{R(a,b)} = \lambda'$ if λ' is not the variable $x_{R(a,b)}$; (3) a was blocked by some ancestor. In all these cases, we can find at least one individual b such that $C(b)$ $x_{C(b)}$ and $R(a, b)$ $x_{R(a,b)}$ is in $\mathcal{A}$, and $t(x_{R(a,b)}, x_{C(b)}) = \lambda$ is in $\mathcal{C}$. By the induction hypothesis, we know that I can interpret $C(b)$ $x_{C(b)}$ and $R(a, b)$ $x_{R(a,b)}$, that is, $C^I(b) = \Phi(x_{C(b)})$ and $R^I(a, b) = \Phi(x_{R(a,b)})$ where $\Phi(x_{C(b)})$ and $\Phi(x_{R(a,b)})$ denote the truth degrees of the variables $x_{C(b)}$ and $x_{R(a,b)}$, respectively. As Φ is a solution to the constraint set $\mathcal{C}$, $\sup_{b \in \Delta^I}\{t(x_{\Phi(C(b))}, x_{\Phi(R(a,b))})\} = \lambda$ holds. Therefore, $\sup_{b \in \Delta^I}\{t(x_{C^I(b)}, x_{R^I(a,b)})\} = \lambda$. On the other hand, based on the semantics of concept conjunction, we have $(\exists R.C)^I(a) = \sup_{b \in \Delta^I}\{t(x_{C^I(b)}, x_{R^I(a,b)})\}$. Therefore, we obtain $(\exists R.C)^I(a) = \lambda$; thus concept assertions of the form $(\exists R.C)(a)$ λ are correctly interpreted by I.

If C is of the form $\forall R.C$, $\mathcal{A}$ contains $\{(\forall R.C)(a) \lambda\}$. Since $\mathcal{A}$ is complete, we know the value restriction rule has been applied. Thus $\{C(b) \ x_{C(b)}\}$ is in $\mathcal{A}$ and $s(\neg x_{R(a,b)}, x_{C(b)}) = \lambda$ is in $\mathcal{C}$ for every individual b with $\{R(a, b) \ \lambda'\}$ in $\mathcal{A}$. $\mathcal{C}$ also contains $x_{R(a,b)} = \lambda'$ if λ' is not a variable. By the induction hypothesis, we know that I can interpret $C(b)$ $x_{C(b)}$ for each b, that is, $C^I(b) = \Phi(x_{C(b)})$ for each b where $\Phi(x_{C(b)})$ denote the truth degree of the variable $x_{C(b)}$. As Φ is a solution to the constraint set $\mathcal{C}$, $\inf_{b \in \Delta^I}\{s(x_{\Phi(C(b))}, \neg x_{\Phi(R(a,b))})\} = \lambda$ holds. Therefore, $\inf_{b \in \Delta^I}\{s(x_{C^I(b)}, \neg x_{R^I(a,b)})\} = \lambda$. On the other hand, based on the semantics of value restriction, we have $(\forall R.C)^I(a) = \inf_{b \in \Delta^I}\{s(x_{C^I(b)}, \neg x_{R^I(a,b)})\}$. Therefore, we obtain $(\forall R.C)^I(a) = \lambda$; thus concept assertions of the form $(\forall R.C)(a)$ λ are correctly interpreted by I.

If C is of the form $\geq nR$, $\mathcal{A}$ contains $\{\geq nR(a) \lambda\}$. Since $\mathcal{A}$ is complete, we know the at-least number restriction rule has been applied. Thus $\{R(a, b_i) \ \lambda | 1 \leq i \leq n\}$ is in $\mathcal{A}$. By the induction hypothesis, we know that I satisfies $R(a, b_i)$ λ with $1 \leq i \leq n$, that is, $R^I(a, b_i) = \lambda$. Thus we can form at least n pairs (a, b_i) for which $R(a, b_i)^I = \lambda$ holds. Therefore, $\sup_{b_1, \ldots, b_n \in \Delta^I, b_i \neq b_j, 1 \leq i < j \leq n} t_{i=1}^n \{R^I(a, b_i)\} = \lambda$. On the other hand, based on the semantics of at-least number restriction, we have $(\geq nR)^I(a) = \sup_{b_1, \ldots, b_n \in \Delta^I, b_i \neq b_j, 1 \leq i < j \leq n} t_{i=1}^n \{R^I(a, b_i)\}$. Therefore, we obtain $(\geq nR)^I(a) = \lambda$; thus the interpretation I satisfies concept assertions of the form $(\geq nR)(a) \lambda$.

If C is of the form $\leq nR$, $\mathcal{A}$ contains $\{\leq nR(a) \lambda\}$. Since $\mathcal{A}$ is complete, we know the at-most number restriction rule has been applied. Thus for each pair b_i, b_j with $j > i$, the inequality $b_i \neq b_j$ is not in A_i^{ε}, the ABox A_i^{ε} is obtained and the constraint set $\mathcal{C}_i$ is obtained by replacing each occurrence of b_j by b_i, and if λ_i is the variable $x_{R(a,b_i)}$, add $\{x_{R(a,b_i)} = \lambda\}$ to $\mathcal{C}_i$. By the induction hypothesis, we know that I can interpret the resultiing n assertions $R(a, b_i) \; x_{R(a,b_i)}$ with $1 \leq i \leq n$, that is, $R^I(a, b_i) = \Phi(x_{R(a,b_i)})$, where Φ denote the truth degrees of the variables $R(a, b_i) \; x_{R(a,b_i)}$ for $(1 \leq i \leq n)$. As Φ is a solution to the constraint set $\mathcal{C}$, we have $\Phi(x_{R(a,b_i)}) \subseteq \lambda$ for $1 \leq i \leq n$. Therefore, $x_{R^I(a,b_i)} = \lambda$ holds for $(1 \leq i \leq n)$. On the other hand, based on the semantics of at-most number restriction, we know if there are at most n pairs (a, b_i) for which $R(a, b_i)^I = \lambda$ holds, we have $(\leq nR)^I(a) = \lambda$. Thus, concept assertions of the form $(\leq nR)(a) \lambda$ are correctly interpreted by I.

$\square$

In order to prove the termination of the $f\mathcal{ALCN}$ reasoning procedure, we first review the definition of $sub(D)$ given in [12]:

1. if D is an atomic concept, then $sub(D) = \{D\}$;
2. if D is of the form $C \sqcap D$, then $sub(D) = \{C \sqcap D\} \cup sub(C) \cup sub(D)$;
3. if D is of the form $C \sqcup D$, then $sub(D) = \{C \sqcup D\} \cup sub(C) \cup sub(D)$;
4. if D is of the form $\exists R.C$, then $sub(D) = \{\exists R.C\} \cup sub(C)$;
5. if D is of the form $\forall R.C$, then $sub(D) = \{\forall R.C\} \cup sub(C)$;
6. if D is of the form $\geq R$, then $sub(D) = \{\geq R\}$;
7. if D is of the form $\leq R$, then $sub(D) = \{\leq R\}$;

From the definition, we know that $sub(D)$ is the closure of subexpressions of D. When testing the consistency of an extended ABox $\mathcal{A}$, the concepts derived from the tableau procedure are restricted to subsets of any concept D (i.e., $sub(D)$) in $\mathcal{A}$. Therefore, we have $sub(\mathcal{A}) = \cup_{\forall D \in \mathcal{A}} sub(\mathcal{D})$.

Lemma 3 *Termination Let $\mathcal{A}$ be an $f\mathcal{ALCN}$ ABox. The tableaux procedure for $f\mathcal{ALCN}$ always terminates when started from $\mathcal{A}$.*

Proof: Let $R_{\mathcal{A}}$ be the set of roles occurring in $\mathcal{A}$. Let $C_{\mathcal{A}} = |sub(\mathcal{A})|$, $n_{\max} = \max\{n| \geq nR \in sub(\mathcal{A})\}$. The termination of our tableau procedure is a consequence of the same properties that ensure termination in the case of the standard $\mathcal{ALCN}$ DL. These properties are shown as follows [14]:

1. The only completion rule that remove assertions from the extended ABox is the at-most number restriction rule, which merges the assertions of an individual b with one of its ancestors a and thus individual b is blocked.

2. New individuals are only generated by the role exists restriction rule and the at-least number restriction rule. For each individual in the extended ABox, the rules can only be applied once. sub($\mathcal{A}$) contains at most s role exists restrictions which

generates at most s successors. Each of these successors can further have $n_{\max}$ edges due to the at-least number restrictions. Therefore, the out-degree of the tree generated from the tableau procedure is bounded by $C_{\mathcal{A}} * n_{\max}$.

3. There is a finite number of possible labels for a pair of nodes and an edge, since concepts are taken from sub($\mathcal{A}$). Thus, there are at most $2^{C_{\mathcal{A}} * n_{\max}}$ possible labels for a pair of nodes and an edge. Hence, if a path is of length at least $2^{C_{\mathcal{A}} * n_{\max}}$, there must exist two nodes along the path that have the same node labels, and hence blocking occurs. Since a path cannot grow longer once a blocking takes place, paths are of length at most $2^{C_{\mathcal{A}} * n_{\max}}$.

$\square$

2.9 Conclusion and Future Work

In this chapter, we propose an extension to Description Logics based on Fuzzy Set Theory and Fuzzy Logic. The syntax and semantics of the proposed Description Logic $f\mathcal{ALCN}$ are explained in detail. We further address different reasoning tasks on $f\mathcal{ALCN}$ knowledge bases. We present a sound and complete reasoning procedure that always terminates and its completion rules.

The $f\mathcal{ALCN}$ DL adopts a norm-parameterized way to cover different logics in the Fuzzy Logic family, currently Zadeh Logic, Lukasiewicz Logic, Product Logic, Gödel Logic, and Yager Logic. Such an approach allows the interpretation of different kinds of uncertain knowledge existing in real world applications. Furthermore, $f\mathcal{ALCN}$ knowledge bases can express fuzzy subsumption of fuzzy concepts of the form $C \sqsubseteq D\ [l, u]$, which allows generalized modeling of uncertain knowledge.

Description Logics constitute a family of descriptive languages with different expressiveness and decidability/efficiency. For reasons of simplicity, our fuzzy Description Logic $f\mathcal{ALCN}$ does not yet include transitive roles, inverse roles and other non-$\mathcal{ALC}$ constructors. We have also considered $\mathcal{ALCHIN}$ as a super language of $\mathcal{ALCN}$ and introduced a fuzzy version $f\mathcal{ALCHIN}$ [36]. Part of our ongoing work considers further fuzzy extensions to more expressive $\mathcal{S}$-style (i.e., $\mathcal{ALCR}^+$) Description Logics.

One of the main practical directions for future work is the implementation of the fuzzy reasoner, which involves a lot of technical designing decisions. We are implementing an $f\mathcal{ALCN}$ reasoner using SWI-Prolog. Our prototype reasoner is based on the $\mathcal{ALC}$ reasoner ALCAS [26] which supports $\mathcal{ALC}$ DL reasoning with an OWL abstract syntax. Our extensions to ALCAS provides functionalities to check consistency as well as fuzzy concept and subsumption entailments of a $f\mathcal{ALCN}$ knowledge base.

References

1. Baader, F., Calvanese, D., McGuinness, D.L., Nardi, D., Patel-Schneider, P.F.: The Description Logic Handbook: Theory, Implementation and Applications. Cambridge University Press, Cambridge, MA (2003)
2. Baader, F., Sattler, U.: An overview of tableau algorithms for description logic. Studia Logica **69**(1), 5–40 (2001)
3. Berners-Lee, T., Hendler, J., Lassila, O.: The semantic web. Scientific American **284**(5), 34–44 (2001). URL http://web.ebscohost.com/ehost/detail?vid=1&hid=102&sid=40d1a318-d0ac-41c6-9854-0ffde44a63eb%40sessionmgr109
4. Bobillo, F., Straccia, U.: A fuzzy description logic with product t-norm. In: Proceedings of the IEEE International Conference on Fuzzy Systems (Fuzz IEEE-07), pp. 652C–657. IEEE Computer Society (2007)
5. Brachman, R.J., Levesque, H.J.: The tractability of subsumption in frame-based description languages. In: Proceedings AAAI-1984, pp. 34–37. AAAI Press (1984)
6. Haase, P., Völker, J.: Ontology learning and reasoning - dealing with uncertainty and inconsistency. In: Proceedings of Uncertainty Reasoning for the Semantic Web, pp. 45–55 (2005)
7. Hájek, P.: Metamathematics of fuzzy logic. Kluwer (1998)
8. Hájek, P.: Making fuzzy description logics more expressive. Fuzzy Sets Syst. **154**(1), 1–15 (2005)
9. Hájek, P.: What does mathematical fuzzy logic offer to description logic?, pp. 91–100. Fuzzy Logic and the Semantic Web, Capturing Intelligence. Elsevier (2006)
10. Hajek, P.: Fuzzy logic. In: The Stanford Encyclopedia of Philosophy. Standford University (2009). URL http://plato.stanford.edu/archives/spr2009/entries/logic-fuzzy/
11. Hollunder, B.: An alternative proof method for possibilistic logic and its application to terminological logics. International Journal of Approximate Reasoning **12**(2), 85–109 (1995)
12. Horrocks, I.: Optimising tableaux decision procedures for description logics (1997). ANNOTE: AKA: Horrocks97b
13. Horrocks, I., Patel-Schneider, P.F., van Harmelen, F.: From $\mathcal{SHIQ}$ and RDF to OWL: The making of a web ontology language. J. of Web Semantics **1**(1), 7–26 (2003)
14. Horrocks, I., Sattler, U., Tobies, S.: Practical reasoning for very expressive description logics. Logic Journal of the IGPL **8**(3), 239–264 (2000)
15. Hsueh-Ieng, P.: Uncertainty management for description logic-based ontologies. Ph.D. thesis, University of Concordia (2008)
16. Jaeger, M.: Probabilistic reasoning in terminological logics. In: Proc. of the 4th Int. Conf. on the Principles of Knowledge Representation and Reasoning (KR94), pp. 305–316 (1994)
17. Koller, D., Levy, A., Pfeffer, A.: P-classic: A tractable probabilistic description logic. In: Proceedings of the Fourteenth National Conference on Artificial Intelligence (AAAI-97), pp. 390–397 (1997)
18. Laskey, K.J., Laskey, K.B., Costa, P.C.G., Kokar, M.M., Martin, T., Lukasiewicz, T.: W3c incubator group report. Tech. Rep. http://www.w3.org/2005/Incubator/urw3/wiki/DraftFinalReport, W3C (05 March, 2008)
19. Lukasiewicz, T.: Expressive probabilistic description logics. Artificial Intelligence **172**(6/7), 852–883 (2008)
20. Martin-Recuerda, F., Robertson, D.: Discovery and uncertainty in semantic web services. In: Proceedings of Uncertainty Reasoning for the Semantic Web, p. 188 (2005)
21. McGuinness, D.L., van Harmelen, F.: Owl web ontology language overview (2004). URL http://www.w3.org/TR/owl-features/
22. Montagna, F., Marini, C., Simi, G.: Product logic and probabilistic ulam games. Fuzzy Sets Syst. **158**(6), 639–651 (2007). DOI http://dx.doi.org/10.1016/j.fss.2006.11.007
23. Motik, B., Grau, B.C., Horrocks, I., Wu, Z., Fokoue, A., Lutz, C.: Owl 2 web ontology language profiles (2009). URL http://www.w3.org/TR/owl2-profiles/#Reasoning_in_OWL_2_RL_and_RDF_Graphs_using_Rules

24. Novák, V., Perfilieva, I., Mockor, J.: Mathematical principles of fuzzy logic. Dodrecht: Kluwer Academic (1999)
25. Sánchez, D., Tettamanzi, A.G.: Fuzzy quantification in fuzzy description logics, pp. 135–160. Fuzzy Logic and the Semantic Web, Capturing Intelligence. Elsevier (2006)
26. Spencer, B.: ALCAS: An ALC Reasoner for CAS. http://www.cs.unb.ca/ bspencer/cs6795swt/alcas.prolog (2006). URL http://www.cs.unb.ca/~bspencer/cs6795swt/alcas.prolog
27. Stamou, G., van Ossenbruggen, J., Pan, J.Z., Schreiber, G.: Multimedia annotations on the semantic web. IEEE MultiMedia **13**, 86–90 (2006). DOI http://doi.ieeecomputersociety.org/10.1109/MMUL.2006.15
28. Stevens, R., Aranguren, M.E., Wolstencroft, K., Sattlera, U., Drummond, N., Horridge, M., Rectora, A.: Using owl to model biological knowledge. International Journal of Human-Computer Studies **65**(7), 583–594 (2007)
29. Stoilos, G., Stamou, G., Pan, J.Z., Tzouvaras, V., Horrocks, I.: Reasoning with very expressive fuzzy description logics. Journal of Artificial Intelligence Research **30**, 273–320 (2007)
30. Straccia, U.: Reasoning within fuzzy description logics. Journal of Artificial Intelligence Research **14**, 137–166 (2001)
31. Straccia, U.: Towards a fuzzy description logic for the semantic web (preliminary report). In: 2nd European Semantic Web Conference (ESWC-05), Lecture Notes in Computer Science, pp. 167–181. Springer Verlag (2005)
32. Tresp, C.B., Molitor, R.: A description logic for vague knowledge. In: Proc. of the 13th Eur. Conf. on Artificial Intelligence (ECAI'98), pp. 361–365 (1998)
33. Yen, J.: Generalizing term subsumption languages to fuzzy logic. In: Proc. of the 12th Int. Joint Conf. on Artificial Intelligence (IJCAI'91), pp. 472–477 (1991)
34. Zadeh, L.A.: Fuzzy sets. Information and Control **8**(3), 338–353 (1965)
35. Zhao, J.: Uncertainty and Rule Extensions to Description Logics and Semantic Web Ontologies, chap. 1, p. 22. Advances in Semantic Computing. Technomathematics Research Foundation (2010). Accepted
36. Zhao, J., Boley, H.: A Reasoning Procedure for the Fuzzy Description Logic fALCHIN. In: Proc. Second Canadian Semantic Web Working Symposium, Kelowna, pp. 46–59 (2009)
37. Zhao, J., Boley, H., Du, W.: Knowledge Representation and Consistency Checking in a Norm-Parameterized Fuzzy Description Logic. In: D.S. Huang, K.H. Jo, H.H. Lee, H.J. Kang, V. Bevilacqua (eds.) ICIC (2), *Lecture Notes in Computer Science*, vol. 5755, pp. 111–123. Springer (2009). URL http://dx.doi.org/10.1007/978-3-642-04020-7

Chapter 3
A Generic Evaluation Model for Semantic Web Services

Omair Shafiq

Abstract Semantic Web Services research has gained momentum over the last few years and by now several realizations exist. They are being used in a number of industrial use-cases. Soon software developers will be expected to use this infrastructure to build their B2B applications requiring dynamic integration. However, there is still a lack of guidelines for the evaluation of tools developed to realize Semantic Web Services and applications built on top of them. In normal software engineering practice such guidelines can already be found for traditional component-based systems. Also some efforts are being made to build performance models for service-based systems. Drawing on these related efforts in component-oriented and service-based systems, we identified the need for a generic evaluation model for Semantic Web Services applicable to any realization. The generic evaluation model will help users and customers to orient their systems and solutions towards using Semantic Web Services. In this chapter, we have presented the requirements for the generic evaluation model for Semantic Web Services and further discussed the initial steps that we took to sketch such a model. Finally, we discuss related activities for evaluating semantic technologies.

3.1 Introduction

Semantic Web Services aim at enabling dynamic service discovery, selection, composition, mediation and invocation of Web services-based on semantic descriptions [6]. There are several realizations that exist for Semantic Web Services, i.e. Web Service Modeling Ontology (WSMO) [6], Web Ontology Language for Services (OWL-S) [15], Semantics for WSDL (WSDL-S) [16] and Semantic Annotations

Department of Computer Science, University of Calgary, Calgary, AB, Canada e-mail: moshafiq[at]ucalgary.ca
Initial work on this paper was carried out when the author was at STI Innsbruck (www.sti2.at).

W. Du and F. Ensan (eds.), *Canadian Semantic Web: Technologies and Applications*, DOI 10.1007/978-1-4419-7335-1_3, © Springer Science+Business Media, LLC 2010

for WSDL (SA-WSDL) [17]. All of these realizations require an execution environment or some toolset in order to process and execute the semantic descriptions, and to perform matchmaking.

Web Service Execution Environment (WSMX) [2] is an execution environment for dynamic discovery, selection, composition, mediation, invocation and execution monitoring of Semantic Web Services (SWS). WSMX is a reference implementation of Web Service Modeling Ontology (WSMO) [6] that acts as conceptual model to describe various aspects of Semantic Web Services. WSMO is based on four major fundamental elements which are namely, Web service descriptions, ontologies, goals and mediators. Web service descriptions are the units of functionality of Web services. Their capabilities describe logically what the Web service can actually offer. Every Web service has a number of interfaces which specify how to communicate with the Web service. Goals provide a means to users to describe its requirements. Ontologies are formal specification of the knowledge domain used by both the Web service descriptions to express its capability, as well as by the Goal to express the desired requirements. Mediators are used to solve different heterogeneity issues, i.e. differences in ontologies used in the description of different Web services and Goals respectively. WSMX is a reference implementation to realize the conceptual model WSMO. WSMX can achieve user's goal by dynamically matching and selecting Web services, mediating the data that needs to be communicated to this service, and finally invoking the Web service.

There have been other reference implementations for like IRS (Internet Reasoning Services), METEOR-S and a set of OWL-S tools. We are not going into the details of these tools, however a comparison can be found can found on some tools in [4]. In this chapter, we will refer to Semantic Web Services realized by WSMO conceptual model and WSMX as its reference implementation because of our expertise and involvement in its development.

The WSMX execution environment is being used in several industrial use-cases, i.e. in [7] it has been used for dynamic supply chain management in Business-to-Business (B2B) scenarios. As Semantic Web Services and its execution environments (i.e. WSMX) are being developed further and started to be adapted by the industry to use it for their solutions, the users of Semantic Web Services have started coming up with several questions like how to measure the usability of Semantic Web Services in many different aspects, i.e. time taken for execution, level of precision of matchmaking results obtained etc. Therefore, we have found the lack of any specific and standard guidelines for such kind of evaluation that could actually be found as normal software engineering practice, i.e. in component-based systems [9]. There are some efforts being made for building a performance model for service-based systems [8]. There exist some methodologies and tools, i.e. Performance Engineering Models and tools for SOA that caters to the growing need for assessing Non-functional requirements for enterprise applications based on SOA-based architectures [8]. It is very important that the impact of SOA on the performance, scalability, availability and the capacity requirements to be studied in detail. Performance engineering in SOA helps customers to move their applications to SOA with ease, assured by the fact that it will continue to perform and help grow their businesses.

There exist a number of tools in this regard, i.e. Jakarta JMeter, Push to Test, Web Performance Services, Mercury Load Runner.

Similarly, based on the related efforts on component- and service-based systems, need for an evaluation model, methodologies and tools for Semantic Web Services is the inspiration of this chapter. Such a model will provide guidelines that will help developers as well users to evaluate the Semantic Web Services tools and applications. The idea is to provide guidelines and sketch out a generic methodology to access functional and non-functional behavior of Semantic Web Services, i.e. to what extent they are able to achieve their required functionality for a particular use-case, and how much effective are the results.

The rest of the paper is organized as follows: section 2 introduces the performance engineering model for component-based systems and their extensions for service-oriented systems. Section 3 discusses the requirements for building such a generic evaluation model and then Section 4 introduces the evaluation model for Semantic Web Services followed by defining its critical evaluation factors. Section 5 assesses its viability by designing the evaluation strategies for evaluation of Semantic Web Services (enhanced with Triple Space Computing to be used as its communication and coordination paradigm), based on the guidelines provided by our proposed evaluation model. Finally, section 6 discusses the relevant activities about evaluation for semantics, services and related technologies followed by conclusions.

3.2 Performance Engineering for Component- and Service-oriented Systems

Performance engineering is defined as, it encompasses the set of roles, skills, activities, practices that are applied to ensure that a solution will be designed, implemented, and operationally supported to meet the non-functional requirements of the system expected by its users and applications [9]. While functional behavior of Semantic Web Services is widely understood as to automate the process of discovery, selection, composition, mediation and execution; non-functional behavior of such systems is not well understood yet. There exist a number of related tools for the evaluation of Component- and Service-based systems, i.e. Jakarta JMeter, Push to Test, Web Performance Services, and Mercury Load Runner.

Software Performance Engineering, as introduced in [10], is a systematic and quantitative approach to construct software systems that meets the performance objectives. It is based on the methodological assessment of performance attributes throughout the lifecycle, e.g. requirements, specification, implementation and maintenance [10]. The basic concept is the separation of the Software Model (SM) from its environment or Machinery Model (MM).

While the work on performance engineering of the component-based systems has become quite mature, several related efforts have been started for performance tuning of service-based systems. Such efforts are referred to as, best-practices for Promoting Scalable Web services. Best-practices for Web services are mainly same as guidelines for developing other distributed systems. There are recommendations to take the overall system performance into account. Optimization techniques have been proposed. Other related efforts for performance engineering or evaluation of service-based systems include caching of SOAP services, Quality of Service for Web services, scaling of SOAP-based Web services, as well as measuring SOAP-based Web service communication overheads [11]. Requirements for optimization techniques have been mentioned in [11] as they must identify and leverage patterns in Web service models, and should be applied to messages at a number of granularities. That must be easy for service developers to understand, implement and use, and to be able to be invoked explicitly or implicitly, and could assume a trust model between the service intermediary as well as the service provide. Based on these guidelines, several optimization techniques, i.e. caching which is a technique that has been used for some time to scale distributed systems, by allowing clients to keep and reuse copies of entities, efficiencies are realized by either the avoidance of data transfer or the avoidance of a round-trip to the server all-together. Another strategy is store-and-forward where some services consistent of submission of a message as request and a brief acknowledgement as resolve. Aggregation is another technique that allows clients to send, or services to receive separate messages from a particular device. This approach allows avoiding the overhead of separately encrypting messages and then submitting and waiting for a response for acknowledgement. [11] also presents optimization techniques that have been identified for applications built on top of Web services.

3.3 Requirements for a Generic Evaluation Model

This section describes the requirements that should be in the evaluation model in order to make it effective and usable to evaluate the semantic technologies, especially Semantic Web Services (SWS). These requirements are namely openness, tools independent, conciseness, preciseness, completeness, based on classical problems, usage of different complexity levels, usage of common benchmarking, and flexible enough to allow remote communication. Each of the requirements is briefly discussed below:

3.3.1 Openness

Openness refers to the systems that are publically available and hence are open to anyone to be accessed and used. In the similar way, the evaluation model as well as strategies should be open enough so that it can be accessed and used by any participant in the related research and industrial community, in order to evaluate their tools. Openness of the evaluation models will also encourage maximum participation from the related community and would also help in comparing different implementations and systems with each other.

3.3.2 Tool Independent

Tool independent refers to something that is not dependent on a particular tool or technology. For example, consider IATA application developed for Ticket bookings and reservation which is dependent for a particular platform and tool to operate. However, the evaluation model and its related tools should not be dependent on a particular tool or implementation. It should be independent and based on standards which are not dependent on any particular tools and implementation. It should well-utilize the openness of Semantics and Web standards, i.e. using XML and standard semantics-based messaging mechanisms to allow communication with all possible implementations.

3.3.3 Conciseness

Conciseness refers explaining something in fewer possible words while keeping the information clear enough. The evaluation model should have concise descriptions of the evaluation techniques so that it could easily be interpreted by participants and should help in avoiding any possible ambiguity in the interpretation by different participants.

3.3.4 Preciseness

Preciseness refers to exact, accurate. As envisioned by Semantic Web Services to allow exact and accurate descriptions of Web services, in the similar manner, the evaluation methodologies should also be defined very precisely to avoid any ambiguity in the interpretation. Even, formal languages, semantic technologies or rule languages can be used to precisely define the evaluation techniques within the evaluation model. This refers to semantically modeling the evaluation model and the evaluation techniques using Ontologies and Rules.

3.3.5 Completeness

Completeness refers to everything included. The evaluation model should have all possible aspects included in it. It would help in allowing evaluation of the tools and implementation from all possible aspects. If evaluation model skips some aspect of evaluation, it can cause overall evaluation of different tools to be invalid.

3.3.6 Based on Classical Problems

Classical problems refer to the problems which are already well-known in the community. The evaluation model and techniques should be based on classical problems and use-cases. The benefit would be that most of the classical problems have been developed by the research community and are mature enough. Therefore, there is less chance of any error or invalidity.

3.3.7 Different Complexity Levels

Complexity levels refer to different levels of complex scenario that the evaluation models or techniques may have. The evaluation model and techniques should be based on different levels of complexity in terms of increasing the level of granularity. It would help in deciding that up to what level a tool can solve the given problem. The level of complexity is further seen two folded. First one is based on functional aspects and second is based non-functional aspects. Complexity based on functional aspects refers that the evaluation model should have different levels of complexity to check the functional aspects of the tool which can be increased step-wise. For example, initially it can ask for basic functionality that the Semantic Web Services tools are supposed to have, and increase it further to maximum, i.e. complete functionality that the tool is supposed to have.

Secondly, complexity based on non-functional aspects refers that the evaluation model should have different levels of complexity to check the non-functional aspects of the tool, whereas the complexity levels can be increased step-wise. For example, initially it can ask for basic for one particular non-functional aspect, i.e. time-taken, and then it can further include more non-functional aspects to increase the complexity level. Following the complexity levels approach would allow testing and evaluating the tools in a debugging manner, and hence evaluating that which tools can perform better and up to what level.

3.3.8 Common Benchmarking

Common benchmarking refers to usage of benchmarking with common understanding of different participants. Different participants and tools may have different levels of performance. For example a tool based on RDF might be much performing better than a tool that is based on OWL-Full, in terms of time consumed to execute the queries. Therefore, it would not be a good idea to evaluate and compare the two tools based on time-consumption. Common evaluation and benchmarking criteria should be used in order to allow semantically correct evaluation and comparisons of tools.

3.3.9 Flexibility to Perform Remote Evaluation

The evaluation test-bed developed from the evaluation model should be flexible enough to allow the evaluation to be performed remotely. This means that the system should exploit the benefits from Service-oriented Architectures and should provide APIs (i.e. Web services) that different tools can implement and have their functionality and performance evaluated. It may not be possible to allow all evaluation procedures run remotely, however, it should be as flexible as possible. Similarly, in some cases the test-bed may require the tools to be available as Web services to be able to invoke them with a query to get answer and then evaluation and compare it. It would specially benefit in making comparison of different available tools for Semantic Web Services, without actually having them installed and configured locally.

3.4 A Generic Evaluation Model for Semantic Web Services

This section presents our proposed generic evaluation model for Semantic Web Services based on different performance engineering aspects:

- How to describe the performance and resource consumption characteristics of services/components in a complex semantic web services architecture?
- How to capture the performance and resource consumption characteristics in an automated way and with minimal overhead?
- How to derive benchmarking applications for Semantic Web Services and describe resource requirements in a hardware independent way?

It is to be noted that the performance engineering aspects of the evaluation model are not just performance with respect to time (i.e. time taken in semantic matchmaking of services), but to identify all possible aspects that are necessary to be considered in the evaluation of Semantic Web Services itself and applications built on top of it. Our proposed evaluation model is based on two major aspects, i.e. (1) lifecycle of Semantic Web Services and (2) the critical factors of evaluation. Therefore, the critical factors are not just considered on the Semantic Web Services as whole, but can also be applied to each any every step within the lifecycle of Semantic Web Services for the sake of insights in the evaluation.

3.4.1 Semantic Web Services Execution Lifecycle

This section describes execution lifecycle of Semantic Web Services that illustrates the steps, relationships and dependencies between various individual steps that are performed as functionality of Semantic Web Services. This section presents the steps in the lifecycle of Semantic Web Services and defines each of them.

3.4.1.1 Service Discovery - S1

The service discovery aims at semantic matchmaking of users request mentioned as a kind of semantic query (i.e. in WSMO notion this is called as Goal), and the semantic description of Web Services. An execution environment of Semantic Web Services takes the user query and matches it (with the help of a reasoner) with all available semantic description of services. Service Discovery uses the Web Services matched in the previous step to access the real services behind such Web service interfaces, finally checking what services fulfill the requester goal. Furthermore, three different approaches in Web service Discovery can be distinguished: Keyword-based Discovery, Lightweight semantic Discovery and Heavyweight semantic Discovery.

3.4.1.2 Service Selection - S2

Selection is the step after the discovery is finished. The selection might be required if there are more than one services matched by the discovery component. When selecting Web services, one and possibly the "best" or the "optimal" Semantic Web Service is to be returned from a set of satisfying matching services. Different variants of services are described by different values of parameters (non-functional properties specific to Web services), such as financial properties, reliability or security.

3.4.1.3 Service Composition - S3

In case, there is no single service that can fulfill the users request, two or more services are possibly to be joined together in the form of a workflow to be able to fulfill the users request. Automatic composition of Web services and reconfiguration of composed Web services are performed by intelligent applications by exploiting the semantic descriptions of services.

3.4.1.4 Service Mediation - S4

Semantic Web Services allow users to specify queries (i.e. Goals) and providers to provide semantic descriptions of services independent of each other, in the web setting. Therefore, there is a possibility that there can be difference in the users request and service provider in terms of syntax, semantics and protocols. Mediation is needed when two heterogeneous entities that do not have a common basis. Semantic Web Services offer support for data and process mediation. Data mediation is based on paradigms of ontology, ontology mapping, and ontology management. Data from different sources are mediated based on their semantic similarities as expressed by their reconciled conceptualizations. Whereas, process mediation is provided when a requester attempts to invoke and execute a Web service of a provider.

3.4.1.5 Service Choreography and Orchestration - S5

Service Choreography refers to formally describe the sequence of steps, that has to be followed by a user, while interacting with a service in order to achieve its goal. Orchestration refers to same, but the interaction is between one service and another service (i.e. when one service communicates with some other service in order to fulfill a users goal).

3.4.1.6 Service Invocation - S6

Semantic Web Service provide semantic descriptions of services, however, end-point Web services are described in well-known standards (i.e. WSDL). After discovering the right service based on semantic description of services, service invocation of the end-point (i.e. actual providers Web service) has to be performed.

3.4.1.7 External Communication - S7

Semantic Web Services act as a middleware between users and the end-point Web services. Users communicates with Semantic Web Services execution environment for precise discovery (and if required other steps) of services. Moreover, SWS execution environment invokes the end-point Web services. The process of interaction of user with SWS execution, and invocation of external end-point Web services is categorized as external communication.

3.4.1.8 Internal Execution Management Time - EM

While executing a users request, the Semantic Web Services execution environment manage the request to get the matchmaking done by discovery process, and if required, to get the selection, mediation, and finally invokes (if-found) the end-point Web service. The process of internal communication and management while executing a users request refer to internal execution management.

3.4.1.9 Overall Execution Time - T

This term refers to all the steps involved in the user request execution by Semantic Web Services execution environment. It includes internal execution management, external communication of users with SWS and SWS with end-point Web services.

3.4.2 Critical Evaluation Factors

This section introduced the identified critical evaluation factors that are to be considered in the proposed evaluation model for Semantic Web Services. The evaluation factors have been proposed while taking into consideration all possible important issues that what Semantic Web Services produce and in return what Semantic Web Services consume. It can be resources in terms of time, computation or data. From functionality side, it can be precision of results obtained from all possible steps of Semantic Web Services, i.e. discovery, selection, composition and so on.

3.4.2.1 Response Time - C1

As name suggests, it refers to the time taken in performing an activity by Semantic Web Services execution environment. It can be either discovery, or selection or composition or any other step mentioned in the Semantic Web Services functional lifecycle. Time taken is measure as the difference in time when an activity was started and when the activity finished.

3.4.2.2 Resource Consumption - C2

It refers to the computation and data resources consumption of a machine where certain activity for Semantic Web Services has been performed. It can be measured as the difference between the resources available at the time of start of activity and the resources available while the activity was being performed. In most of the cases, the resource consumption varies from time to time during the processing of an activity. Therefore, we consider average of the variation. In this case, it can be referred to as average resource consumption.

```
Percentage Resource Consumption = [ ( Resources while
execution of an activity - Resource before
started of activity ) / Resource before
started of activity ] * 100 .
```

For example, if 12 Mb data is available at hard disk, and during the execution of an activity, it consumes 4 Mb of data, the resource consumption of the activity will

```
be [ ( 12   4 ) 12 ] * 100 = 66.66 percent
```

3.4.2.3 Resource Availability - C3

It refers to the free/available resources (both computation as well as data) at a particular instance of time. It can be measured as the computation and data resources available. Since it heavily varies at operating system and hardware of the machine, and the time of performed activity is much shorter total system up time, therefore, we recommend not to have an average measure of resource availability, but to calculate it for a particular instant of time, i.e. when an activity is to be started.

Moreover, resource availability for a particular activity can also be calculate by taking a difference in the resource availability before the start of the activity, and the recourse availability while the activity was in execution.

3.4.2.4 Service Availability - C4

Previous section refers to the availability of physical resources. However, here by service availability, we mean the availability of the software service (i.e. discovery service, selection service etc.). It can be measured as availability of the instance of service for a particular duration of time. For example, within one hour, a discovery service was invoked one time that it took 6 minutes for the discovery services to perform the matchmaking. In that case, the service availability will be calculated as percentage of the time taken in execution the activity for a given duration of time. The exact formula is presented below:

```
Percentage service availability =
( Time taken in execution /
Total Time ) * 100 .
```

3.4.2.5 Meaningfulness of Results - C5

The term meaningful refers to the correctness, consistency, and completeness of results obtained from the functions of Semantic Web Services execution environment. Each of the aspect (i.e. correctness, consistency and completeness) has been defined below for our case.

There is no automated way to measure the completeness, consistency and completeness of the results except with human intervention. As human (i.e. system developer or administrator) have to see the results obtained and compare it with the expected results based on the data (i.e. semantic descriptions) available for Semantic Web Services).

3.4.2.6 Correctness of Results - C6

It refers to the precision of results obtained from the functionality of Semantic Web Services execution environment. In theoretical computer science, correctness of an activity (service discovery, for example) is asserted when it is said that the output of the activity is exactly as expected. If required, one can also measure total correctness which requires the activity to terminate and partial correctness which requires that if an answer is returned, it will be correct.

3.4.2.7 Completeness of Results - C7

The term completeness refers to the consideration of all possible data that was available to generate the answer by an activity. For example, result of service discovery will be complete if the SWS execution environment uses all service descriptions that are considered to be matched.

3.4.2.8 Consistency of Results - C8

The term consistency refers to validity of a result with respect to already available knowledge and domain information. For example in the domain it is known about some facts, and the result of an activity generated that negates some already existing fact will be called as inconsistent result. As mentioned, the meaningfulness of results (i.e. completeness, correctness and consistency) cannot be measured automatically, and required human intervention of measure its degree of meaningfulness. Below we recommend some guidelines to evaluate the correctness, completeness and consistency of answers obtained from Semantic Web Services. These recommendations are based on inspiration of proposal given for ranking answers from Semantic Web reasoners in [12]. Based on the above mentioned ranking of answers, following are the possibilities that the answer can be further categorized based on the results obtained from Semantic Web Services execution environment, i.e. Intended answer: if the answer of the SWS is same as the expected answer; Counter-intuitive answer: if the answer if completely opposite to the expected answer; Cautious answer: if expected answer is accepted or rejected, but SWS answer is undetermined; Reckless Answer: if SWS answer is accepted or rejected whereas the expected answer is undetermined.

3.4.2.9 Degree of Decoupling - C9

It refers to the level of decrement in unnecessary connection between two components or processes. The more two components or processes are disconnected or separated (both logically and physically) without effecting the required/necessary communication. It can be calculated as the amount of time the two components spend in communication with each other out of overall time for execution.

Based on the Semantic Web Services execution life-cycle as well as the critical evaluation factors, the first version of evaluation model is given below. It depicts the overall Evaluation model as a sort of traceability matrix. Each of the steps in execution life-cycle of Semantic Web Services is given in columns, whereas each of the critical evaluation factors is mentioned in rows. Evaluation has been identified for each of the step in execution life-cycle with respect to each of the critical evaluation factor. The evaluation model further shows additional columns of Internal Execution Time and Overall Execution Time, which is are derived columns from previous columns. The overall execution time is derived as sum of the time taken at each of the steps in Semantic Web Services execution life-cycle. We could further derive internal execution time by subtracting time taken at each step of Semantic Web Services execution life-cycle from the overall execution time.

It leads us to design precise formulae and further detail our strategies within the proposed evaluation model, for each step of execution of Semantic Web Services with respect to the critical evaluation factor. We will further devise precise formulae for calculation of each activity against each evaluation factor. It also motivates us to utilize semantic technologies for precise modeling and execution of the evaluation strategies, i.e. by using ontologies and rules, and hence a comprehensive Semantic Web Service Evaluation Toolkit that is based on our proposed generic evaluation model for Semantic Web Services. It may have each of the evaluation strategies precisely modeled using semantic and rule languages as required. It may further utilize Service-oriented Architecture to build services that use our proposed evaluation strategies for performing the evaluation of Semantic Web Services tools and infrastructures. Hence, it provides us an easy and standard way to measure the Semantic Web Service infrastructures and provide us necessary benchmarking support for it.

The figure 3.1 shows each step of the Semantic Web Services execution life-cycle in columns and critical evaluation factors in rows. Each of the steps in execution life-cycle of Semantic Web Services mentioned as S1, S2 up to S7. Similarly, each of the evaluation factors is mentioned as C1, C2 up to C9. This initial sketch of a generic evaluation model can be further detailed by investigating the applicability of each of the evaluation factor on each of the step of execution of Semantic Web Services.

Our prescribed critical evaluation factors as well as identified steps in the execution of Semantic Web Services help us in heading towards a generic evaluation model for Semantic Web Services where each of the critical evaluation factors is mapping against each of the steps in Semantic Web Services execution life-cycle. Our next steps are to define precise, however generic formulas for each of the critical evaluation factors, i.e. Resource consumption in service discovery, Service availability in service composition, time taken in internal execution management, response time in external communication and so on. These guidelines are based on the formals for each of the critical evaluation factors against each of the step at Semantic Web Services execution life-cycle.

Furthermore, these critical evaluation factors have helped us in improving the evaluation of Semantic Web Service execution environment enabled with Triple Space Computing [1] against the one using typical SOAP based communication protocol [3] (i.e. the first one uses Simple Object Access Protocol (SOAP) over HTTP as underline communication protocol, whereas other uses Triple Space Computing (TSC) as underline communication infrastructure where communication can

	Semantic Web Service execution life-cycle								
	Service Discovery S1	Service Selection S2	Service Composition S3	Service Mediation S4	Service Choreography and Orchestration S5	Service Invocation S6	External Communication S7	Internal Execution Management EM = T − (S1+S2 ... S7)	Overall Execution Time T
Response Time C1	C1 for S1	C1 for S2	C1 for S3	C1 for S4	C1 for S5	C1 for S6	C1 for S7	C1 for EM	Response time for Overall Execution
Resource Consumption C2	C2 for S1	C2 for S2	C2 for S3	C2 for S4	C2 for S5	C2 for S6	C2 for S7	C2 for EM	
Resource Availability C3	C3 for S1	C3 for S2	C3 for S3	C3 for S4	C3 for S5	C3 for S6	C3 for S7	C3 for EM	
Service Availability C4	C4 for S1	C4 for S2	C4 for S3	C4 for S4	C4 for S5	C4 for S6	C4 for S7	C4 for EM	
Meaningfulness of Results C5	C5 for S1	C5 for S2	C5 for S3	C5 for S4	C5 for S5	C5 for S6	C5 for S7	C5 for EM	
Correctness of Results C6	C6 for S1	C6 for S2	C6 for S3	C6 for S4	C6 for S5	C6 for S6	C6 for S7	C6 for EM	
Completeness of Results C7	C7 for S1	C7 for S2	C7 for S3	C7 for S4	C7 for S5	C7 for S6	C7 for S7	C7 for EM	
Consistency of Results C8	C8 for S1	C8 for S2	C8 for S3	C8 for S4	C8 for S5	C8 for S6	C8 for S7	C8 for EM	
Degree of decoupling C9	C9 for S1	C9 for S2	C9 for S3	C9 for S4	C9 for S5	C9 for S6	C9 for S7	C9 for EM	

Fig. 3.1 Proposed Generic Evaluation Model for Semantic Web Services

be carried out by reading and writing triples over a global, shared virtual space). The evaluation strategies include comparing resource availability when Web Service Execution Environment (WSMX) schedules a user Goal to execute it. Analyzing performance matrices with concurrent execution of users Goals, comparing communication overhead (when reading and writing RDF triples over the shared space vs. direct message exchange, comparing the time taken in distributed service execution (i.e. different WSMX systems interconnected with each other forming a distributed cluster), comparing time saved by applications during Goal execution and comparing time saved in resource retrieval.

3.5 Using the Evaluation Model for Semantic Web Services based on TSC

In this section, we present evaluation of Semantic Web Services based systems after integrating it with a new communication and coordination paradigm called as Triple Space Computing (TSC) [1]. This work was carried out in parallel, while we were working on the generic evaluation model of Semantic Web Services and hence is relevant to mention.

Triple Space Computing (TSC) [1] is a new communication and coordination paradigm based on semantic extension of the tuple-space computing. Semantic Web Services have been adapted to use the Triple Space Computing paradigm for their communication and coordination.

This section presents viability and usage of our proposed Semantic Web Services evaluation model to evaluate the one case of Semantic Web Services. The case for evaluation is based on comparison of Semantic Web Services execution environments using different underline communication infrastructures. The first one uses Simple Object Access Protocol (SOAP) over HTTP as underline communication protocol, whereas other uses Triple Space Computing (TSC) as underline communication infrastructure where communication can be carried out by reading and writing triples over a global, shared virtual space [5].

On the basis of our proposed generic evaluation model for Semantic Web Services, we have been able to come up with following useful test cases to evaluate the Semantic Web Services (enabled with Triple Space Computing) with the one based on SOAP-over-HTTP communication protocol.

3.5.1 Comparing Resource Availability

While WSMX component manager schedules the Goal execution by coordinating the between the components, Triple Space enables the WSMX manger to be released from waiting for response and makes it available to facilitate scheduling of other incoming Goals execution requests while previous Goal is already executing. From this evaluation strategy, we can perform the evaluation by submitted Goals to WSMX and checking for availability of WSMX manager to schedule other upcoming Goal execution requests. This refers to C3 (Resource Availability) for Internal Execution Management in our proposed generic evaluation model for Semantic Web Services.

3.5.2 Analyzing Performance on Concurrent Execution of Goals

Based on the comparison of resource availability and consumption, in this evaluation strategy we can compare the overall execution time taken by WSMX Manager. The comparison has to be done with the WSMX manager operating on SOAP based communication and the WSMX manager using Triple Space Computing middleware. This refers to overall execution time in our proposed generic evaluation model for Semantic Web Services.

3.5.3 Comparing Communication Overhead

While performing the components management over Triple Space, the WSML [6] descriptions are converted into RDF Named Graphs and then are published on Triple Space. It involved some extra steps to be performed than typical message based communication of WSML description. These extra steps include conversion of WSML description in the form of objects in memory, into RDF Named Graphs, publishing RDF Named Graphs over Triple Space, retrieving RDF Named Graphs from Triple Space, as well as converting RDF Named Graph back to memory object. Hence, these extra steps enforce some overhead on the communication of two communicating components. In this evaluation strategy, we can analyze and to have an idea about the overhead that is caused in write and read of data from Triple Space. This refers to internal execution management in our proposed generic evaluation model for Semantic Web Services.

3.5.4 Communication Overhead vs. Time Saved in Multiple Goal Execution

In the above mentioned evaluation strategies, we analyzed the behavior of increase in availability of resources and increase in the performance of overall Goal execution by WSMX while using Triple Space Computing for its internal components management. At the same time, we can also analyze the overhead caused by required transformation of WSML data into RDF, communicated between the components of WSMX during Goal execution. This refers to overall execution time in our proposed generic evaluation model for Semantic Web Services.

3.5.5 Comparing Time Taken in Distributed Service Execution

WSMX has been envisioned to run as interconnection of other WSMX nodes over Triple Space. The communication and coordination of different WSMX systems over Triple Space will help the WSMX in providing distributed service discovery, selection, composition, mediation and invocation. The communication model used in the current implementation of WSMX is synchronous. WSMX is dealing with reasoning, therefore, immediate responses are usually not available which is reason for such high response latency being network congestion and slow processing. In such situations, the synchronous communication will be costly as it forces the system to remain idle until the response is available. Triple Space serves as a communication channel between WSMXs by introducing a-synchronicity between communicating parties. The Triple Space supports purely asynchronous communication that optimizes performance as well as communication robustness, especially in the webscale distributed coordination. This comparison strategy aims to compare the time taken in Goal execution different WSMX systems together, coordinated by SOAP based messages as well as Triple Space. This also refers to measure and compare overall execution time in different scenarios.

3.5.6 Comparing Time Saved by Applications while Executing a Goal

WSMX-TSC [3] integration envisions decoupling between the user invoking WSMX with a Goal and WSMX itself. A goal may take some significant amount of time in execution WSMX might have to match the Goal with large number of Web service descriptions. It might also need to use selection, composition and mediation mechanisms. In the mean while, it is important for the user application providing Goal to WSMX not to hang-up until the Goal execution has been completed which can be the case if a message based communication mechanism is used between the communication of user and WSMX. User can however avoid this situation having a thread-based approach (i.e. to run a separate thread invoking WSMX) but all kind of users (i.e. light-weight users) can not afford it. Therefore, the WSMX gets this support at middleware level when users communicate with it via Triple Space. The comparison strategy aims to compare the time that a WSMX user can save (to perform other tasks, or at least be available to handle any further request) during the Goal execution by WSMX. This refers to overall execution time as well as internal execution time in our proposal model for Semantic Web Services.

3.5.7 Comparing Time Saved in Resource Retrieval by WSMX

The WSML based Web service descriptions, Goals, Mediators and Ontologies can be grounded to Triple Space. The storage of the semantic data in RDF will help in enhancing and fastening the process of accessing the data afterwards. For instance, in the current discovery mechanism of WSMX, the WSML reasoners have to reason on each and every Web service description available in the local repositories which takes significant amount of time. When the Web service descriptions will be stored over Triple Space, the template matching based simpler reasoning will be used as a first step in order to filter-out the most relevant and possibly required Web service descriptions. The filtered Web services descriptions based on template based matching over Triple Space are retrieved and converted back to WSML to be reasoned over by WSML reasoners. It makes the process of discovery simpler and faster by performing reasoning operation only on relevant Web service descriptions rather than all. Based on this assumption, this comparison strategy can help to compare the time taken in resource retrieval by the Resource Manager of WSMX with and with-out using Triple Space. This refers to resource availability in our proposed evaluation model.

These are the initial comparison factors that we managed to come up with, while adapting Semantic Web Services to use Triple Space Computing for communication and coordination. It lead us to conclude that there are no standardized tools or methodologies or any other kind of standard guidelines that are available to help in evaluation and comparison of Semantic Web Services tools. Hence, we presented our proposal and initial ideas about having a generic evaluation model accordingly.

3.6 Related Work

Apart from the performance-engineering models and tools for Semantic Web Services, there have been different initiatives to come up a common platform. It will help to test and evaluate different solutions for Semantics and related technologies (also including Semantic Web Services) based on real-world usage scenarios. These initiatives can also be major deriving forces towards standardized guidelines for evaluation semantic technology (and hence specifically also Semantic Web Services). Most commonly known efforts are described below:

3.6.1 Semantic Web Challenge

Semantic Web Challenge http://challenge.semanticweb.org aims at applying Semantic Web techniques in building online end-user applications that integrate, combine and deduce information needed to assist users in performing tasks. Intentionally, the challenge does not define specific task, data set, application domain or technology to be used because the potential applicability of the Semantic Web is very broad. Instead, a number of minimal criteria have been defined which allow people to submit a broad range of applications. In addition to the criteria, a number of specific desires have been formulated. The more desires are met by the application, the higher the score will be. The Semantic Web Challenge expects applications to use RDF, RDF schema and OWL. The core evaluation model of Semantic Web Challenge focuses on evaluation of benefits of semantic technologies used, scalability of applications through semantics and the use of dynamic data.

3.6.2 Semantic Web Services Challenge

Semantic Web Services Challenge (SWSC) http://www.sws-challenge.org aims to evaluate the ability of Semantic Web Services based applications in automating the process of mediation, choreography and discovery processes between Web services. The approach is to provide a set of problems that participants solve. Participants self-select which scenario problems and sub-problems they would like to attempt to solve. Solutions are verified by Challenge staff. In addition, it attempts to evaluate the level of effort of the software engineering technique used in going from a problem to a sub-problem.

3.6.3 Semantic Service Selection (S3)

Semantic Service Selection (S3) Content http://www.dfki.de/ klusch/s3 aims at comparative evaluation of the performance of OWL-S, SAWSDL, and WSMO based service matchmaking tools on the basis of different test collections. The performance evaluation matrices include classic average query response time and resource usage. It provides different test collections of services and related queries under different categories of applications.

3.6.4 IEEE Web Services Challenge

IEEE Web Services Challenge http://insel.flp.cs.tu-berlin.de/wsc06 addresses syntactic as well as semantic matching based on the Web Services Description Language (WSDL) and the usage of XML Schema type inheritance. In the syntactical challenge participants are required to identify and compose services which interfaces are described in WSDL. For the matching of services the input and output messages of a service are used. A more detailed technical description of the syntactic and semantic matching is available under Technical Description. Applications are evaluated for design and functional capabilities of their software. The evaluation considers the correctness of the approach with regard to the provided results as well as the performance of the system. The competition is mainly based on the capabilities of service discovery and composition.

3.6.5 SEALS Evaluation Campaigns

SEALS (Semantic Evaluation at Large Scale) http://www.seals-project.eu is a European Commissions FP7 funded project that focuses on building platform, methodology, tools and technologies to evaluate the semantic technologies. The goal of the SEALS project is to provide an independent, open, scalable, extensible and sustainable infrastructure (which may be called as SEALS Platform) to allow remote evaluation of semantic technologies, hence providing an objective comparison of the different existing semantic technologies.

The SEALS Platform aims to provide an integrated set of semantic technology evaluation services and test suites. It is planned to be used in two public and worldwide evaluation campaigns. The results of these evaluation campaigns will be used to create semantic technology roadmaps identifying sets of efficient and compatible tools for developing large-scale semantic applications.

3.6.6 STI International Test Beds and Challenges Service

Semantic Technology Institute (STI) International Test Beds and Challenges Service [13], provides test beds and challenges for evaluating, testing, demonstrating, and comparing semantic technologies. The aim is to bring the related research and industrial community together and provide them a common platform and to offer sophisticated and commonly accepted metrics for evaluating the technical quality of new technology developments as well as for assessing their capabilities in real-world problem solving. For this, STI assembles and develop methodologies, use-cases, and test environments for several fields of semantic technology developments. These can be used to validate research results, to compare different technologies, to demonstrate the benefits of semantic technologies to industry and to other interested parties, and to build interwoven communities of researchers and developers.

The test-beds offered aims to cover Semantics related tools, i.e. Ontology Engineering, Semantic storage systems (i.e. RDF stores and other metadata serialization tools), semantic reasoning systems, ontology matching, as well as semantic tools and technologies for describing and using Web services.

3.6.7 International Rules Challenge at RuleML

The International Rules Challenge is one of the key parts of the RuleML (Rule Markup Language, http://ruleml.org) Symposium, with the idea of evaluating rule-based applications developed in the university, government, and industry sectors (e.g., [14]). The challenge seeks for best practice solutions, e.g., design patterns and architecture models, case studies, and experience reports describing interesting solutions, use-cases, and benchmarks. It further solicits evaluations of rule-based systems, tools for manipulating rules and related data in existing or emerging standards (e.g., RuleML, RIF, etc.), commercial rule-based system implementations, or engineering methods for the development and deployment of rule-based solutions. It has a broad focus on evaluating the functionality of rule-based applications and the usefulness of rules.

3.7 Conclusions and Future Work

In this extended version of chapter, we presented the revised version of generic evaluation model for Semantic Web Services and prescribed critical evaluation factors like time taken, resource consumption, resource availability, service availability and correctness of results etc. The critical evaluation facts have been discussed with respect to each step of Semantic Web Services execution lifecycle, to be able to perform detailed and specific evaluations. The guidelines of the evaluation model can be considered for the evaluation of Semantic Web Services infrastructures and the applications built on top of it. It will help the potential users and the customers to evaluate Semantic Web Services while using it in their B2B solutions. We further presented the requirements for building such a generic evaluation model. We also showed the viability of the proposed evaluation model to be used to design the evaluation strategies for comparing Semantic Web Services with the one integrated with Triple Space Computing paradigm for enhanced communication and coordination.

Our next steps are to further detail our strategies within the proposed evaluation model, for each step of execution of Semantic Web Services with respect to the critical evaluation factors. We will further devise precise formulas for the calculation of each activity against each evaluation factor. Furthermore, we want to use the evaluation model to come up with the guidelines for non-technical users and administrators of applications built on top of Semantic Web Services. It further motivates us to use semantic technologies for precisely modeling and executing the evaluation strategies, i.e. by using ontologies and rules, which may lead us towards Semantic Web Service Evaluation Toolkit that provides with an easy and precise way to measure the Semantic Web Services infrastructures and provide necessary benchmarking support for it.

Acknowledgments.

The work has been partially funded by FIT-IT (Forschung, Innovation, Technologie Informationstechnologie) research program by Austrian Government, under the project TSC (Triple Space Computing), and European Commission, under FP6 STREP TripCom (Triple Space Communication) Project.

References

1. D. Fensel, Triple-space computing: Semantic Web Services based on persistent publication of information: In Proceedings of the IFIP International Conference on Intelligence in Communication Systems, INTELLCOMM 2004, Bangkok, Thailand, November 23-26, 2004.
2. C. Bussler et. al., Web Service Execution Environment (WSMX), W3C Member Submis-sion, June 2005. Available at http://www.w3.org/Submission/WSMX
3. O. Shafiq, M. Zaremba and D. Fensel, "On communication and coordination issues of Semantic Web Services", in the proceedings of IEEE International Conference Web Services (ICWS 2007), July 9-13, 2007, Salt Lake City, Utah, USA.
4. O. Shafiq, M. Moran, E. Cimpian, A. Mocan, M. Zaremba and D. Fensel, "Investigating Semantic Web Services execution environments: A comparison between WSMX and OWL-S tools", in proceedings of 2nd International Conference on Internet and Web Applications and Services (ICIW 2007), May, 2007, Morne, Mauritius.
5. O. Shafiq, R. Krummenacher, F. Martin-Recuerda, Y. Ding, D. Fensel, "Triple Space Computing middleware for Semantic Web Services", The 2006 Middleware for Web Services (MWS 2006) Workshop at 10th IEEE International Enterprise Computing Conference (EDOC 2006), 16-20 October 2006, Hong Kong.
6. D. Roman, U. Keller, H. Lausen, J. de Bruijn, R. Lara, M. Stollberg, A. Polleres, C. Feier, C. Bussler, and D. Fensel: Web Service Modeling Ontology, Applied Ontology, 1(1): 77 - 106, 2005.
7. A. Wahler, E. Oren, B. Schreder, A. Balaban, Mich. Zaremba, Mar. Zaremba, "Demonstrating WSMX: Least Cost Supply Management", WIW 2004, 1st WSMO Implementation Workshop, held at Frankfurt, Germany, September 2004.
8. D. Karastoyanova, "A Methodology for Development of Web Service-based Business Processes", at 1st Australian Workshop on Engineering Service-Oriented Systems (AWESOS 2004), Australian Software Engineering Conference - ASWEC, April 2004, Melbourne, Australia.
9. A. Bertolino, R. Mirandola: Towards Component-Based Software Performance Engineering, in Proceedings of the 6th ICSE Workshop on Component-Based Software Engineering, held at Portland, Oregon, USA May, 2003.
10. C. U. Smith, Performance Engineering of Software Systems, Addison-Wesley, 1990.
11. M. Nottingham, Web Service Scalability and Performance with Optimizing Intermediaries, W3C workshop on Web services: Position papers 11-12 April 2001, San Jose, CA, USA.
12. Z. Huang, F. van Harmelen, and A. ten Teije, Reasoning with Inconsistent Ontologies, in the proceedings of International Joint Conference on Artificial Intelligence (IJCAI 2005), July 2005, held at Edinburgh, Scotland.
13. STI (Semantic Technology Institute) International Test Beds and Challenges Services. http://testbeds-challenges.sti2.org
14. Y. Hu, C. Yeh, W. Laun, G. Governatori, J. Hall, A. Paschke (editors): "RuleML-2009 Challenge", in proceedings of the 3rd International RuleML-2009 Challenge, collocated with the 3rd International Symposium on Rules, Applications and Interoperability (RuleML-2009), Las Vegas, Nevada, USA, November 5-7, 2009. CEUR Proceedings, Volume 549. http://sunsite.informatik.rwth-aachen.de/Publications/CEUR-WS/Vol-549

15. David Martin (editor), "OWL-S: Semantic Markup for Web Services", W3C Member Submission, 22 November 2004. Available at `http://www.w3.org/Submission/OWL-S`
16. R. Akkiraju, J. Farrell, J. Miller, M. Nagarajan, M. Schmidt, A. Sheth, K. Verma, "Web Service Semantics - WSDL-S", W3C Member Submission, 7 November 2005, `http://www.w3.org/Submission/WSDL-S/`
17. Joel Farrell and Holger Lausen, "Semantic Annotations for WSDL and XML Schema", W3C Recommendation, 28 August 2007. Available at `http://www.w3.org/TR/sawsdl`

Chapter 4
A Modular Approach to Scalable Ontology Development

Faezeh Ensan and Weichang Du

Abstract The increasing desire for applying semantic web techniques for describing large and complex domains demanded scalable methods for developing ontologies. Modularity is an emerging approach for developing ontologies that leads to more scalable development process and better reasoning performance. In this chapter, we describe the interface-based modular ontology formalism and its capabilities for developing scalable ontologies. We present an extension to OWL-DL as well as tool support for creating scalable ontologies through the formalism. Furthermore, we introduce a set of metrics for evaluating modular ontologies and argue how these metrics can be applied for analyzing the scalability and reasoning performance of ontologies. We investigate a number of case studies from real-world ontologies, redesign them based on the interface-based modular formalism and analyze them through the introduced metrics.

4.1 Introduction

Semantic web techniques and ontologies have been increasingly applied to real-world problems and domains in the recent years. The Ontology for Biomedical Investigations (OBI)[32], the Gene and Gene products ontology [5] and the Earth and environmental terminologies (SWEET Ontologies) [2] are some samples of the developed large ontologies for describing complex domains. The emerging desire for applying semantic web techniques has lead to developing numerous techniques, algorithms and methodologies for ontology development and management [11, 10]. Until recently the research works for developing and managing ontologies mostly followed a monolithic approach. In [13], different frameworks for designing and

Faezeh Ensan
University of New Brunswick, Fredericton, NB, Canada, e-mail: m4742@unb.ca

Weichang Du
University of New Brunswick, Fredericton, NB, Canada, e-mail: wdu@unb.ca

W. Du and F. Ensan (eds.), *Canadian Semantic Web: Technologies and Applications*,
DOI 10.1007/978-1-4419-7335-1_4, © Springer Science+Business Media, LLC 2010

maintaining one or more monolithic ontologies have been discussed and analyzed. For instance, Text-To-Onto [24] and OntoLearn [26] are frameworks for learning ontologies from text resources and web documents. PROMPT [27] and Oasis [33] have been designed to help ontology developers manage existing domain ontologies and provide capabilities for ontology merging and mapping. In [17], different ontological methodologies have been reviewed. These methodologies define necessary phases and criteria for the ontology development process [14].

The main drawbacks of the monolithic approach for developing ontologies are its poor support for scalability and reusability and also its low reasoning performance especially in the case of large and complex ontologies. Complex domains and problems may need large and complex ontologies. This complexity emerges when the development of ontologies is carried out by different groups of experts around the world. The integration and synchronization of the distributed developed parts of an ontology as well as management, evolvement and version control of a large ontology is problematic. Moreover it is rather hard for a human expert to understand the main features of a complex ontology or describe it for non-expert users. This problem affects the reusability of developed ontologies. A complex ontology can hardly be reused in another related domain or project. Furthermore, since there does not exist any clear components, the whole complex structure should be understood, analyzed and imported even for reusing a small part of the ontology.

Large knowledge bases and a huge number of individual and inclusion axioms may have a negative effect on the performance of reasoning engines that verify and validate ontologies. A small update in adding or deleting a simple axiom may require processing the whole knowledge base for potential arisen inconsistencies. In addition, for answering a query, a reasoning engine should process the whole knowledge base even if the posed query was related to just a small part of the ontology.

Developing ontologies in a modular manner has been investigated in recent years as an alternative to the monolithic approach for providing more scalable design and better reasoning performance. Through the modular approach, a modular ontology is defined as a set of ontology modules where these modules can be integrated through various proposed formalisms. A number of modularity formalisms [7, 6, 8, 22] have been designed. These formalisms mostly provide new extensions to existing description logics syntax and semantics in order to make automated reasoning over ontology modules feasible. The objective of these formalisms is to allow ontology modules to evolve independently and the reasoning be performed only on the relevant parts of the knowledge base.

In [15, 16], we have introduce the Interface-Based modular ontology Formalism (IBF) for developing modular ontologies. IBF is designed based on the notion of interfaces and the exploitation of queries for retrieving the ABox assertions from ontology modules. Through this formalism, ontology modules can be developed independently of each others' language and signature at development time and be integrated at configuration time. Furthermore, this formalism supports a reliable mechanism for separating local (private) definitions and axioms of a module from the (public) global ones and hence endows ontology modules with a kind of black-box behaviour.

Analogous to the field of modular programming in software engineering, we can evaluate modular ontologies that are developed though a formalism and the formalism itself using a range of criteria such as encapsulation, cohesion and coupling. By encapsulation we mean the support for ontology modules to hide their detail knowledge base and axioms and offer the required parts to other ontology modules. In [15] we argue that contrary to most existing modularity formalisms, IBF supports knowledge encapsulation. IBF supports for ontology modules to define their main contents using well-defined interfaces, such that their knowledge bases can only be accessed by other modules through these interfaces. Through ontology interfaces, a group of people can understand the main features of complex ontologies and use them for their modelling purposes even though the number and size of the ontologies are growing. Additionally, high cohesion in ontology modules lead to better reusability and hence better support for scalability. Low coupling has positive effect on reasoning performance where a reasoning engine needs to only take into account the smaller number of ontology modules while processing a query or verifying an ontology module.

The objective of this chapter is to provide application support for creating scalable ontologies through the interface-based modular ontology formalism and also introduce a variety of methods for evaluating these ontologies. Our contributions can be enumerated as follows:

- We introduce an extension of Web Ontology Language (OWL), which supports the interface-based modular ontology formalism. We show that this extension can be used for developing ontology modules, interfaces and modular ontologies. In addition, we present an extension to the SWOOP [21] ontology editor which can be exploited for developing interface-based modular ontologies. We describe a new reasoner for IBF based modular ontologies, which is designed as an extension to the existing reasoning engines such as Pellet [31].
- We introduce three set of metrics for evaluating encapsulation, cohesion and coupling in interface-based modular ontologies. These metrics are driven from the ontology structure elements. We discuss how the structure of ontology modules can affect the modularity nature of an ontology.
- Considering four real-world ontologies from Protege ontology library [1] as case studies, we explain the modular design of these ontologies using the interface-based modular ontology formalism. Furthermore, we analyze these ontologies using the introduced modularity metrics and discuss how IBF leads to better support for scalability in the design of these ontologies.

The rest of this chapter is organized as follows: in section 4.2, we describe the Interface-Based modular ontology formalism in more detail. In Section 4.3, we introduce our extension to OWL and SWOOP for supporting IBF though different examples. Section 4.4 discusses the driven metrics for evaluating modular ontologies and especially IBF ontologies. Section 4.5 investigates four different case studies and presents the result of their evaluation. Section 4.6 gives some related works and finally section 4.7 concludes the chapter and gives some venues for future work.

4.2 Interface-Based Modular Ontologies

4.2.1 The Formalism

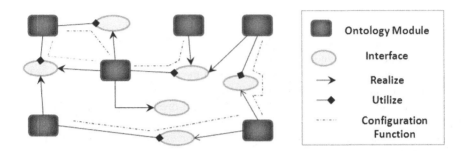

Fig. 4.1 A modular ontology which is defined through the interface-based formalism

In [15, 12] we have introduced the Interface-Based modular ontology Formalism (IBF) for developing modular ontologies. Through this formalism, a modular ontology is defined as a set of ontology modules and interfaces where an interface is a set of concept and role names and their inclusion axioms and a module is an ontology in any description logic language. An ontology module can either *realize* or *utilize* an interface. A realizer module should provide definitions and assertions for roles and concepts of a specific interface. On the other hand, a utilizer module augment its knowledge base with the definitions and assertions provided by the other (realizers) modules. In the definition of modular ontologies, there exist also a *configuration function* which specifies which utilizer and realizer modules should be connected. This formalism offers a main contribution. By the introduction of the notion of interfaces, ontology modules can communicate through interfaces and not directly, which is an important step to reduce the tightly-coupled-ness of ontologies. In addition, interfaces can be exploited to enable the practical integration of modules in a modular ontology. Figure 4.1 shows the main components of the formalism.

In [16], we introduced the *augmented semantic* for ontology modules in IBF. The proposed formalism uses epistemic or conjunctive queries to retrieve all individuals of interfaces' concepts and roles from a realizer module and augments the domain of the utilizer module with these individuals. The specifics of IBF can be found in [15].

4.2.2 IBF: Scalability and Reasoning Performance

In the following, we enumerate how IBF improves scalability in the design and management of ontologies and leads to better reasoning performance.

- Based on the notion of interfaces, the complexity of each ontology module can be hidden from the other ontologies. Consequently, each ontology module can be developed, managed, evaluated and validated independently while its complexity does not influence the management of other parts of ontology. This nature facilities complexity management in large ontologies.
- The introduction of interfaces facilitates understanding the features of an ontology. Understandability of ontology modules leads to better management and reuse. Through well-defined interfaces, ontology modules can express their content, hence human experts as well as automatic ontology search engines can easily find the appropriate ontologies that fulfill their requirements.
- After augmenting a module with appropriate individuals from other modules, reasoning engines are not required to take into account the other modules' knowledge bases anymore. Consequently, the reasoning would be considerably more efficient compared with the situation when the whole union of all knowledge bases should be processed.

4.3 OWL Extension and Tool Support for the Interface-Based Modular Ontology Formalism

OWL-DL has emerged as a popular logic-based language for representing web ontologies. In this section, we investigate the exploitation of IBF for creating OWL-DL ontologies, even though, theoretically, this formalism can be used for developing modular ontologies with any subset of the DL representation languages.

Each ontology can be treated as an ontology module in IBF. These modules can exploit or realize a set of interfaces. An interface is itself an OWL ontology whose elements have been more particularized by means of one or more realizer modules.

In the following, we use an example from the tourism domain to illustrate the main features of IBF. This example shows a modular combination of three ontology modules: 1) the *Activity* ontology 2) the *Accommodation* ontology and 3) the *Destination* ontology which defines different appropriate destinations for tourists based on the information that is made available by the activity and accommodation ontologies. The modular ontology is designed considering the monolithic ontology 'travel' which is depicted in [3] and will be more analyzed in Section 5.

We model each of these ontologies in different OWL files and connect them using the notion of interfaces. The Destination ontology uses the knowledge bases of the Activity and Accommodation ontology modules. Consequently, it should use the interfaces that have been realized by the two other ontologies. In this example, suppose that there are two interfaces: *activityInterface* and *accoInterface* which stand for two interfaces about activities and accommodations, respectively. Both of the *activityInterface* and *accoInterface* interfaces are simple ontologies that are represented in OWL files and include a subset of the concepts and roles of the activity and accommodation ontologies.

We extended OWL syntax with two new ontology properties: *useInterface* and *realizeInterface*, analogous to the definition of *owl:imports*. *useInterface* and *realizeInterface* are followed by the ID of interfaces that they use and realize, respectively.

The knowledge bases of the Activity and Accommodation ontologies are illustrated in Figure 4.2. *activity.owl* realizes the *activityInterface*:

```
<owl:Ontology rdf:about="">
    <ibf:realizeInterfaces rdf:resource=
    "&IBFModularOntology;acctivityInterface.owl"/>
</owl:Ontology>
```

where `&"IBFModularOntology;activityInterface.owl"` is the URI of the *activityInterface* interface.

Similarly, *accommodation.owl* realizes the *accoInterface* interface:

```
<owl:Ontology rdf:about="">
    <ibf:realizeInterfaces rdf:resource=
    "&IBFModularOntology;accoInterface.owl"/>
</owl:Ontology>
```

where `&"IBFModularOntology;accoInterface.owl"` is the URI of the *accoInterface* interface.

The Destination ontology utilizes these two interfaces:

```
<owl:Ontology rdf:about="">
    <ibf:useInterfaces rdf:resource=
        "&IBFModularOntology;accoInterface.owl"/>
    <ibf:useInterfaces rdf:resource=
        "&IBFModularOntology;activityInterface.owl"/>
</owl:Ontology>
```

Figure 4.3 show the knowledge bases of the interfaces *accoInterface* and *activityInterface*.

Notice that Activity and Accommodation ontology modules can realize interfaces other than *activityInterface* and *accoInterface* with more concepts and roles. In other words, an ontology can describe itself through different interfaces with different levels of abstraction. Consequently, a utilizer module can explore different interfaces and select the most appropriate ones for its particular requirements.

Destination ontology module contains `hasAccommodation`, a role whose range is the concept `Accommodation` from the *accoInterface* interface and `has Activity`, a role whose range is `Activity` from the *activityInterface* interface:

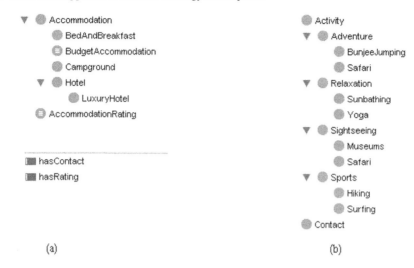

Fig. 4.2 Accommodation (a) and Activity (b) ontology modules

Fig. 4.3 accoInterface and activityInterface interfaces in the Travel modular ontology

```
<owl:ObjectProperty rdf:about="#hasAccommodation">
    <rdfs:domain rdf:resource="#Destination"/>
    <rdfs:range rdf:resource="&accInterface.owl;
       Accommodation"/>
  </owl:ObjectProperty>

  <owl:ObjectProperty rdf:about="#hasActivity">
    <rdfs:domain rdf:resource="#Destination"/>
    <rdfs:range rdf:resource="&activityInterface.owl;
            Activity"/>
  </owl:ObjectProperty>
```

Using these roles, the Destination ontology can specify the type of accommodations and also the activities provided by a particular destination. In addition, it can define new concepts using these roles as well as the concepts which are provided by interfaces. For example, the destination ontology defines the BudgetHotel Destination as a specific type of tourist destination, which has a budget accommodation:

```
   </owl:Class>
   <owl:Class rdf:ID="BudgetHotelDestination">
     <owl:equivalentClass>
       <owl:Class>
         <owl:intersectionOf rdf:parseType="Collection">
           <owl:Class rdf:about="#Destination"/>
           <owl:Restriction>
             <owl:onProperty>
               <owl:ObjectProperty rdf:about=
                "#hasAccommodation"/>
             </owl:onProperty>
             <owl:someValuesFrom>
               <owl:Class>
                 <owl:intersectionOf rdf:parseType="Collection">
                   <owl:Class rdf:about="&accInterface.owl;
                    BudgetAccommodation"/>
                   <owl:Class rdf:about="&accInterface.owl;
                        Hotel"/>
                 </owl:intersectionOf>
               </owl:Class>
             </owl:someValuesFrom>
           </owl:Restriction>
         </owl:intersectionOf>
       </owl:Class>
     </owl:equivalentClass>
   </owl:Class>
```

As another example, `RetireeDestination` can be defined as a destination whose accommodation has three star rating and offers sightseeing activities:

```
<owl:Class rdf:ID="RetireeDestination">
    <owl:equivalentClass>
      <owl:Class>
        <owl:intersectionOf rdf:parseType="Collection">
          <owl:Class rdf:about="#Destination"/>
          <owl:Restriction>
            <owl:someValuesFrom>
              <owl:Restriction>
                <owl:onProperty>
                  <owl:ObjectProperty rdf:about="&accInterface;
                      hasRating"/>
                </owl:onProperty>
                <owl:hasValue rdf:resource="&accInterface;
                       ThreeStarRating"/>
              </owl:Restriction>
            </owl:someValuesFrom>
            <owl:onProperty>
              <owl:ObjectProperty rdf:about=
                "#hasAccommodation"/>
            </owl:onProperty>
```

```
    </owl:Restriction>
    <owl:Restriction>
      <owl:onProperty>
        <owl:ObjectProperty rdf:about="#hasActivity"/>
      </owl:onProperty>
      <owl:someValuesFrom>
        <owl:Class rdf:about=
         "&activityInterface.owl;Sightseeing"/>
      </owl:someValuesFrom>
    </owl:Restriction>
  </owl:intersectionOf>
 </owl:Class>
</owl:equivalentClass>
</owl:Class>
```

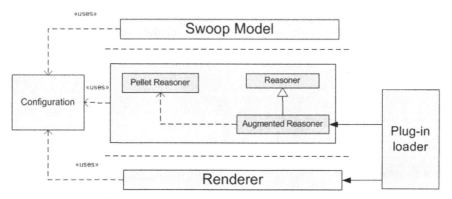

Fig. 4.4 A new extension to the architecture of Swoop for supporting interface-based modular ontologies

For implementation purpose, we perform two tasks. First, we extend OWL-DL with '*useInterface*' and '*realizeInterface*' ontology properties, in order to allow ontology modules use or realize a set of interfaces. Second, we extend the architecture of the Swoop ontology editor and browser in order to be able to work with interfaces and perform reasoning on the modular ontologies based on the semantics described earlier.

Swoop [21] is an ontology browser and editor which is tailored for OWL ontologies. It provides a convenient environment for manipulating multiple ontologies. The architecture of Swoop is comprised of three components: Model, Reasoning and Rendering. In addition, it consists of a plug-in loader which loads the appropriate reasoner or renderer in the environment. We modify the architecture of Swoop by introducing an augmented reasoner as well as a configuration object which can be shared among different layers of the architecture. Figure 4.4 depicts the modified architecture of the Swoop ontology editor.

As it has been illustrated in Figure 4.4, the augmented reasoner can be defined as an extension to any existing reasoner available for Swoop. The augmented reasoner augments the knowledge base of the ontology module with the result set of the epistemic or conjunctive queries posed to the modules which realize its required interfaces before performing a reasoning task. The augmented reasoner uses the capability of performing epistemic queries from Pellet for doing its augmentation process. It uses the configuration component in order to recognize the appropriate realizer modules.

We also modify the Model component of the Swoop architecture such that it provides capabilities for loading and working with interfaces as well. Using the extended OWL-API, the new version of Swoop supports loading interfaces and configuring modular ontologies in such a way that for each ontology module the users can select a realizer module for each of the interfaces it uses. Figure 4.5 shows a snapshot of the modified Swoop environment for creating a modular ontology.

As it can be seen it this figure, a user can graphically see the configuration of the modular ontology through the newly introduced tab: 'Configuration'. Moreover, clicking on the 'Configure Module' button, a pop-up menu is shown to the user that contains the list of all modules and for each selected module, the list of all interfaces it uses and for any selected interface the list of its realizer modules. The users can use this menu to change the configuration of a modular ontology.

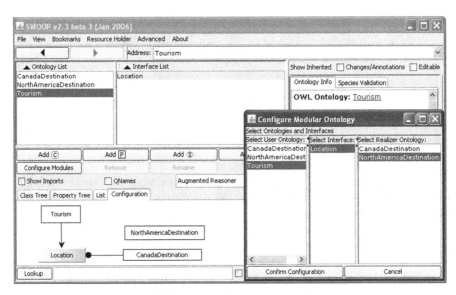

Fig. 4.5 Interface-based modular ontologies in Swoop

4.4 Evaluating IBF Modular Ontologies

The emerging desire for developing ontologies in a modular manner increases demands for having reliable metrics for evaluating modular ontologies. These metrics are distinguishable from the ontology evaluation techniques and metrics [29] that evaluate the correctness and completeness of a given ontology. Through modularity metrics, the reusability, maintainability, evolvability and scalability of ontology modules should be evaluated and analyzed.

In this section, we introduce a set of metrics for the evaluation of 'cohesion', 'coupling' and 'knowledge encapsulation' in modular ontologies and especially those which are developed through the interface-based modular ontology formalism. Through the cohesion metric, we evaluate how well the elements of an ontology module are related to each other. Understanding and maintaining an ontology module that has a set of unrelated concepts and roles is complicated. Furthermore, it is difficult to situate such ontology modules in different problem statements, for describing different domains of discourse. The coupling metric evaluates the interdependency of different ontology modules in a modular ontology. A loosely-coupled modular ontology can evolve more efficiently, in view of the fact that a module can evolve with insignificant affect on other ontology modules.

By knowledge encapsulation we evaluate how the content of the knowledge base of an ontology module is represented to other ontology modules. Ontology modules with higher encapsulation can evolve and update their knowledge base while this change is mostly hidden from foreign ontologies. In addition, it is easier for domain experts to understand the main features of an ontology modules while the unnecessary knowledge has been hidden. Moreover, as we have shown in [15] knowledge, encapsulation in IBF leads to polymorphism in ontologies i.e. a concept can be defined from different perspectives. Hence, different ontology modules can use a concept while the exact meaning of that concept is subject to more specialization in the future.

In the following, the terms ontology ontology module are used interchangeably.

4.4.1 cohesion

For measuring cohesion, we specify a set of elements in the structure of ontologies that represent a type of similarity between ontology constituents as follows:

1. *Hierarchical class relationships*: a class that is subsumed by another class in the ontology has similarity to its parent. This subsumption may be direct or indirect. For estimating the extent of this type of similarity in an ontology, we use the number of direct and indirect hierarchical class links.
2. *Object properties*: two sets of classes that are defined to be the domain and range of an object property are associated with each other. For counting this type of similarity between ontology classes, we compute the multiplication of the do-

main size and the range size of every object property. This measure shows how many classes have been associated through the particular object property. Indeed, it is necessary to sum up these measures for all existing object properties in the ontology.

3. *Hierarchical role relationships*: contrary to the previous items that measure the similarity of ontology classes, this measure estimates the similarity of ontology roles. The hierarchical role relationships measures the similarity of roles that are directly or indirectly subsumed by each other. In order to estimate this type of similarity, we count the number of direct and indirect hierarchical role links.

The cohesion metric is a number between 0 and 1, where a larger amount represents an ontology with higher similarity degrees. The Equations [1] 4.1 and 4.2 show the metrics that measure the ontology cohesion reasoned by the hierarchical class and role relationships. In order to calculate these metrics, we compute the ratio of the Number of Direct Hierarchal Relationships between Classes and Roles ($NdHC$ and $NdHR$, respectively) over the number of all potential hierarchal relationships that may exist. For an ontology with NC classes, there may exist at most $1/2(NC^2 - NC)$ subsumption relationships. Similarly, for an ontology with $NRoles$ Roles, there may exist at most $1/2(NRoles^2 - NRoles)$ subsumption relationships. The indirect class and role hierarchical relationships are counted by $NidHC$ and $NidHR$, respectively. For counting indirect hierarchical relationships between two given classes A and B, we assumed that A is indirectly subsumed by B, iff A is not directly subsumed by B, but the knowledge based implies $A \sqsubseteq B$. Notice that the resulting value of Equations 4.1 and 4.2 are between 0 and 1.

$$Hierarchical\ Class\ Cohesion(HCC) = \frac{2 \times (NdHC + NidHC)}{NC^2 - NC} \qquad (4.1)$$

$$Hierarchical\ Role\ Cohesion(HRC) = \frac{2 \times (NdHR + NidHR)}{NRoles^2 - NRoles} \qquad (4.2)$$

Equation 4.3 shows the cohesion metric which is obtained from the similarity of classes that are involved in object properties. $NdC(r_i)$ and $NrC(r_i)$ represent the number of ontology classes in the domain and range of the role r_i. The multiplication of these numbers results in the all associated classes through the role r_i. All these numbers have been summed up in the numerator of the fraction in the Equation 4.3 to obtain the number of all associated classes in an ontology. The denominator of the fraction represents the total number of classes that can be associated via object properties in the best case.

As an example, suppose we want to calculate the object property cohesion in the ontology which is depicted in Figure 4.6 (a). According to the figure, two roles, $R1$ and $R2$ exist when the domain of $R1$ and $R2$ includes class D and their ranges consist of the classes B and C for $R1$ and C for $R2$. The number of classes which have been associated through the role $R1$ is equal to $(NdC(R1) = 2) \times (NrC(R1) = 1) = 2$. Similarly for $R2$, the number of associated classes is equal to $NdC(R2) = 1) * (NrC(R2) = 1) = 1$. Figure 4.6 (b) shows all possible

---

[1] All the notations used in the equations are defined in Table 4.8 in Appendix.

association links that could exist among different classes through the roles R1 and R2. As it can be seen in the figure, in a supreme high-cohesion situation, there could be the $R1$ and $R2$ links between D and C, D and B, and B and C.

$$Object\ Property\ Cohesion(OPC) = \frac{2 \times \sum_{i=1}^{NRoles} NdC(r_i) \times NrC(r_i)}{NRoles \times (NC^2 - NC)} \quad (4.3)$$

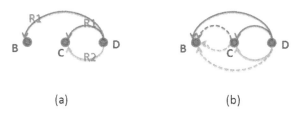

(a)   (b)

Fig. 4.6 An example for object property cohesion: (a) associated classes, (b) all potential association links

The cohesion of an ontology is calculated by a weighted mean of the discussed cohesion measures as follow:

$$Cohesion = \frac{\alpha \times HCC + \beta \times HRC + \delta \times OPC}{\alpha + \beta + \delta} \quad (4.4)$$

The values of the coefficients specify the impact of each type of hierarchical class, hierarchical role or object property cohesion in the overall cohesion metric. In our case studies that are illustrated in the next section, we choose a larger value for α and β compared with δ. The reason is that hierarchical relationships means stronger similarity between ontological elements and also the value of object property cohesion is not considerable in our selected ontologies because of the small number of role numbers compared with all existing association links that could exist.

4.4.2 coupling

By means of the coupling metric, we estimate the inter-dependency of different ontology modules. We specifies different resources for coupling between two ontology modules as follows:

1. *Hierarchical class dependency*: a class in an ontology is directly or indirectly defined as a subclass of another class from an external ontology. For measuring the hierarchical class dependency in an ontology module, we count all direct or indirect hierarchical class relationships to foreign ontologies.
2. *Object property dependency*: the domain or range of a role in an ontology includes classes from external ontologies. In order to estimate this type of depen-

dencies, we count the number of roles that associate external classes to local ones.

3. *Hierarchical role dependency*: a role in an ontology is directly or indirectly defined as a sub role of an external role. For measuring the hierarchical role dependency, similarly to the hierarchical class dependency, we count all direct or indirect hierarchical role relationships to foreign ontologies.

4. *Axiom dependency*: an ontological element is associated to an external element through an inclusion axiom. For example, in the general inclusion axiom $A \sqsubseteq B \sqcup \exists R.C$, B R and C have been associated with A. When one side of an axiom includes an external role or class, it results in the axiom dependency.

The coupling metric is a number between 0 and 1, where a lower value for the coupling metric means more desirable modularity and lower inter-dependency between ontology modules. Equations 4.5 and 4.6 show the metrics that measure the ontology coupling caused by by the hierarchical class and role dependencies. In order to calculate these metrics, we use the ratio of the number of direct hierarchical class dependencies and indirect hierarchical dependencies between local classes and external classes ($NedHC$ and $NeidHC$, respectively) over the number of all existing direct hierarchical class dependencies and indirect hierarchical class dependencies that could possibly exist between local and external clasees, respectively. Similarly we use the ratio of the number of direct hierarchical role dependencies and indirect hierarchical role dependencies between local and external roles($NedHR$ and $NeidHR$, respectively) over the number of all existing direct hierarchical class dependencies and hierarchical role dependencies could possibly exit between local and external roles, respectively. For object property dependency, we define Equation 4.7, where the nominator of the fraction $NeRoles$ is the number of all roles that have an external class in their domain or range and the denominator is the number of all existing roles in the ontology.

$$Hierarchical\ Class\ Coupling\ (HCCp) = 1/2 \times (\frac{NedHC}{NdHC} + \frac{NeidHC}{NidHC}) \qquad (4.5)$$

$$Hierarchical\ Role\ Coupling\ (HRCp) = 1/2 \times (\frac{NdHR}{NedHR} + \frac{NeidHR}{NidHR}) \qquad (4.6)$$

$$Object\ Property\ Coupling\ (OPCp) = \frac{NeRoles}{NRoles} \qquad (4.7)$$

Equation 4.8 show the axiom coupling metric. Here, $LS(axm)$ and $RS(axm)$ mean the size of the left and right sides of the axiom axm, respectively. Moreover, $LSE(axm)$ and $RSE(axm)$ mean the number of foreign (external) elements in the left and right sides of the axiom axm, respectively. $externalAssociation Number(axm)$ represent the number of all external ontological elements that have been associated through the axiom axm to the internal elements. In the equation, all external association numbers for all axioms are summed up and are divided to the number of all association among all internal or external elements that are caused by ontological axioms. This ratio is a number between 0 and 1 such that when all associated elements are internal the coupling would be 0 . The coupling metric is in its worst case 1 when all axioms associate the ontological classes to the external roles and and classes. Figure 4.7 shows an example of the axiom coupling. In the figure 4.7 (a), the concept A in the first ontology module is defined as a sub concept of $\exists R.C$, where R is a role in *ontology module 1* and C is a class from the second ontology module. Based on this inclusion axiom, A has dependencies to R and C (figure 4.7 (b)), while C is an external element. In this example, based on the inclusion axiom, there are 2 dependencies between ontological elements. While one dependency is to a forign element. Consequently, the value of the axiom coupling metric is equivalent to $(1/2)$.

$$Axiom\ Coupling\ (ACp) = \frac{\sum_{i=1}^{N\,Axioms} external\,Association\,Number(axm_i)}{\sum_{i=1}^{N\,Axioms} LS(axm_i) \times RS(axm_i)} \quad (4.8)$$

where

$external\,Association\,Number(axm) =$
$LSE(axm_i) \times RS(axm_i) + LS(axm_i) \times RSE(axm_i) - LSE(axm_i) \times RSE(axm_i)$

Take into account that logically, there may exist some axioms that do not necessarily result in a dependency. For example from the expression $A \sqsubseteq \neg B \sqcup B$, it is not inferred that A is dependent on B nor $\neg B$. As another example from $A \sqsubseteq A \sqcup B$, we can not conclude that A is dependent on B. For estimating coupling, we first apply a pre-processing on inclusion axioms and remove all tautologies and all axioms that have similar logical consequences. Subsequently, we count the number of dependent elements for calculating the coupling measure.

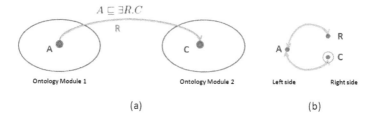

Fig. 4.7 An example for axiom coupling

Finally the overall coupling metric is defined as a weighted mean of the four introduced coupling measures:

$$coupling = \frac{\alpha * HCCp + \beta * HRCp + \gamma * OPCp + \delta \times ACp}{\alpha + \beta + \gamma + \delta} \quad (4.9)$$

4.4.3 Knowledge Encapsulation

Knowledge encapsulation measures the capability of the formalism to hide the internal knowledge base. In the case of IBF, for a chain of connected ontology modules that represent a modular ontology, the interface concepts and roles are not hidden and can be accessed by other modules. We estimate the knowledge encapsulation measure by counting interface concepts and roles and obtaining a ratio of this number over the total number of classes and roles. Equation 4.10 shows the knowledge encapsulation metric in interface-based modular ontologies. In this equation NC_{MO} and $NRoles_{MO}$ represent the number of all classes and roles in all ontology modules which involve in a modular ontology. In addition NiC_{MO} and $NiRoles_{MO}$ denotes the number of all interface classes and roles in a modular ontology.

$$Knowledge\ Encapsulation\ (KE) = 1 - \frac{NiC_{MO} + NiRoles_{MO}}{NC_{MO} + NRoles_{MO}} \qquad (4.10)$$

As an example, consider calculating the KE metric for the modular ontology which is depicted in Figure 4.8.

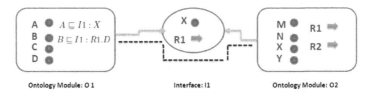

Fig. 4.8 An example for estimating the knowledge encapsulation metric

According to this figure, the modular ontology is consist of two ontology modules $O1$ and $O2$ and an interface $I1$, where $O1$ utilizes the class and role of the interface $I1$ in its inclusion axioms and $O2$ realizes this interface. The number of classes in the modular ontology is equal to 8 (4 in $O1$ and 4 in $O2$), the number of roles in the modular ontology is 2. There exist one class (X) and one role ($R1$) that are visible to other ontology modules through interface $I1$. KE for this modular ontology is equal to 1-2/8=0.75.

4.5 Case Studies

In this section, we show the evaluation of four ontologies from [1] based on the modularity evaluation metrics that we introduced in the previous section. These ontologies are all monolithic ones. We redesign them using the interface-based modularity formalism and evaluate and compare them. Take into account that since coupling and knowledge hiding for monolithic ontologies do not have a clear meaning, we only compare the cohesion metrics of IBF ontologies regarding to the original monolithic versions.

4.5.1 IBF Modular Ontologies

The first example is the famous wine-food ontology from [4]. Originally, there exit two ontologies: *food* and wine, where the food and wine ontologies import each other using the *owl:imports* statement. *owl:imports* brings all ontological elements of the reference ontology to the referring one. We design an IBF based modular ontology for representing the wine and food knowledge bases in a modular manner. A notable point in our redesigns is that our goal is not to decompose an existing monolithic ontology to a modular one and keep the reasoning consequences. Instead we start a new design and development process. However, for the purpose of comparison, we limit our new design such that the modular ontology has the ontological elements of the monolithic one. Figure 4.9 shows that the modular ontology of wine and food:

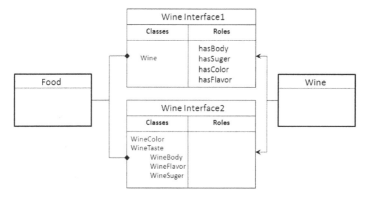

Fig. 4.9 An IBF-based design for Wine and Food ontologies

We designed two interfaces for the wine ontology. *Wine Interface1* represents the wine concept and four of its object properties and *Wine Interface2* denotes the notions of colors and tastes for wine. The food ontology makes use of these interface elements in its knowledge base for defining new concepts.

The second case study is the music set of ontologies from [30]. Figure 4.10 shows the modular ontology we have designed for it using the interface-based modular ontology formalism. We defined three interfaces for each of Time, keys and Event ontologies. The Event ontology realizes the Event interface while it utilizes `Temporal Entity` from the Time interface. Time interface itself is realized by the Time ontology module. The Music ontology utilizes both Keys and Event interface in its internal knowledge base. Our modular design is an alternative to the original design where the Event ontology imports the whole knowledge base of the Time ontology, and Music ontology imports the whole knowledge bases of the Event and Keys ontologies.

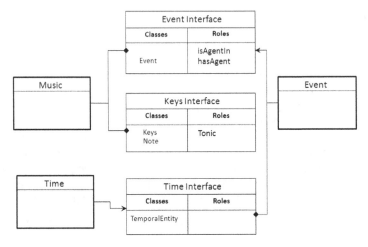

Fig. 4.10 An IBF-based design for music ontologies

The third set of ontologies we have selected for the purpose of evaluation are the SWEET ontologies. Semantic Web for Earth and Environmental Terminology (SWEET) [2] is a NASA founded project for providing ontologies for modeling various Earth science. We chose the "Earth Realm" ontology from the SWEET 1.0 version and redesign it using interfaces and ontology modules based on IBF. The Earth Realm ontology imports four ontologies: 'Property', 'Numerics', 'Space' and 'Substance'. Despite importing the whole knowledge bases of these four ontologies, Earth Realm just uses a limited number of their ontological elements. Figure 4.11 shows the IBF modular ontology that we have designed for this situation. In this figure, there exist four interfaces related to the four ontologies. The Property, Numerics, Space and Substance ontology modules have not been shown in the figure but they realize their corresponding interfaces. The Earth Realm is the utilizer of all these ontologies. A considerable point in this figure is that we made use of generalization between interfaces. Some of the concepts of the Space Interface have subclass-superclass relationships with some classes of the Numeric ontology. For instance, `Layer- Boundary` form Space ontology is defined as a sub concept of `layer` from the Numeric ontology. Accordingly, we defined the *Space-Numeric* interface that extends both space and numeric ontologies with the inclusion axiom of `Layer-Boundary ⊑ Boundary`. The Earth Realm uses this interface, in order to have the relationships between space and numerics elements.

And finally, the last ontology is the Travel ontology which is thoroughly discussed in Section 4.3. This ontology is a simple, small ontology that does not have any import statements. we redesign it by recognizing this fact that the destination,

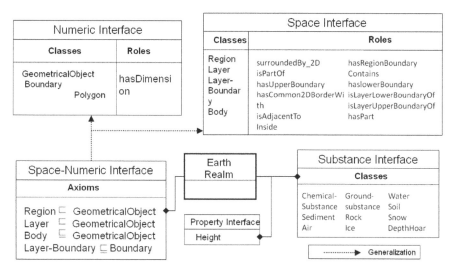

Fig. 4.11 An IBF-based design for SWEET ontologies

accommodation and activities are three semi-independent parts of the ontology that can be modeled as separate ontology modules. The Destination ontology module exploits the Activity and Accommodation concepts and roles to define appropriate tourist destinations.

4.5.2 IBF Ontologies Analysis

In this section, we analyze the four introduced modular ontologies though the modularity metric. Figure 4.12 shows the value of the cohesion metric of IBF-based modular ontologies and also the original ontologies. We use the average of overall cohesion metrics of constituent ontology modules in the modular ontologies and also the average cohesion metric of connected ontologies in the monolithic ontologies for the purpose of comparison and depiction in the diagram. The only exception in all following diagrams is the SWEET ontology. Since we redesigned only the Earth Realm ontology through IBF, we illustrate the value of the metrics only for this ontology module.

According to this figure, we can see that the cohesion metric has been improved through the IBF-based redesign, specially in the case of SWEET and travel modular ontologies. The accommodation and activity in the travel ontology are completely independent of each other and also independent form the destination part. Accordingly, separating them from each other results in better cohesion metrics. We can conclude that the reasoning performance will be considerably improved in the modular version of travel ontology. In the case of SWEET ontology, because of the huge number of class numbers, the overall cohesion metric is low. Nonetheless, the

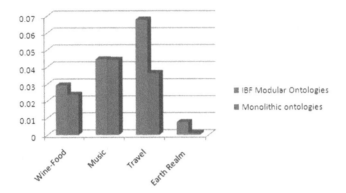

Fig. 4.12 The value of cohesion metric for sample modular ontologies

difference between two cohesion metrics show the significant improvement of the modular design.

Figure 4.13 shows the value of different coupling metrics in four modular ontologies.

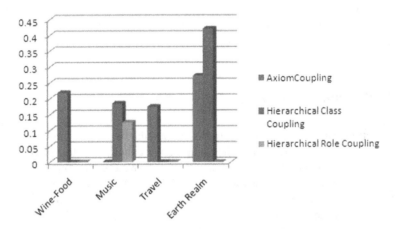

Fig. 4.13 The value of coupling metric for sample modular ontologies

A gold standard design for a modular ontology is when its cohesion metric has a large value while its coupling metric is low. However, reaching this goal is not easy for all ontologies. For example the Earth Realm ontology module suffers from a high coupling metric specially for the hierarchical dependencies. It is as a result of a large number of classes that are defined to be subsumed directly or indirectly by interface concepts.

Figure 4.14 illustrates the knowledge encapsulation metric for four developed modular ontologies. According to this figure, Earth Realm ontology reaches a very well knowledge encapsulation level. Accordingly, all utilized ontologies like Units, Numerics and Time can be evolved and change their internal knowledge base with very few impact on the design of Earth Realm ontology. On the contrary, the Travel ontology does not provide a good level of knowledge encapsulation. Consequently, the evolution or replacement of ontology modules is not efficient.

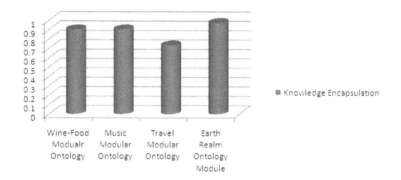

Fig. 4.14 The value of knowledge encapsulation metric for sample modular ontologies

4.6 Related Work

In [35], scalability in the filed of ontologies is defined as providing valid reasoning support for complex domain and comprehensive axioms and concepts. The authors in [35] introduce a modular design for the 'Value Added Tax', VAT ontology, and argue that this design can improve the scalability of the ontologies. Ontology modularization is also emphasized in [23] as an approach for improving scalability and reasoning performance.

Modularity provides stronger support for knowledge reuse, parallel and more efficient reasoning in the ontology development process. In [25], two types of scalability in ontologies are discussed that can be achieved by modularization. First, scalability for information retrieval, that needs a type of modularization that limits the search space for a given query. Second, scalability for evolution and maintenance for which , modularization should be in a way that reduces the propagation of changes from an evolving ontology to other parts.

[34] provides a survey of modular ontology formalisms. It characterizes the scalability of a formalism by its reasoning performance in the case of large ontologies. Analogous to our work which is presented here, [34] defines a number of features for modular ontologies. It enumerate reusability, encapsulation, loose coupling ,self containment, reasoning scalability and reasoning support as criteria for evaluating modular ontologies. However it does not introduce any metrics for estimating these

features. Accordingly, modularity formalisms are analyzed through the introduced features instead of modular ontologies. Different modular ontology formalisms are hence categorized under 'well', 'partially', 'fairly', or 'low' support for the modularity features.

In [9], a set of evaluation metrics for ontologies are introduced. These metrics are concerned with different perspectives of an ontology like its authority, history, comprehensiveness, richness and etc. In [18], three approaches, structural, functional and usability-related, are explained for the purpose of ontology evaluation and validation. [18] introduces a set of metrics such as depth, breadth and leaf and sibling distribution for the structural measure. All these metrics are calculated using the ontology graph elements.

[20] and [28] talk about the cohesion and coupling metrics in ontologies. It is discussed that the number of root classes, leaf classes and also the average depth of inheritance tree of leaf nodes in an ontology represent its cohesion. Furthermore, the number of external classes, reference to external classes, and also the number of included references in an ontology highlighted as set of effective elements for coupling of an ontology.

The coupling and cohesion metrics that introduced in this chapter for modular ontologies consider the depth of the ontology graph and its root and leaf classes, implicitly. While they take into account other perspectives of an ontology like its role similarities, axiom dependencies, direct and indirect hierarchical dependencies between ontologies and hierarchical role dependencies.

4.7 Conclusion

In this chapter, we presented language and application support for the interface-based modular ontology formalism (IBF). We also presented a set of metrics for evaluating modular ontologies. We analyzed a number of case studies and real world ontologies using the introduced metrics.

We designed four modular ontologies for real-world applications and domains based on IBF. We investigated their modularity features like cohesion, coupling and knowledge encapsulation. We showed that the interface-based modular ontologies enjoy a better cohesion metrics compared with the monolithic ones. High cohesion in ontology modules lead to better reusability and hence better support for scalability. We also analyzed the coupling and knowledge encapsulation of sample modular ontologies. IBF improves loose coupling and knowledge hiding of ontologies by connecting ontologies through interfaces instead of importing approach. This feature leads to better understandability and reusability of ontology modules and therefore improves scalability in the process of ontology development.

References

1. Protege ontology library (2008). http://protegewiki.stanford.edu/index.php/
2. Semantic web for earth and environmental terminology (sweet) (2008). http://sweet.jpl.nasa.gov/
3. Travel ontology (2008). Http://protege.cim3.net/file/pub/ontologies/travel/travel.owl
4. Wine-food ontologies (2008). Http://www.w3.org/TR/2004/REC-owl-guide-20040210/wine.rdf and http://www.w3.org/TR/2004/REC-owl-guide-20040210/food.rdf
5. Ashburner, M., Ball, C.A., Blake, J.A., Botstein, D., Butler, H., Cherry, J.M., Davis, A.P., Dolinski, K., Dwight, S.S., Eppig, J.T., Harris, M.A., Hill, D.P., Issel-Tarver, L., Kasarskis, A., Lewis, S., Matese, J.C., Richardson, J.E., Ringwald, M., Rubin, G.M., Sherlock, G.: Gene ontology: tool for the unification of biology. the gene ontology consortium. Nat Genet **25**(1), 25–29 (2000)
6. Bao, J., Caragea, D., Honavar, V.: Modular ontologies - a formal investigation of semantics and expressivity. In: R. Mizoguchi, Z. Shi, F. Giunchiglia (eds.) ASWC, vol. 4185, pp. 616–631 (2006)
7. Bao, J., Slutzki, G., Honavar, V.: A semantic importing approach to knowledge reuse from multiple ontologies. In: AAAI, pp. 1304–1309 (2007)
8. Borgida, A., Serafini, L.: Distributed description logics: Assimilating information from peer sources. J. Data Semantics **1**, 153–184 (2003)
9. Burton-Jones, A., Storey, V.C., Sugumaran, V., Ahluwalia, P.: A semiotic metrics suite for assessing the quality of ontologies. Data Knowl. Eng. **55**(1), 84–102 (2005)
10. Corcho, O., Fernandez-Lopez, M., Gomez-Perez, A.: Methodologies, tools and languages for building ontologies: where is their meeting point? Data Knowl. Eng. **46**(1), 41–64 (2003). DOI http://dx.doi.org/10.1016/S0169-023X(02)00195-7
11. Ding, Y., Foo, S.: Ontology research and development. part 1- a review of ontology generation. Journal of Information Science **28**(2), 123–136 (2002)
12. Ensan, F.: Formalizing ontology modularization through the notion of interfaces. In: EKAW, pp. 74–82 (2008)
13. Ensan, F., Du, W.: Towards domain-centric ontology development and maintenance frameworks. In: the Nineteenth International Conference on Software Engineering and Knowledge Engineering (SEKE), pp. 622–627 (2007)
14. Ensan, F., Du, W.: Formalizing the role of goals in the development of domain-specific ontological frameworks. In: 41st Hawaii International International Conference on Systems Science (HICSS-41), p. 120 (2008)
15. Ensan, F., Du, W.: An interface-based ontology modularization framework for knowledge encapsulation. In: International Semantic Web Conference (2008)
16. Ensan, F., Du, W.: A knowledge encapsulation approach to ontology modularization. Knowledge and Information Systems (2009). DOI 10.1007/s10115-009-0279-y
17. Fernandez-Lopez, M., Gomez-Perez, A.: Overview and analysis of methodologies for building ontologies. Knowl. Eng. Rev. **17**(2), 129–156 (2002). DOI http://dx.doi.org/10.1017/S0269888902000462
18. Gangemi, A., Catenacci, C., Ciaramita, M., Lehmann, J.: A theoretical framework for ontology evaluation and validation. In: SWAP (2005)
19. Grau, B.C., Horrocks, I., Kazakov, Y., Sattler, U.: Just the right amount: extracting modules from ontologies. In: WWW '07: Proceedings of the 16th international conference on World Wide Web, pp. 717–726. ACM, New York, NY, USA (2007). DOI http://doi.acm.org/10.1145/1242572.1242669
20. H., Y., A.M., O., L., E.: Cohesion metrics for ontology design and application. Journal of Computer Science **1**(1), 107–113 (2005)
21. Kalyanpur, A., Parsia, B., Sirin, E., Grau, B.C., Hendler, J.A.: Swoop: A web ontology editing browser. J. Web Sem. **4**(2), 144–153 (2006)
22. Kutz, O., Lutz, C., Wolter, F., Zakharyaschev, M.: E-connections of abstract description systems. Artif. Intell. **156**(1), 1–73 (2004)

23. Lefort, L., Taylor, K., Ratcliffe, D.: Towards scalable ontology engineering patterns: lessons learned from an experiment based on w3c's part-whole guidelines. In: AOW '06: Proceedings of the second Australasian workshop on Advances in ontologies, pp. 31–40 (2006)

24. Maedche, A., Staab, S.: Ontology learning for the semantic web. Intelligent Systems, IEEE **16**(2), 72–79 (2001)

25. Menken, M., Stuckenschmidt, H., Wache, H., Serafini, L., Tamilin, A., et al.: Report on modularization of ontologies. Tech. rep., The Knowledge Web Network of Excellence (NoE), Deliverable D2.1.3.1 (2005)

26. Navigli, R., Velardi, P.: Learning domain ontologies from document warehouses and dedicated web sites. Comput. Linguist. **30**(2), 151–179 (2004). DOI http://dx.doi.org/10.1162/089120104323093276

27. Noy, N.F., Musen, M.A.: The prompt suite: interactive tools for ontology merging and mapping. Int. J. Hum.-Comput. Stud. **59**(6), 983–1024 (2003)

28. Orme, A.M., Yao, H., Etzkorn, L.H.: Coupling metrics for ontology-based systems. IEEE Software **23**(2), 102–108 (2006). DOI http://doi.ieeecomputersociety.org/10.1109/MS.2006.46

29. Porzel, R., Malaka, R.: A task-based approach for ontology evaluation. In: P. Buitelaar, S. Handschuh, B. Magnini (eds.) Proceedings of ECAI 2004 Workshop on Ontology Learning and Population. Valencia, Spain (2004)

30. Raimond, Y., Abdallah, S., Sandler, M., Giasson, F.: The music ontology. In: International Conference on Music Information Retrieval (2007)

31. Sirin, E., Parsia, B., Grau, B.C., Kalyanpur, A., Katz, Y.: Pellet: A practical owl-dl reasoner. Web Semantics: Science, Services and Agents on the World Wide Web **5**(2), 51–53 (2007)

32. Smith, B., Ashburner, M., Rosse, C., Bard, J., Bug, W., Ceusters, W., Goldberg, L.J., Eilbeck, K., Ireland, A., Mungall, C.J., Leontis, N., Rocca-Serra, P., Ruttenberg, A., Sansone, S.A., Scheuermann, R.H., Shah, N., Whetzel, P.L., Lewis, S.: The obo foundry: coordinated evolution of ontologies to support biomedical data integration. Nat Biotech **25**(11), 1251–1255 (2007)

33. Song, G., Qian, Y., Liu, Y., Zhang, K.: Oasis: A mapping and integration framework for biomedical ontologies. In: CBMS '06: Proceedings of the 19th IEEE Symposium on Computer-Based Medical Systems, pp. 611–616 (2006)

34. Wang, Y., Bao, J., Haase, P., Qi, G.: Evaluating formalisms for modular ontologies in distributed information systems. In: RR, pp. 178–193 (2007)

35. Zhao, G., Meersman, R.: Architecting ontology for scalability and versatility. In: OTM Conferences (2), pp. 1605–1614 (2005)

4.8 Appendix

Notation	Explanation
NdHC	Number of direct hierarchal relationships between classes in the ontology module
NidHC	Number of indirect hierarchal relationships between classes in the ontology module
NdHR	Number of direct hierarchal relationships between roles in the ontology module
NidHR	Number of indirect hierarchal relationships between roles in the ontology module
NdC(R)	Number of domain classes for role R
NrC(R)	Number of range classes for role R
NRoles	Number of roles in the ontology module
NC	Number of classes in the ontology module
NedHC	Number of direct hierarchal relationships between local classes in the ontology module and external classes from foreign ontologies
NeidHC	Number of indirect hierarchal relationships between local classes in the ontology module and external classes from foreign ontologies
NedHR	Number of direct hierarchal relationships between local roles in the ontology module and externals role from foreign ontologies
NeidHR	Number of indirect hierarchal relationships between local roles in the ontology module and external roles from foreign ontologies
NeRoles	Number of roles that have an external class in their domain or range
LS(amm)	Number of the left elements of the axiom axm
RS (axm)	Number of the left elements of the axiom axm
LSE (axm)	Number of external elements in the left side of the axiom axm
RSE(axm)	Number of external elements in the right side of the axiom axm
NAxioms	Number of the axioms in an ontology
NiC_{MO}	Number of classes in all of existing interfaces in a Modular Ontology (MO)
NC_{MO}	Number of classes in all ontology modules that form a modular ontology
$NiRoles_{MO}$	Number of roles in all of existing interfaces in a Modular Ontology
$NRoles_{MO}$	Number of roles in all ontology modules that form a modular ontology

Table 4.1 List of notations which are used in the equations

Chapter 5
Corporate Semantic Web: Towards the Deployment of Semantic Technologies in Enterprises

Adrian Paschke, Gökhan Coskun, Ralf Heese, Markus Luczak-Rösch, Radoslaw Oldakowski, Ralph Schäfermeier, and Olga Streibel

Abstract The amount of information that companies have to produce, acquire, maintain, propagate, and use has increased dramatically over the last decades. Nowadays, companies seek more capable approaches for gaining, managing, and utilizing knowledge, and the Semantic Web offers promising solutions. While the global Semantic Web still remains an unfulfilled vision for the present, the Corporate Semantic Web idea aims at bringing semantic technologies to enterprises. The expected results are a competitive advantage for enterprises using semantic technologies and a boost for the evolution of the global Semantic Web.

5.1 Introduction

The transition from manufacturing to information economies and the progressive globalization of markets pose new challenges to enterprises. The amount of information that companies have to produce, acquire, maintain, propagate, and use has increased dramatically. While technologies and tools that help collaborating and structuring content, such as tagging, wikis, blogs, and collaboration platforms are in place, companies seek more capable approaches for gaining, managing, and utilizing knowledge required for their business processes. The amount, the heterogeneity, and the multimodality of data remain problematic aspects in the integration of data sources, presentation of information, and the extraction of knowledge.

In this regard, the Semantic Web offers promising solutions but also poses new challenges. The principal aspect of the Semantic Web is a shift away from the focus on data and documents towards their actual informational content and a machine-readable representation of it [3] by the means of ontologies. In the context of the Semantic Web, an ontology is a formal specification of a conceptualization and allows inference engines to derive and make explicit new information which is already implicitly contained in it.

AG Corporate Semantic Web, Freie Universität Berlin, Germany

W. Du and F. Ensan (eds.), *Canadian Semantic Web: Technologies and Applications*, DOI 10.1007/978-1-4419-7335-1_5, © Springer Science+Business Media, LLC 2010

As a result of the need for better knowledge management in corporate settings Corporate Semantic Web (CSW) aims at establishing semantic technologies in enterprises. By focusing on the controlled environment, in contrary to the global Semantic Web, it avoids facing unresolved problems like scalability, broader adoption of commonly shared ontologies, and trust issues. Therefore, the potential in many industrial application scenarios and the short-term practicability in closed enterprise settings merits continued work, although semantic technologies are relatively young and gaps in standards and implementations exist.

The rest of this chapter is organized as follows. Section 5.2 introduces application domains we have identified in close cooperation with our industrial partners. Based on the cooperation we derived real world gaps between corporate contexts and the application of ontologies which are described in section 5.3. In section 5.4 the three research areas of CSW are introduced that concertedly close the identified gaps and aim at applying semantic technologies in the enterprise world. These three research areas are then presented in detail in sections 5.5, 5.6, and 5.7. Finally, the conclusion and an outlook is presented in section 5.8.

5.2 Application Domains for a Corporate Semantic Web

Derived from interviews with our industrial cooperation partners we see two major application domains for corporate semantic technologies in the enterprise area:

1. Automated Semantic (Business) Processes Management
   The assumption behind Business Process Management (BPM) is that the uniqueness of an enterprise lies in the way how it manages and executes its business processes. Accordingly, business processes are the most valuable asset of an enterprise. Modern BPM often directly builds IT Service Management (ITSM) which describes the change of information technology (IT) towards service and customer orientation, and IT Infrastructure Management (ITIM) which focuses on planning and efficient and effective delivering of IT services and products while meeting quality of service and security requirements. Corporate Semantic Web (CSW) technologies for semantic business process management (SBPM) provide scalable methods and tools for the machine-readable representation of knowledge, especially rules as a means for declaratively describing business rules and IT policies, and ontologies as a means of capturing a domain of discourse such as a business vocabulary which, for example, might be used in semantic business processes and Semantic Web Services (SWS).

2. Knowledge Management
   In particular in the realm of corporate collaboration tools, Semantic Web technologies will support semi-automatic knowledge evolution and dynamic access to and integration of distributed, heterogeneous information sources and knowledge consolidation – for example, for trend, enterprise structure, and problem recognition. This will enable the mapping from corporate data and human expert information into explicit knowledge and finally into corporate wisdom stored

e.g. in semantic organizational memories supporting e.g. sophisticated semantic search for organizational knowledge.

From the aforementioned interviews we have identified the following common applications and objectives for the utilization of semantic technologies in corporate environments:

- Intelligent Semantic Search
  Objectives:

  - improved relevance of search results with higher precision and recall
  - processing of relations between different search results
  - determining of non explicit, unknown correlations
  - automated navigation structures, e.g. for visual navigation of research results in the ontology graph
  - personalized and contextual semantic search

- Declarative Knowledge Representation
  Objectives:

  - separation of concerns by separating content from meaning and presentation
  - declarative processing decoupled from the application logic
  - overcome problems of heterogeneous information integration
  - (automated) linking to other relevant information
  - (end) user control including personalization and customization

- Knowledge Transfer and Dissemination
  Objectives:

  - right knowledge at the right time, at the right place / for the right person(s)
  - capture expert and organizational knowledge (organizational memory)
  - collaborative work supported by shared knowledge
  - detection of relevant information and situations and triggering of adequate reactions
  - reuse and utilization of knowledge (e.g. in departments, with partners, for customers)

- Advanced Agile Enterprise IT Service Management and Business Process Management
  Objectives:

  - enhanced automation in discovery, configuration and composition of appropriate process components, information objects, and services
  - automated mediation between different heterogeneous interfaces and abstraction levels via business ontologies
  - targeted complex queries on the process space and flow
  - higher quality of service through improved semantic IT Service Management, e.g. by semantic web services and rule-based SLA monitoring
  - much more agile business process management via (business) rules

While declarative knowledge representation technologies and tools, such as semantic tagging, wikis, blogs, and collaboration platforms, help collaborating and structuring shared distributed content, companies are also seeking more capable approaches for gaining, managing, and utilizing knowledge required for their agile business processes and dynamic enterprise service networks. Often this requires integration of knowledge-intensive work flows and human activities. Typically, this is problematic due to the purely syntactic functional interface descriptions. For instance, there is a semantic gap between the two worlds - human / knowledge representation vs. automated services and processes management. Corporate Semantic Web technologies allow discovering and transforming existing information into relevant knowledge of practical consequences, trigger automated reactions according to occurred complex events/situations, and derive answers and decisions from distributed information sources. Hence, these technologies are means to bridge between the two worlds.

5.3 Gaps

Early manifestations of Semantic Web technologies which have their roots in the realm of artificial intelligence and inference systems were complex, expensive to run and maintain and not very business-user friendly. Improved technology providing enhanced usability, scalability and performance, as well as less costly maintenance and better understanding of the underlying inference systems makes the current generation of Semantic Web technologies more usable for its application in enterprise settings. However, there are still a number of challenges that have to be taken into account when employing a semantic technologies.

In [9] four bottlenecks for the adoption of ontologies in the public web have been discussed. [15] has identified further cost- and process-related problems restraining the application of ontologies in the industrial area. Considering Delteil's "Semantic Web Business Gaps" [6] combined with the findings from our conducted interviews with industry partners the following four gaps between corporate contexts and the application of ontologies can be identified:

(G1) Academic orientation gap: Research on ontologies is predominantly oriented to scientific-formed problems. Being mainly considered as the background artifact of Semantic Web applications instead of flexible means for knowledge representation and data integration, processes and tools for ontology creation only address developers with academic background, but rarely the usability needs of business end-users. There are only few early adopters which allow the construction of real-world use cases. But, lasting developments and advanced outreach to industry [6] have not taken place, yet. This is partially caused due to the lack of ongoing financial support after project funding periods end.

(G2) Application maturity gap: In consequence of G1 only very few tools reach a mature development state and become ready for productive use which explicitly address business end-users. Additionally, an adequate comparability for mature tools is missing because only few valuable benchmarks exist for those (e.g. [4]) and transparent benchmark standards are not reached yet. This fact yields a reasonable suspiciousness of computational performance of large-scale ontology-based applications.

(G3) Process gap: Most current ontology engineering methodologies focus on ontologies for worldwide or at least inter-corporate application domains ([8], [18], [12], [16]). They do not cover cost-effective creation and management of knowledge in small and mid-size companies and neglect the application dependence of ontology development. Based on software engineering life cycles many of them ignore the agility of knowledge engineering processes. Methodologies which respect this agility are needed . Several case studies try to prove the applicability of current well-researched methodologies [20] but are not adequate regarding industrial problems in the corporate context.

(G4) Cost-benefit-estimation gap: Since the current methodologies do not respect the increased agility of knowledge evolution and since cost-estimation models are derived from software engineering approaches, there is a strong need for companies to estimate the cost-benefit-ratio of ontology-based information systems. This is a difficult task because individually engineered ontologies have to integrate all parts of corporate knowledge while applications using those ontologies only fulfill some special purposes. A single application can hardly valorize the effort of the ontology engineering task. Thus, it is hard to start the application of ontology-based information systems as a step-by-step process - in contrast to conventional information systems, e.g., Web 2.0 tools.

5.4 Corporate Semantic Web

Corporate Semantic Web addresses both the consumer and the producer side, where consumers and producers might be humans as well as automated services, for example, in business processes and enterprise service networks. This also includes the adequate engineering, modeling, negotiation and controlling of the use of the (meta)data and meaning representations in a (collaborating) community of users or services in enterprise settings where the individual meanings as elements of the internal cognitive structures of the members become attuned to each others' view in a communicative / interaction process. This allows dealing with issues like ambiguity of information and semantic choices, relevance of information, information overload, information hiding and strategic information selection, as well as positive and negative consequences of actions (for example, in a decision making process).

Corporate Semantic Web has two intended meanings:

1. (Collaborative) work flows/processes, communication and knowledge management based on an infrastructure for enterprise networks which uses Semantic Web technologies.
2. Corporate = entrepreneurial usages of Semantic Web technologies (also with respect to total costs and return on investment)

Corporate Semantic Web aims at delivering innovative concepts and solutions for the management of knowledge in electronically organized enterprise environments. It focuses on the development and application of semantic technologies in controlled environments as well as the propagation of novel solutions for knowledge acquisition, provision, and management in corporate contexts (cf. Fig. 5.1).

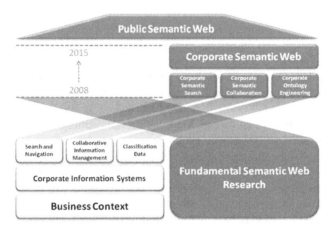

Fig. 5.1 Evolution of the public Semantic Web based on results from Corporate Semantic Web research

The identified gaps (challenges of CSW) are addressed by three research areas:

1. Corporate semantic engineering improves the facilitation of agile ontology engineering to lessen the costs of ontology development and, especially, maintenance.
2. Corporate semantic collaboration focuses the human-centered aspects of knowledge management in corporate contexts.
3. Corporate semantic search is settled on the highest application level of the three research areas and at that point it is a representative for applications working on and with the appropriately represented and delivered background knowledge.

All three parts work together in an integrative Corporate Semantic Web life cycle loop where (1) semantic information is extracted from the existing corporate data (Semantic Search), (2) semantic knowledge such as corporate ontologies or business rules are engineered from this information and semantic-enriched information objects are created (Semantic engineering), and (3) used in collaborative processes and in knowledge-intensive decisions (Semantic Collaboration). These collaborative processes are again semantically analyzed to produce further information bits and in a new loop (1-2-3) are, for example, used to personalize the search and collaboration context.

Corporate Ontology Engineering aims on closing the gaps G3 and G4 by realizing ontology engineering in an evolutionary, aspect-oriented and cost-effective way which respects the agility and various aspects of the knowledge engineering and business processes. It comprises investigation on methodologies and tools regarding versioning, modularization and integration of ontologies and rule bases. While modular reuse and integration of existing ontologies reduce the cost and the time to deployment, efficient versioning allows for evolutionary improvement and refinement.

The goal of *Corporate Semantic Collaboration* is to close the gap G1 and G4 by extending the ontology engineering process to domain experts as well as knowledge managers. The evolution of ontologies is enabled by modeling knowledge in a collaborative way using easy-to-use collaborative modeling tools. Mining user activities additionally extends the corporate knowledge by observing users and deriving new knowledge from their work flows.

Finally, the third research area is *Corporate Semantic Search* which aims at closing gap 2. It investigates easy information discovery in both semantic as well as non-semantic data. Utilizing innovative semantic search techniques to facilitate deep analysis of available information by analyzing complex relationships in non-semantic data (i.e. trend mining) as well as providing users with personalized access to corporate information, results of this research will prepare the ground for various semantic-based applications.

5.5 Corporate Ontology Engineering

In modern economy the success of companies strongly depends on their ability to rapidly adopt new achievements into their business processes. The quick creation of economic value from knowledge is essential. But, classic enterprise applications and software systems are based upon static information systems and database solutions. They are not able to reflect dynamics of knowledge and cannot enable the agile adoption of new achievements into the business processes. They are mainly developed for very special purposes aiming at meeting some functionalities and requirements of the company.

Knowledge-based applications are built upon knowledge bases (KB), which allow to manage declarative knowledge, that is to create, modify, and delete knowledge stored in the KB. Such applications are able to take new knowledge immediately into consideration and are therefore a very promising approach to displace classic data based and application dependent software systems. Being able to handle dynamics and power of knowledge they are the key for flexible business processes.

In the Semantic Web ontologies are an important means for representing knowledge. They provide a shared understanding of a domain of interest. In a corporate environment, ontologies describe terms and their interrelation relevant to business context. In order to adopt ontologies in corporate environments by closing the previously mentioned gaps, there is a need for a new methodology to create and maintain ontologies for corporate settings. Such a methodology has to keep the corporate setting in view. That is, it has to meet the following requirements

- The influence of the ontology development and maintenance process on the work flow of domain experts have to be minimized to avoid negative influence on their productivity. (R1)
- The already existing and running system must not be disturbed. (R2)
- The ontology has to evolve with the progress of the company. (R3)
- The need for ontology engineers have to be minimized to reduce costs. (R4)

As a solution approach we proposed the early stage of the Corporate Ontology Lifecycle Methodology (COLM). Being focused on corporate settings it inherently closes gap G1 and will prepare the ground for new knowledge based applications (G2). It reflects the agility of knowledge engineering (R3) processes and brings application dependency through the concrete definition of the application environment and the business needs (G3).

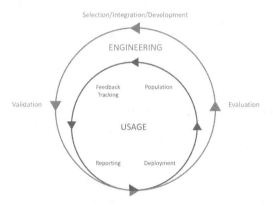

Fig. 5.2 The Corporate Ontology Lifecycle Methodology COLM

COLM consists of two different cycles, namely the usage cycle and the engineering cycle, and seven phases. By splitting the development process into the mentioned parts it allows an intuitive understanding of raising costs and provides a cost-sensitive evolution of knowledge in form of ontologies. Enabling cost-benefit-estimation it closes the gap G4 and fulfills the last requirement listed above (R4).

5.5.1 Modularization and Integration Dimensions of COLM

Ontology modularization and integration allows less investment costs by modular reusability of existing ontologies and easy management as well as maintenance by improving understandability through well sized ontology modules. It is in different ways integrable into the lifecycle. As illustrated and mentioned previously COLM facilitates cost estimation in the run-up of cost-intensive evolution steps. The modularization and integration dimensions of COLM helps to decrease investment costs as well as the operational costs and supports to realize ontology adoption to the corporate environment by keeping the incentives of a company in view.

At the very beginning of COLM during the selection and integration phases it is reasonable to look for existing ontologies for the sake of reusability, because developing ontologies from scratch is a very cumbersome and time-consuming task. Expecting candidate ontologies which perfectly fit into the targeted system is unrealistic, some customization will be necessary in order to adapt candidate ontologies and make them useful. At this point modularization is an important mechanisms to allow reusability even if the candidate ontologies are not usable in their original form. The possibility of extracting only relevant parts of existing ontologies and integrate them in order to achieve a useful ontology decreases investment costs drastically and makes ontology application realistic and really attractive for companies.

Modularization during the lifetime of ontologies is also possible. This can be done based upon diverse aspects. In the feedback tracking and reporting phases, the closed and controlled corporate environment allows obtaining information as relevance of concepts and relationships regarding departments and application. It also enables to observe the evolution of the ontology and allows to identify vague parts which change very often and well-established parts which change less frequently.

Finally, in case of context-sensitive and ontology-based applications, which are able to define ontology requirements, an additional aspect of ontology modularization is possible. During the deployment phase, while application need to load ontologies, optimized modules regarding the application context, can be identified and extracted in real-time. This would lead to personalization and increased efficiency of the ontology usage, because loading needless parts and wasting storage as well as computing power can be avoided.

5.5.1.1 Technical Concept

In the following we will demonstrate functional components within a corporate environment which are necessary to realize modularization and integration of ontologies in order to meet the aforementioned goals. Figure 5.3 illustrates the relevant parts of the overall system architecture and shows the interrelation between them.

The Ontology Engineering Editor is a front end application for ontology engineers and knowledge managers. It is a tool to create, load, visualize and modify ontologies directly. The Ontology Discovery & Integration component has access to the local ontology repository as well as the publicly available repositories as Watson, Swoogle etc. According to ontology requirements and based upon module descriptions it is able to find and integrate ontology modules. These requirements can be defined manually by ontology engineers using the Ontology Engineering Editor or automatically by Semantic (Web) Applications. The Modularization component of the Ontology Framework is capable of module extraction and ontology partitioning. According to feedbacks from the Feedback Repository it can partition the ontology automatically.

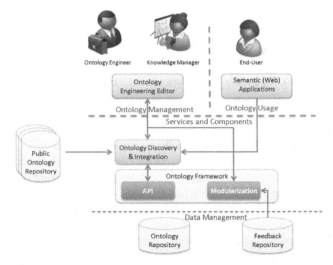

Fig. 5.3 Technical Components for Ontology Modularization and Integration

5.5.2 Versioning Dimensions of COLM

Efficient ontology versioning is a key enabler for the agile evolution of ontologies in the setting of enterprise information system infrastructures. It facilitates the management of various coexisting representations of corporate knowledge which is used by heterogeneous applications.

Our SVoNt approach for ontology versioning incorporates into the overall approach of COLM as the central back end component which encapsulates the ontology repository. Combined with other parts of the COLM ontology management framework the whole development, update, release and access chain is handled by this system.

The versioning of ontologies is important when continuously evolving ontologies are in focus. For our work we state two aspects as the most relevant reasons why the continuous evolution of ontologies is indispensable in context of corporate ontology engineering. First, there will ever be artifacts which change necessarily over time and influence the knowledge represented in corporate ontologies, e.g. the product portfolio or the department structure. Second, using or re-using a rudimentary existing ontology in the domain of discourse can lessen the costs for initial ontology development. Furthermore, we also adopt two base perspectives in which ontology versioning has to be applicable. The first one is the perspective of the vendor of ontologies and ontology-based services or software and the second one is the perspective of the user of ontologies as part of his information systems infrastructure.

Existing approaches yielded valuable results with focus on tracking of changes, change detection and calculation of the so called ontology diff (or semantic diff) to facilitate efficient and conflict free versioning mechanisms. However, an approach which provides commit and rollback of ontology versions on the concept level is missing. Such an approach can upgrade the distributed development and evolution of ontologies effectively and thus it is in focus of our work.

According to the aforementioned requirements we adopt the requirements R2 (the already existing and running system must not be disturbed) and R4 (the need for ontology engineers have to be minimized to reduce costs) and derive the following specific ones for the design and implementation of an ontology versioning solution which is applicable in the corporate context flexibly.

1 The system has to deploy the actual ontology version(s) to various applications directly. (related to R2)
2 The system has to be usable for non-experts in the field of ontology engineering. (related to R4)
3 The system has to be usable with other tools than dedicated ontology engineering applications. (related to R4)

With reference to requirement R4 we state that other people beside *ontology engineers* have to access the ontology version history and derive the users which form the relevant target group for our system. From a technical perspective, these people are *software engineers* and in some cases *IT administrators* or *IT managers*. They check out the actual ontology versions to verify that the modeled knowledge is conform with the requirements of the software systems which use it. That means they search for necessary ontology primitives and structural aspects of the conceptualization, e.g. essential properties or depth of the hierarchy.

5.5.2.1 Design of the SVoNt Version Control System for OWL Ontologies

We decided to set up on top of the well-known version control system SVN which is typically used for versioning of source codes in software engineering contexts. Thus, the selection of SVN fulfills requirement (2) perfectly from a non-technical point of view. To facilitate ontology versioning in the sense of all of the mentioned requirements, the text-based approach of SVN has to be extended to act on semantic structures of OWL ontologies and finally integrated into an ontology management framework which handles the access to appropriate ontology versions for distributed applications.

We implement an extension of the classical SVN approach for the server and the client side as it is depicted in Figure 5.4.

On the server side we wrapper the SVoNt server architecture around the classical SVN server architecture and keep all functionalities of the classical SVN system working as before. Internally, we add two major components which facilitate the additional functionality, namely consistency checks and generation of the ontology diff. The former supports the detection of of semantic inconsistencies when a new version is committed to the system and results an alert and avoids the commitment in case of a failure. The latter is applied after the consistency of the committed version is approved and provides the semantic distinction of the endmost and the

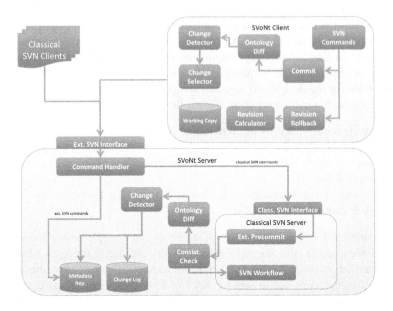

Fig. 5.4 The SVoNt architecture

new ontology version. From the set of differences we calculate a set of granular change operations and store them into a change log.

Our server side approach allows the use of any classical SVN client since we kept all actions and commands working as before. However, we implement a special SVoNt client as well which will provide

- the visualization of revision numbers on concept level,
- the partial commit of selected sets of changed concepts and
- concept-oriented rollback to former revisions.

To do that the SVoNt client accesses the SVoNt server change log and retrieves information about the atomic changes. A special tree view will provide an intuitive visualization as it is commonly familiar from the SVN visualization of source code repositories.

5.6 Corporate Semantic Collaboration

In this section we describe the conceptual design of a light-weight ontology editor. In contrast to existing ontology editors and our work on ontology engineering, we focus on developing an easy-to-use editor for non-experts in engineering of ontologies. Thus, we concentrate on the usage cycle of the ontology lifecycle (cf. COLM in Section 5.5) and primarily address the needs of domain experts. But the editor also supports ontology engineers as it also gathers feedback about changes in the ontology. The feedback is analyzed by ontology engineers to improve the quality of the ontologies and deploy a new release of them.

Figure 5.5 highlights the relationship of the editor to the components presented in the Sections 5.5 and 5.7. These components allow to access ontologies (ontology framework), to keep track of user interaction (feedback tracking), and to assist a user in modeling ontology concepts (matching framework).

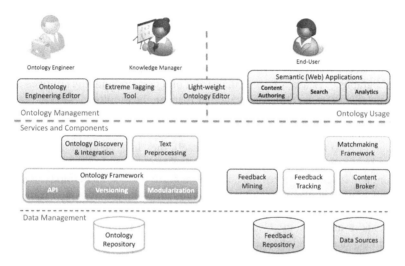

Fig. 5.5 Overview of the architecture

In a first step to design an ontology editor we compiled a list of user groups operating ontology engineering tools and a list of operations to handle ontologies. Compiling these lists we assumed that ontology engineers have already made basic design decisions on the ontology model and a first version of it is in productive use. The employees of a company are in charge of extending the ontology.

In this section we first describe functionality of the planned editor and identify user groups. Afterwards, we specify the architecture and sketch the working plan.

5.6.1 Editor Functionalities

The list below gives an overview of operations on an ontology. Some of these operations may require a deeper technical understanding of ontology engineering than other one. We indicate the level of required technical knowledge with '+' signs, ranging from ' +' (low) to ' +++' (high). In addition, further operations are conceivable, but we omitted them, because they require a too high technical knowledge. Please note, that we do not make any assumptions on the procedure of applying changes to the ontologies. For example, the changes may be immediately permanent and visible to all or have to be reviewed by a knowledge engineer.

Search concepts   A user searches for concepts in the ontologies that correspond to a given a search term. If context information of the user are available, the search engine considers them for ranking the results. (+)

Navigate   Starting from a concept users navigate through an ontology along relations. Context information are used to narrow the offered navigation paths. (+)

Add concepts/relations   A user adds a new concept to an ontology by typing a word into a form field. Tthe system will help him to find the right place for it in the ontology and to create relations to other concepts. (++)

Remove concepts/relations   Delete concepts and relations from an ontology. (++)

Move subgraphs   A user changes the parent of a concept and, thus, moves a concept together with its children to another place in the ontology. (+++)

Tag concepts   Tagging of concepts aims at putting concepts into context and, therefore, it pursues a similar goal as creating relations between concepts. Although tags do not need to be concepts itself, they help an ontology engineer to understand the meaning of a concept and decide on its placement. (+)

Comment and discuss   Users can add comments to parts of an ontology to discuss the meaning of concepts and relations and to adapt the ontology accordingly. (+)

Add data using a pattern   Ontology design patterns are templates for creating new elements in an ontology. Users fill in and submit a pattern-based form and the system populates the information to the ontology. (++)

Manage design patterns   A user can create, modify, and delete ontology design patterns that can be used by other users to populate and modify ontologies. (+++)

However, the system has always to ensure that all data is still in a consistent state after modifications by users. To add a concept, for example, it has to verify that this concept does not already exist in the target ontology. If it does, it has to execute some procederes to solve this conflict, e.g., automatically disambiguate the meaning using context information. A more challenging situation arises if a user moves a subgraph, because it may affect many other concepts, e.g., all subclasses.

5.6.2 User Groups

Methodologies for ontology engineering such as HCOME [10], METHONTOLOGY [11], and OTK methodology [17], refer to the user groups *ontology engineers, experienced users, knowledge managers,* and *system designers.* In the usage cycle of COLM, we distinguish between user groups influencing the further development of ontologies. Depending on background knowledge and experience of users we consider the following main groups:

Application user   Application users are not aware of the usage of ontologies in the system; for them the functionality of the application stands in the focus. Thus, they are not directly involved in ontology engineering, but provide implicitly feedback to ontology engineers by just using the application.

Ontology user   This group mainly uses ontologies read-only as a vocabulary (e.g., to annotate content). From their point of view on ontologies they are especially able to judge the adequateness of the domain model. Their comments and discussions are valuable feedback for knowledge managers and ontology engineers.

Knowledge manager   Knowledge managers maintain ontologies and, thus, they are not only using or commenting but actively modifying them. A knowledge manager may be responsible for the complete ontology or only for a part of it, e.g., an ontology module modeling a particular department of a company. The changes of ontology managers may be subject of reviews by ontology engineers.

Ontology engineer   Ontology engineers have a deep understanding of modeling ontologies, formats, technologies, and methodologies. Typically, they are no experts of the application domain. However, in contrast to knowledge managers, he has to consider the complete ontology and the dependencies between its modules.

In literature, the role of domain experts is often mentioned. From our viewpoint, domain experts are a group of persons that may belong to all mentioned groups. Thus, we do not list them separately.

Derived from the tasks of the mentioned groups in the engineering process, we associate a set of operations with them that they typically perform (Table 5.1).

User Group	Operations	Level
Application user	no operations in cause of indirect ontology usage	–
Ontology user	search, navigate, comment, discuss, tag concepts, use design pattern	(+)
Knowledge manager	all operations of ontology users, modify the ontology, manage design pattern	(++)
Ontology engineer	all operations	(++)

Table 5.1 User groups and their typical operations

5.6.3 Design of the Light-weight Ontology Editor

Designing a light-weight ontology editor we focus in the first step on the user group consisting of ontology users. In a second step, we will extend the functionality of the editor to support knowledge managers. The group of application users is not considered since they do not directly interact with the ontology, instead the system collects feedback of them. Ontology engineers, in contrast, need a dedicated tool to manage ontologies efficiently (see Section 5.5). Figure 5.6 puts the leight-weight ontology editor into the context of the overall system architecture of the CSW project. Users interact with this editor which in turn interacts with the extreme tagging tool or backend components, i.e., feedback tracking, matchmaking framework, text preprocessing, and the ontology API (cf. Section 5.7).

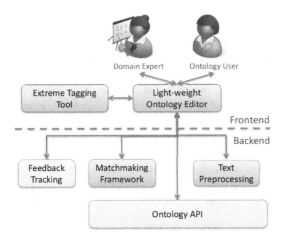

Fig. 5.6 Architecture of the light-weight ontology editor

Using the *extreme tagging tool* [19] a knowledge manager can collaborate with domain experts and obtain new concepts for an application domain. The feedback tracking component is responsible for collecting feedback of the interaction between users and ontology editor. A knowledge manager, for example, can analyze the feedback to discover concepts that are often searched but are currently not modeled.

The *matchmaking framework* is a central component for the ontology editor. It is used for the following tasks:

- Search (similar) concepts to use for performing a task, e.g., annotate documents.
- Check that a concept is not already modeled when a user wants to create it.
- Suggest potential parent concepts for a newly created concept.

To improve the results of invoking the matchmaking framework may use information from external data sources, e.g., Zemanta Semantic API[1], OpenCalais[2] and DBpedia[1]. The *text preprocessing* component is an auxiliary means to help the user to recognize concepts that are already contained in the ontology or to suggest new concepts. Thus, a user saves time, because he does not try to add already existing concepts. Finally, the *ontology API* allows the ontology editor to access and modify the ontology. The component implementing this API guarantees that changes to the ontology are performed consistently.

In Figure 5.7, we present the components of the ontology editor. We distinguish between user interface components (upper part) and core components (lower part).

---

[1] http://www.zemanta.com/

[2] http://www.opencalais.com/

We design two kinds of user interfaces, a Web based editor and a embedded Web based editor. While the purpose of the *Web based editor* is to support the task of ontology management, the *embedded Web based editor* enables a user to make changes to the ontology on the fly. For example, if a user wants to annotate content of a wiki page with concepts then he does not need a full-featured ontology editor but only a few functionalities, e.g., a search field or suggestions for annotations.

While we implement the Web based editor as a standard Web application, we consider to use an RDF JavaScript API (cf. [7]) for the embedded Web based editor. This API allows an integration of semantic technologies into a webpage by modifying RDF models on the client side and synchronizing them with a server.

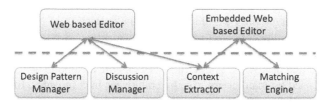

Fig. 5.7 Components of the light-weight ontology editor

The ontology editor invokes functionalities of core components such as design pattern manager, discussion manager, context extractor, and annotation engine. These components in turn access services and components of the architecture depicted in Figure 5.5. The *design pattern manager* provides operations on ontology design patterns as described in Section 5.6.1. Furthermore, it extracts RDF data from completed patterns for further processing. The *discussion manager* handles user discussions about concepts and relations of the ontologies, keeps track of arguments, and supports the process of decision-making. Implementing this feature, we found inspiration in DILIGENT [13] supporting controlled discussions besides others. The *context extractor* is responsible for detecting the current context of a user, e.g., to improve the quality of suggestions for placing new concepts into an ontology. The *matchmaking engine* searches for concepts that are related to a given search term. This feature is also used to find concepts for annotating texts and to suggest potential parents for a new concept and relations to existing concepts.

5.7 Corporate Semantic Search

As business oriented research concentrating on the Semantic Web organized within corporate structures, Corporate Semantic Web covers a wide spectrum of innovative scientific and application oriented solutions for research problems in a corporate context. In the previous chapters, we explained two fundamental pillars of the Corporate Semantic Web research. In this chapter, we introduce the last research pillar.

Based on advantages of Corporate Ontology Engineering and Corporate Ontology Collaboration, the Corporate Semantic Search brings new ideas and methods for realizing high quality search tasks in the corporate context.

5.7.1 Search in Non-Semantic Data

The preservation and advancement of corporate ontologies insist on ontology learning and ontology population. These crucial tasks can be accomplished by semi-automatic search for ontology concepts, complex relations between them, and instances in corporate text collections. From this point of view, the working package *search in non-semantic data* should deal with the extraction of "semantics" from the corporate text collections. Yet mostly, this "semantics" is not explicit assigned to the documents in corporate text collections. Texts are given in electronic form, in best case formatted in XML. Besides, there is a *tagging* technique which is the most common way used by many users, also by employees in companies, for annotating knowledge and information. Tagging helps in understanding the meaning of information being tagged. Combining both: search in text collections and tagging, we can satisfy the need for extracting "semantics" from texts and create an automatic approach for "understanding" given text from a text collection.

5.7.1.1 Collecting Knowledge with Extreme Tagging Approach

Automatic generation of relations between individual words is still a problem. The current approaches of computer linguistics do not produce satisfactory results. Therefore, people should be involved in this process. Previous tagging methods produce no precise specification of the relations. Each word is linked with another, without assigning the relation a more precise meaning. The Extreme Tagging System (ETS) approach [19] allows to tag the relations. ETS extends the common tagging method with an enrichment of the tags with a meaning. This can give the relations better semantics than just "is associated with", e.g. A "is part of" B or X "is a" Y. With the help of tags we can now use various graph algorithms to generate ontologies. We developed our first concept for generating semantic relations from folksonomy tags[3]. In this approach, partitions of tag graphs are generated. Using these partitions ambiguities and synonyms can be found and polysems can be discovered.

Algorithmic extraction of semantic relations out of folksonomies Problems with "Semantics" based on Tags[14] There are two main problems that emerged in social tagging: Ambiguity- which means having more than one meaning for a tag- reduces the precision of a keyword based search in folksonomy tags. Therefore users search-

---

[3] Many thanks to Mike Rohland, FU Berlin

ing for *atlas* retrieve relevant resources to *world atlas*, as well as results for *Atlas Mountains* in Africa. Synonymy- which means equal or similar meaning of tags- reduces the quantity of the resultset of a keyword based search in folksonomy tags. Users searching for *titan* should retrieve *atlas* as well, since due to mythology *Atlas* is an examplar of a *titan*. In addition to folksonomies, our concept of Extreme Tagging Systems (ETS) as an extension of common folksonomy allows to tag tags and to tag emerged relations between tags X,Y: 'X $\langle is - tagged - with \rangle$ Y'. Extreme tagging extends folksonomy graphs by adding semantics to tags. It enables the use of user's own concepts in description of the meaning, e.g. the use of their "subjective" synonyms. This is useful for generating personal ontologies from the ETS graph. However, these advantages bring obstacles in realizing ETS, which are: the high user interaction in the tagging process and the user-specific language used for tags and relation descriptions like users' synonyms. aETS is based on a four-stepped process. Using the data contained in a folksonomy, our method develops an ontology built upon semantic relations between folksonomy tags. In the preparation phase the Jaro-Winkler-algorithm is used on the set of tags to unify the spelling of the tag occurrences via gathering all different spelling forms of each tag. In the disambiguation phase, a bipartite graph is established for each tag that should be disambiguated (*dis-tag*). The bipartite graph contains *users: u* and *entities: e* as vertices. Tagging of an *e* with the *dis-tag* by *u* is represented by an edge in the graph. Applying one-mode projection to the bipartite graph results in a new graph where vertices are represented by entities *e* and edges between them are transformed from tagging edges of the bipartite graph. The transformation reduces the graph by omitting *u* (entities tagged with the dis-tag by the same user are connected with the edge). It allows for representing tagged entities as a network of vertices due to users who tagged these entities with the dis-tag. Applying the Girvan-Newman-algorithm for cluster determination to the transformed graph determines clusters in the graph; hence it determines possible meanings of the *dis-tag*. Entities that are included in one cluster are considered as possible synonyms. In the synonym extraction step the cosine similarity between each of the tags is used to determine synonyms. In the generating ontology step the extracted semantic relations are recorded as an ontology. The aETS method has been prototypically implemented in Ruby and tested relying on Delicious[4] user tags. The first evaluation of aETS shows very promising results of extracting semantic relations out of tags.

eXTS is realized so far as a web application for Apache Tomcat. In order to achieve an easy distribution of the software, we use HSQL DB as storage for the tags. This allows us to keep the database within the releases, so no external database is necessary. Furthermore, the communication between the JSP front-end and the back-end is completely encapsulated by web services. So it is possible for us to use a central authority to gather the tags from various places. This can also be turned off, so eXTS can run locally and do not forward the data to the central authority. Currently, only a simple user permission system implemented. This allows only

---

[4] http://delicious.com/

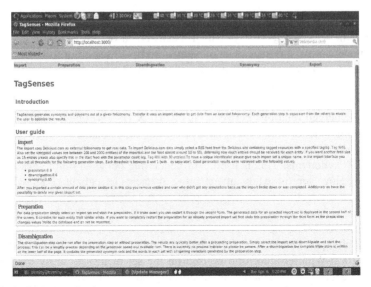

Fig. 5.8 TagSenses application

registered users to tag words and assign their tags an association that are then stored in RDF files. In a later phase, we plan to connect eXTS to the Tagsenses system mentioned above. For the evaluation we plan to test the eXTS with an expert group in order to collaborative generate lightweight ontologies that can be apply to the preprocessing process described in the following subsection.

5.7.1.2 Preprocessing Texts by Parsing and Chunking

The aim of the preprocessing component is to automatically generate triplets (trenary, syntactic relations) from a natural language text so that RDF-Tripels can be then generated from these triplets. We evaluated several tools and methods for their capability to fulfill our goal.

First, we started with the evaluation of scientific reports and implementations concerning information-retrieval and concept mining from texts. These concepts use in general methods from computer linguistics. Almost all of these tools and papers apply to English which has has a different syntax than German. German is not as explored as English, but today several works are in progress. So we cannot use the approaches directly but as a lead to our goal. Today only proof of concepts exits, but with interesting approaches. They distinguish between statistic and syntactic processes and between noun and verb based processes.

The text in statistic processing is mostly classified with the TF-IDF (Salton) method to make an approximate statement about the content and to find to most significant words. After that, the text is sentence wise processed and noun-noun, noun-adjective or noun-verb tuples are extracted. If such a tuple occurs very often, you can say, these two words belong together. This method can be improved, if you implicate synonyms for the words of the tuples. But in these methods, the syntax of the processed sentences is not regarded, so this can lead to wrong results. However, you will find many connections between the words (low precision, high recall). The biggest advantage of statistical methods is their language independence. Furthermore, entities can be recognized with regular expressions. Call numbers or salutations have usually the same structure; you can create an expression to find all entities in a specific domain. This entities gain a higher weight and you extract the tuples over relations of these words.

Syntactic methods are the other approach. Approaches from computer linguistic like POS-tagging are used here. The parsers for syntax-trees base on POS-taggers, because they have to know information about the particular words. You can identify dependencies between the words of the sentence in the created syntax trees and assign attributes to nouns (adjectives) or verbs (adverbs). Regular expressions, which are created for the particular language (e.g. X is part of Y; X, Y, Z are related to A), are also used to find relations between concepts. The biggest problem of syntactic methods is the dependency on the language to parse. A parser for English cannot be used to parse German texts. The parsers have often the problem to create the whole tree but identified relations are usually accurate. So, they have in difference to pure statistic algorithms a high precision but a low recall. The syntactic concept extraction is based on the so called tree-tagger. Our biggest problem at the evaluation was the low distribution of German in the computer linguistic. We found only two suitable parsers. First, the University of Stanford works on a project, which is available for free. This tagger was original developed for English, but there exist projects, which port it to other languages like Chinese or German. These ports do not work satisfyingly at this moment. The other result was a commercial product from Connexor. This tagger delivers far better results than the Stanford-parser and enriches the output with much more information. It finds the tempus and the casus of a word if it is not in its baseform. Connexor provides a web based form to test its product. The results look sophisticated.

The connection between preprocessing component and extreme tagging tool is a promising approach in order to retrieve triples out of preprocessed texts.

5.7.2 Semantic Search Personalization

In the Web context, Baldoni et al. define the personalized access to Web data as *"the process of supporting the individual user in finding, selecting, accessing, and retrieving Web resources (or meaningful sub-sets of this process)"* [2]. User adapted services or applications require a user profile describing his or her preferences in order to be able to select the set of relevant information. Additionally, personalized systems require some form of representation of their application domain. Ontologies have the potential to fulfill this role by providing formalized machine-readable means for meaningful representation of both users and domain resources.

Whereas the research fields of corporate ontology engineering and corporate semantic collaboration, presented in previous sections, focus on formalizing enterprise knowledge in form of ontologies, this section concentrates on providing users within the corporate context, both internal (employees) and external (customers, business partners, etc.), with personalized access to this information. For realizing personalized search, however, there is a need for an architecture component which determines the similarity between user preferences and domain resources. In this section, we present a flexible domain-independent Semantic Matchmaking Framework for calculating semantic similarity of information objects represented as arbitrary RDF graphs, thus being applicable in a wide range of scenarios.

5.7.2.1 Semantic Matchmaking Framework

The implementation of a domain-specific application architecture supporting personalized search based on user profiles requires a suitable component for ranking of resources with respect to user preferences. The process of finding best alternatives for a given user profile is called matchmaking. Such a component should offer application developers a ready-to-use tool allowing a fast implementation of the matchmaking logic, thereby reducing the cost of the overall application development. The key requirements for such a tool are:

- **domain-independent generic architecture**
  being able to handle various corporate resources and user profiles regardless of the underlying data schema (ontology T-Box)
- **flexibility**
  i.e. offer various matchmaking techniques for different kinds of object properties
- **extensibility**
  i.e. provide interfaces for implementation of new (domain specific) matchmaking techniques
- **traceability**
  i.e. deliver a detailed explanation of the matchmaking result together with the similarity ranking

Given these requirements, we designed a flexible Semantic Matchmaking Framework for calculating semantic similarity of multi-attributive and multi-dimensional information objects (as depicted in Figure 5.9) represented as arbitrary RDF graphs with concepts from an underlying corporate or domain ontology. In the corporate context, such information objects may represent, on the one hand, enterprise resources like products, services, employees, business partners, documents (including metadata), etc. On the other hand, they may represent user profiles. In general, the framework can be applied in a wide range of use case scenarios ranging from product/service recommender systems to expert finder systems.

Depending on the type and semantics of object attributes or dimensions the framework should deliver different kinds of matchmaking techniques, for example:

- **string-based**

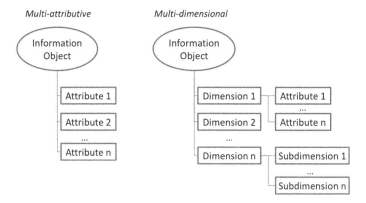

Fig. 5.9 Multi-attributive and Multi-dimensional Information Objects

Calculating the similarity of two string values represented by RDF Literals. This includes comparing keywords, searching for keywords (and their synonyms) in texts, searching for Named Entities, or applying Natural Language Processing techniques.

- **numeric**

  Used to determine similarity of two numeric values. A good application example for this matching technique is the comparison of a product price some person is willing to pay (p_q) with the actual product price (p_r). For all $p_r > p_q$ the similarity shall decrease with increasing p_r. However, beyond a certain value (upper bound) where p_r would be unacceptably high the similarity shall equal 0.

- **taxonomic**

  Applied for matching attribute values represented by resources from a common taxonomy. In this case, the similarity between two concepts c_1 and c_2 can be determined based on the distance $d(c_1, c_2)$ between them, which reflects their respective position in the concept hierarchy. Consequently, the concept similarity is defined as: $sim(c_1, c_2) = 1 - d(c_1, c_2)$. For the calculation of the distance between concepts different distance functions may be applied.

  As example, consider the method presented in [21] where every concept in a taxonomy is assigned a milestone value. Since the distance between two given concepts in a hierarchy represents the path over the closest common parent (ccp), the distance is calculated as $d(c_1, c_2) = d_c(c_1, ccp) + d_c(c_2, ccp)$ where $d(c_n, ccp) = milestone(ccp) - milestone(c_n)$. The milestone values are calculated with an exponential function: $milestone(n) = \frac{0.5}{k^{l(n)}}$ where k is a factor greater than 1 indicating the rate at which milestone values decrease along the hierarchy. It can be assigned different values depending on the hierarchy depth.

  This formula implies two assumptions: (1) the semantic difference between upper level concepts is greater than between lower level concepts (in other words: two general concepts are less similar than two specialized ones) and (2) that the distance between "brothers" is greater than the distance between "parent" and "child". As an example, we determine the distance between two concepts: *Java*

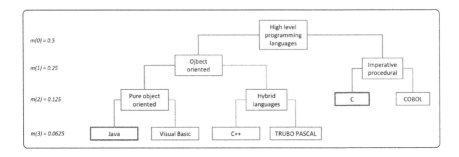

Fig. 5.10 Example of a Skill Taxonomy

and *C*. Figure 5.10 shows a snippet of a simple taxonomy together with milestone values (with $k = 2$) for the corresponding hierarchy levels (in brackets). Since the closest common parent is *High level programming languages*, the distance between *Java* and *C* is calculated as follows:

$d(Java, C) = d(Java, High\ level\ programming\ languages) + d(C, High\ level\ programming\ languages) = (0.5 - 0.0.0625) + (0.5 - 0.125) = 0.8125$. Consequently, the similarity between these two concepts equals: $sim(Java, C) = 1 - 0.8125 = 0.1875$. This value is much smaller than in the case of the evidently more related concepts *Java* and *VisualBasic* for which $sim(Java, VisualBasic) = 0.875$.

- **rule-based**
  Which given a set of pre-defined rules determine the similarity between complex object dimensions. Consider, for example, an expert finder scenario in which, while searching for experienced Java programmers, only those candidates would receive a high ranking whose skill matches the concept *Java*, and additionally have already worked in projects for which *Java* skills were required.
- **(geo)location-based**
  For performing vicinity search given two locations (cities, street names, etc.) as strings or geo coordinates.
- **collaborative filtering**
  Taking into account not only a given user profile but also preferences of similar users, with respect to a particular attribute or dimension to be matched.

As depicted in Figure 5.11, the Matchmaking Framework plays a key role in realizing Web applications supporting personalized search in corporate data. In a given use case scenario, through a domain-specific Web interface , users provide their query and preferences which are represented in RDF using concepts from an underlying corporate or domain ontology. As next, a user profile is merged with the use-case-specific matchmaking configuration delivered by the application administrator. It includes, among others, the selection and mapping of attributes/dimensions

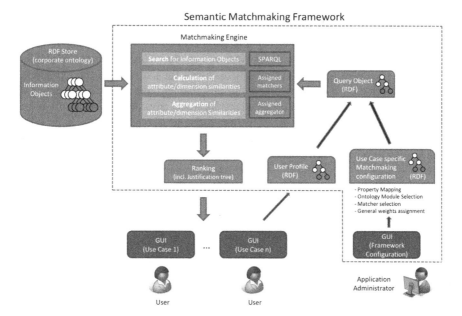

Fig. 5.11 Architecture of the Semantic Matchmaking Framework

in user profiles with the semantically corresponding attributes/dimensions in corporate information objects to be matched, together with information about which matching techniques should be applied for computation of each attribute/dimension similarity. The aggregated RDF graph is then passed (as query object) to the Matchmaking Engine.

The process of matchmaking is carried out by the engine in three steps. First, the information objects to be matched, together with all relevant background knowledge (e.g. concept taxonomies), are retrieved from the RDF store. The access to RDF data is realized with *Jena - the Semantic Web Framework for Java* [5]. As next, for each information object, the engine computes the attribute/dimension similarities by invoking appropriate matchers implementing a certain matching technique specified by the application administrator. Finally, all attribute/dimension similarities are aggregated into an overall similarity score for a particular information object. The output of the engine is a ranking of information objects for a given user profile with additional information containing the explanation of the matchmaking process for each single object. The result is rendered in an appropriate format and presented to the user via the application-specific Web interface.

5.8 Conclusion and Outlook

Nowadays, companies seek more capable approaches for gaining, managing, and utilizing knowledge, and the Semantic Web offers promising solutions. While the global Semantic Web remains an unfulfilled vision for the present, the Corporate Semantic Web idea, which we presented in this chapter, aims at bringing semantic technologies to enterprises. The expected results are an advantage in competition for enterprises using semantic technologies. In this chapter, we have discussed promising application domains of Semantic Web technologies in enterprises. In terms of a gap analysis we have introduced the main four challenges towards a Corporate Semantics Web and have identified the three corresponding research areas which address these challenges. Our ongoing research activities in these areas, focusing on the application of semantic technologies within controlled environments, contribute to the further maturing of Corporate Semantic Web technologies.

However, the Semantic Web technology has not arrived in the corporate world, yet. Incentives need to be provided to encourage in-house adoption and integration of these new Corporate Semantic Web technologies into the existing IT infrastructures, services and business processes. Decision makers on the operation, tactical and strategic IT management level need to understand the impact of this new technological approach and its adoption costs and return on investment.

Therefore, companies will have in mind the economical justifiability of the deployment of new technologies. One of the next steps in Corporate Semantic Web research will be to develop methods for cost estimation of ontology development processes, ontology use, and ontology maintenance that are adaptable to different corporate environments.

Furthermore, methods for evaluating existing ontologies with regard to enterprise relevant usage criteria are needed. Early adopters deploying application-oriented solutions for improving their competitive advantages through enhanced knowledge management of semantically rich data will demonstrate incentives for further corporations to follow and thereby accelerate the realization of a global Semantic Web.

Acknowledgements This work has been partially supported by the "InnoProfile-Corporate Semantic Web" project funded by the German Federal Ministry of Education and Research (BMBF) and the BMBF Innovation Initiative for the New German Länder - Entrepreneurial Regions.

References

1. Auer, S., Bizer, C., Lehmann, J., Kobilarov, G., Cyganiak, R., Ives, Z.: DBpedia: A nucleus for a web of open data. In: Proceedings of the 6th International Semantic Web Conference and 2nd Asian Semantic Web Conference (ISWC/ASWC2007), *Lecture Notes in Computer Science*, vol. 4825, pp. 715–728. Springer Verlag, Berlin, Heidelberg (2007). URL http://iswc2007.semanticweb.org/papers/715.pdf
2. Baldoni, M., Baroglio, C., Henze, N.: Personalization for the semantic web. In: N. Eisinger, J. Maluszynski (eds.) Reasoning Web, *Lecture Notes in Computer Science*, vol. 3564, pp.

173–212. Springer (2005)
3. Berners-Lee, T., Hendler, J.: The semantic web. a new form of web content that is meaningful to computers will unleash a revolution of new possibilities. Scientific American Magazine pp. 34–43 (2001)
4. Bizer, C., Schulz, A.: Berlin sparql benchmark bsbm. Tech. rep., Freie Universität Berlin (2008). URL http://www4.wiwiss.fu-berlin.de/bizer/BerlinSPARQLBenchmark/
5. Carroll, J.J., Dickinson, I., Dollin, C., Reynolds, D., Seaborne, A., Wilkinson, K.: Jena: implementing the semantic web recommendations. In: WWW Alt. '04: Proceedings of the 13th international World Wide Web conference on Alternate track papers & posters, pp. 74–83. ACM, New York, NY, USA (2004). DOI http://doi.acm.org/10.1145/1013367.1013381
6. Delteil, A., Cuel, R., Louis, V.: Knowledge web technology roadmap. Tech. rep., University of Trento, Italy (2007)
7. Dietzold, S., Hellmann, S., Peklo, M.: Using javascript rdfa widgets for model/view separation inside read/write websites. In: Proceedings of the 4th Workshop on Scripting for the Semantic Web (2008). URL http://www.semanticscripting.org/SFSW2008/papers/15.pdf
8. Fernandez-Lopez, M., Gomez-Perez, A., Juristo, N.: Methontology: from ontological art towards ontological engineering. In: Proceedings of the AAAI97 Spring Symposium, pp. 33–40. Stanford, USA (1997)
9. Hepp, M.: Possible ontologies: How reality constrains the development of relevant ontologies. IEEE Internet Computing 11(1), 90–96 (2007)
10. Kotis, K., Vouros, G.A.: Human-centered ontology engineering: The hcome methodology. Knowl. Inf. Syst. 10, 109–131 (2006)
11. Mariano Fernandez and Asuncion Gomez-Perez and Natalia Juristo: Methontology: from ontological art towards ontological engineering. In: Proceedings of the AAAI97 Spring Symposium Series on Ontological Engineering, pp. 33–40. Stanford, USA (1997)
12. Pinto, H.S., Tempich, C., Staab, S., Sure, Y.: Distributed engineering of ontologies (diligent). In: S. Stuckenschmidt, S. Staab (eds.) Semantic Web and Peer-to-Peer, pp. 301–320. Springer (2005)
13. Pinto, S., Tempich, C., Staab, S., Sure, Y.: Semantic Web and Peer-to-Peer, chap. Distributed Engineering of Ontologies (DILIGENT), pp. 301–320. Springer Verlag (2006)
14. Rohland, M., Streibel, O.: Algorithmic extraction of tag semantics. In: FIS2009: Proceedings of the 2nd international Future Internet Symposium, Berlin, 2009, pp. –. LNCS, Subseries: Computer Communication Networks and Telecommunications, Springer Verlag (2009)
15. Simperl, E.P.B., Tempich, C.: Ontology engineering: A reality check. In: R. Meersman, Z. Tari (eds.) OTM Conferences (1), *Lecture Notes in Computer Science*, vol. 4275, pp. 836–854. Springer (2006)
16. Suarez-Figueroa, M.C., de Cea, G.A., Buil, C., Dellschaft, K., Fernandez-Lopez, M., Garcia, A., Gomez-Perez, A., Herrero, G., Montiel-Ponsoda, E., Sabou, M., Villazon-Terrazas, B., Yufei., Z.: Neon methodology for building contextualized ontology networks. Tech. rep., Universidad Politecnica de Madrid (2008)
17. Sure, Y., Studer, R.: On-to-knowledge methodology — expanded version. Tech. Rep. 17, Institute AIFB, University of Karlsruhe (2002)
18. Sure, Y., Studer, R.: On-to-knowledge methodology - expanded version. Tech. rep., Institute AIFB, University of Karlsruhe, Germany (2002)
19. Tanasescu, V., Streibel, O.: Extreme tagging: Emergent semantics through the tagging of tags. In: L. Chen, P. Cudré-Mauroux, P. Haase, A. Hotho, E. Ong (eds.) ESOE, *CEUR Workshop Proceedings*, vol. 292, pp. 84–94. CEUR-WS.org (2007)
20. Tempich, C., Simperl, E.P.B., Luczak, M., Studer, R., Pinto, H.S.: Argumentation-based ontology engineering. IEEE Intelligent Systems 22(6), 52–59 (2007)
21. Zhong, J., Zhu, H., Li, J., Yu, Y.: Conceptual graph matching for semantic search. In: Proceedings of the 10th International Conference on Conceptual Structures (ICCS), pp. 92–196. Springer-Verlag, London, UK (2002)

Chapter 6
Semantic Service Matchmaking in the ATM Domain Considering Infrastructure Capability Constraints

Thomas Moser, Richard Mordinyi, Wikan Danar Sunindyo, and Stefan Biffl

Abstract In a service-oriented environment business processes flexibly build on software services provided by systems in a network. A key design challenge is the semantic matchmaking of business processes and software services in two steps: 1. Find for one business process the software services that meet or exceed the BP requirements; 2. Find for all business processes the software services that can be implemented within the capability constraints of the underlying network, which poses a major problem since even for small scenarios the solution space is typically very large. In this chapter we analyze requirements from mission-critical business processes in the Air Traffic Management (ATM) domain and introduce an approach for semi-automatic semantic matchmaking for software services, the "System-Wide Information Sharing" (SWIS) business process integration framework. A tool-supported semantic matchmaking process like SWIS can provide system designers and integrators with a set of promising software service candidates and therefore strongly reduces the human matching effort by focusing on a much smaller space of matchmaking candidates. We evaluate the feasibility of the SWIS approach in an industry use case from the ATM domain.

6.1 Introduction

Safety-critical systems and business processes, e.g., in the Air Traffic Management (ATM) domain, have to become more flexible to implement changes due to new business environments (e.g., mergers and acquisitions), new standards and regulations. Typical examples for such business processes are the life-cycle support of flights, consisting of a variety of completely different acitivies such as air surveil-

Thomas Moser
Christian Doppler Laboratory, Software Engineering Integration for Flexible Automation Systems, Vienna University of Technology, Austria
e-mail: thomas.moser@tuwien.ac.at

W. Du and F. Ensan (eds.), *Canadian Semantic Web: Technologies and Applications*,
DOI 10.1007/978-1-4419-7335-1_6, © Springer Science+Business Media, LLC 2010

lance while the flight is airborne as well as the supply of catering goods. A promising approach follows the service-oriented architecture (SOA) paradigm that builds flexible new systems for business processes based on a set of software services provided by system nodes in a network. A key design challenge is the matchmaking of business processes and software services, i.e., finding the software services that a) best meet the requirements of the business processes under consideration and b) can be implemented with the available network capabilities. The solution space is typically large even for small problems and a general semantic solution to enable comprehensive tool support seems infeasible.

To provide a SOA solution for a set of business processes, meaning to identify suitable software services for business processes, designers and system integrators need to overcome 3 integration challenges that build on each other:

1. Technical integration connects networked systems that use heterogeneous technologies, i.e., different protocols, operational platforms, etc. Current technical integration approaches like Enterprise Service Bus (ESB) [6] or Service Oriented Architecture (SOA) [31] need manual configuration on the technical detail level and tool support is typically focused on a single technology or vendor.

2. Semantic integration translates data content and format between systems that use heterogeneous semantics, i.e., different terminologies for service names, data formats, etc. For semantic integration, there is no standard or framework available, making the semantic transformations between multiple services inefficient and expensive.

3. Business process support builds on technically and semantically integrated systems that provide software services the business process needs to fulfil its goal. The system integrator has to select software services that really match the requirements of the business process, and check whether the infrastructure capabilities can support the communication requirements of the chosen solution.

Large business process and software service integration networks consist of hundreds of integration nodes; changes of software service properties and network capabilities make the correct and efficient identification of feasible business process and software service pairs a recurring complex and error-prone task. Current service matchmaking approaches focus on either technical or semantic integration issues [48], while business process support is, to our knowledge, missing. Tool support for matchmaking of business processes and software services need to make the requirements of business processes and software services as well as the capabilities of software services and the underlying infrastructure understandable for machines.

In previous work, we introduced a systems integration approach, the "system-wide information sharing" (SWIS) approach (see Figure 6.1). The SWIS framework explicitly models the semantics of integration requirements and capabilities using a machine-understandable notation (semantic integration) [35]; and the connectors and transformations between heterogeneous legacy systems (technical integration) to simplify systems integration (business process support) [34].

In this chapter, we describe the semantic matchmaking of business processes and software services and the optimization of the integration solution with re-

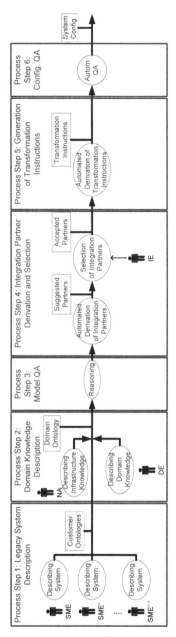

Fig. 6.1 Overview SWIS systems integration approach.

spect to available network capabilities. Semantic matchmaking uses the machine-understandable SWIS models to describe business process and software service requirements and software service and network capabilities to derive 2 results: 1. Provide sets of possible software services for each business process; 2. Optimize the set of selected software services with multiple objectives (e.g., costs, delay) while observing the capabilities of the underlying network infrastructure, a variation of the knapsack problem [27]. We evaluate the feasibility of the SWIS approach in a use case from the ATM domain.

The remainder of this chapter is structured as follows: Section 6.2 summarizes related work, Section 6.3 motivates the research issues, while Section 6.4 describes the use case. Section 6.5 elaborates the semantic service matchmaking approach and the optimization of the integration solution. Section 6.6 evaluates the approach using a case study and discusses the results with regard to the research issues. Finally, Section 6.7 concludes and identifies further work.

6.2 Related Work

This section summarizes related work on technical integration, semantic integration with semantic web services, and service matchmaking with multi-objective optimization.

6.2.1 Technical Integration

Technical system integration is the task to combine networked systems that use heterogeneous technologies to appear as one big system. There are several levels at which system integration could be performed [2], but there is so far no standardized integration process that explains how to integrate systems in general.

System integration can require changes [21] in the actual business policy of a company not only due to the emerging communication needs between multiple computer systems but also due to the communication requirements which have to be established between business units. Therefore, integration can have strong implications on the company as improper integration solutions can lead to considerable inefficiency. Another integration challenge is to keep sufficient control over the involved applications as in most cases integration developers have only limited control over these applications, e.g., legacy systems.

Typical integration solutions focus only on either the semantic heterogeneity (i.e., heterogeneity on service level, e.g., heterogeneous service descriptions, message data fields or service policies) or technical heterogeneity (i.e., heterogeneity on network level, e.g., different technologies or protocols). There is, to our knowledge, no existing approach or concept that takes into consideration both technical and semantic heterogeneities at the same time. In order to cope with technological heterogeneity on service level a homogeneous middleware technology approach [16] could be used for syntactical transformation between services, while the semantic heterogeneity of services could be addressed by means of a common data schema [19]. Heterogeneity on network level may be addressed by using so called adapters transforming messages between each used combination of middleware technologies. However, in order to provide an effective continuous integration solution in this environment, both integration levels (i.e. service and network level) need to be addressed in a mutual way.

The derived limitations for such kinds of integration approaches are on the one hand the need for a common data schema [19], which is often a hard and time consuming procedure, if not even impossible in integration scenarios with several different stakeholders. On the other hand, the need for integration over heterogeneous middleware technologies with different APIs, transportation capabilities, or network architecture styles implies the development of static and therefore inflexible wrappers between each combination of middleware technologies, and thus increases the complexity of communication. Traditional approaches for integration of business services can be categorized [6] into: Hub and spoke (EAI brokers) vs. distributed integration, and coupled vs. separated application and integration logic. In the following, using current technology concepts for each category a brief discussion about their advantages and disadvantages with respect to the described scenario is given.

Application servers [16] are capable of interoperating through standardized protocols, however tind to tightly couple together integration logic and application logic. Additionally, as the name suggests a server based architecture style is used for integration and as such has proven to be inconvenient for the scenario. Traditional EAI brokers [6], some of them built upon application servers, use a hub-and-spoke architecture. This approach on the one hand has the benefit of centralized functions such as the management of business rules or routing knowledge, but on the other hand does not scale well across business unit or departmental boundaries, although it offers clear separations between application, integration and routing logic. Message-oriented Middleware [41] is capable of connecting application in a loosely coupled manner but requires low-level application coding intertwining integration and application logic. The resulting effort and complexity of implementing an integration platform with the support for any kind of existing middleware technologies and protocols therefore is considerably high. To enable transparent service integration, the Enterprise Service Bus (ESB) provides the infrastructure services for message exchange and routing as the infrastructure for Service Oriented Architecture (SOA) [31]. It provides a distributed integration platform and clear separation of business logic and integration logic. It offers routing services to navigate the requests to the relevant service provider based on a routing path specification. Routing may be [6] itinerary-based, content-based, conditional-based defined manually [45] or dynamic [51]. In both cases the drawback is the minimal support for considering all functional and non-functional requirements of all service connections in the system. Dynamic configuration focuses mainly on creating a route for a special business case. Using manual configuration, a system integrator has to rely on his expertise, thus the high number of service interactions may get complex and the configuration error-prone. This may lead to routes that are configured in a way in which their influence on other business interactions is not fully known. As a consequence, business interactions may mutually violate their non-functional business requirements, such as message delivery within a specific time frame otherwise the message may be still useful but not up-to-date any more. Additionally, dynamic configuration may not cope with e.g. node failures fast enough due to missing routing alternatives, therefore possibly violating the same type of non-functional business service requirements.

6.2.2 Semantic Integration with Semantic Web Services

Semantic Integration is defined as the solving of problems originating from the intent to share data across disparate and semantically heterogeneous data [19]. These problems include the matching of ontologies or schemas, the detection of duplicate entries, the reconciliation of inconsistencies, and the modelling of complex relations in different sources [38]. Over the last years, semantic integration became increasingly crucial to a variety of information-processing applications and has received much attention in the web, database, data-mining and AI communities. One of the most important and most actively studied problems in semantic integration is establishing semantic correspondences (also called mappings) between vocabularies of different data sources [11].

Doan and Halevy [10] summarize the research on semantic integration in the database community. There, the matching of two database schemas requires deciding if any two elements of both schemas match, meaning that they refer to the same real-world concept. Typical challenges include the efficient extraction of semantic information, unreliable clues for matching schema elements (e.g., element names, types, data values, schema structures and integrity constraints), incomplete schema and data clues, and subjective matching depending on the application. Rule-based matching techniques use hand-crafted and/or probabilistic rules to exploit schema information for the identification of mappings. Rule-based matching techniques are relatively inexpensive and fairly fast since the typically operate only on schemas and not on data instances. But this is also their main drawback, as they cannot exploit data instances effectively, even though the instances can encode a wealth of information. Additionally, in many cases effective matching rules are simply too difficult to hand craft. Learning-based matching techniques consider a variety of machine learning techniques to exploit both schema and data information. There is also a growing realization that schema- and data-related evidence in two schemas being matched often is inadequate for the matching process, leading to the inclusion of external evidences beyond the two current schemas to the matching process. The key idea here is that a matching tool must be able to learn from past matches. Goh [18] identified three main categories of semantic conflicts in the context of data integration that can appear: confounding conflicts, scaling conflicts, and naming conflicts. The use of ontologies as a solution option to semantic integration and interoperability problems has been studied over the last 10 years. Wache et al. [49] reviewed a set of ontology-based approaches and architectures that have been proposed in the context of data integration and interoperability.

Noy [37] identified three major dimensions of the application of ontologies for supporting semantic integration: the task of finding mappings (semi-)automatically, the declarative formal representation of these mappings, and reasoning using these mappings. There exist two major architectures for mapping discovery between ontologies. On the one hand, the vision is a general upper ontology which is agreed upon by developers of different applications. Two of the ontologies that are built specifically with the purpose of being formal top-level ontologies are the Suggested Upper Merged Ontology (SUMO) [36] and DOLCE [17]. On the other hand, there are approaches comprising heuristics-based or machine learning techniques that use various characteristics of ontologies (e.g., structure, concepts, instances) to find mappings. These approaches are similar to approaches for mapping XML schemas or other structured data [5], [9]. The declarative formal representation of mappings is facilitated by the higher expressive power of ontology languages which provide the opportunity to represent mappings themselves in more expressive terms. There exists a large spectrum of how mappings are represented. Bridging axioms relate classes and properties of the two source ontologies and can be seen as translation rules referring to the concepts of source ontologies and e.g., specifying how to express a class in one ontology by collecting information from classes in another ontology. Another mapping representation is the declarative representation of mappings as instances in an ontology. This ontology can then be used by tools to perform the needed transformations. Then a mapping between two ontologies constitutes a set of instances of classes in the mapping ontology and can be used by applications to translate data from the source ontology to the target. Naturally, defining the mappings between ontologies, either automatically, semi-automatically, or interactively, is not a goal in itself. The resulting mappings are used for various integration tasks: data transformation, query answering, or web-service composition, to name a few. Given that ontologies are often used for reasoning, it is only natural that many of these integration tasks involve reasoning over the source ontologies and the mappings.

Rosenthal et al. [44] extend the concept of semantic integration to semantics management, which has the goals of easing data sharing for both new and old systems, of ensuring that needed data is actually collected, and of maximizing over time the business value of an enterprise's information systems. To reach these goals, new areas of useful semantic agreements need to be produced proactively, helping enterprises to satisfy new requirements and also reducing costs by reducing unneeded semantic and representation diversities. Additionally, not only the needs of technology-savvy system integrators need to be considered, but also other roles (e.g., enterprise owners, architects, end users and developers) need assistance to have a greater shared understanding of what the data means. Finally, the definition of "semantics" need to be broadened, to describe what data instances are collected and desired (as in publish/subscribe systems), not just concept definitions and relationships.

Uschold and Gruninger [47] identified four main categories of ontology application to provide a shared and common understanding of a domain that can be communicated between people and application systems [14]: Given the vast number of non-interoperable tools and formats, a given company or organization can benefit greatly by developing their own neutral ontology for authoring, and then developing translators from this ontology to the terminology required by the various target systems. To ensure no loss in translation, the neutral ontology must include only those features that are supported in all of the target systems. The trade-off here is loss of functionality of some of the tools; since certain special features may not be usable. While it is safe to assume there will not be global ontologies and formats agreed by one and all, it is nevertheless possible to create an ontology to be used as a neutral interchange format for translating among various formats. This avoids the need to create and maintain O(N2) translators and it makes it easier for new systems and formats to be introduced into an existing environment. In practical terms, this can result in dramatic savings in maintenance costs - it has been estimated that 95% of the costs of enterprise integration projects is maintenance [42].

There is a growing interest in the idea of Ontology-Driven Software Engineering, in which an ontology of a given domain is created and used as a basis for specification and development of some software. The benefits of ontology-based specification are best seen when there is a formal link between the ontology and the software. This is the approach of Model-Driven Architecture (MDA) [32] created and promoted by the Object Modeling Group (OMG) as well as ontology software which automatically creates Java classes and Java Documents from an ontology. A large variety of applications may use the access functions of the ontology. Not only does this ensure greater interoperation, but it also offers significant cost reduction for software evolution and maintenance. A suite of software tools all based on a single core ontology are semantically integrated for free, eliminating the need to develop translators. To facilitate search, an ontology is used as a structuring device for an information repository (e.g., documents, web pages, names of experts); this supports the organization and classification of repositories of information at a higher level of abstraction than is commonly used today Using ontologies to structure information repositories also entails the use of semantic indexing techniques, or adding semantic annotations to the documents themselves. If different repositories are indexed to different ontologies, then a semantically integrated information access system could deploy mappings between different ontologies and retrieve answers from multiple repositories.

The promise of Web Services and the need for widely accepted standards enabling them are by now well recognized, and considerable efforts are underway to define and evolve such standards in the commercial realm. In particular, the Web Services Description Language (WSDL) [8] is already well established as an essential building block in the evolving stack of Web Service technologies, allowing the specification of the syntax of the input and output messages of a basic service, as well as of other details needed for the invocation of the service. WSDL does not, however, support the specification of workflows composed of basic services. In this area, the Business Process Execution Language for Web Services (BPEL4WS)

[22], has the most prominent status. With respect to registering Web services, for purposes of advertising and discovery, Universal Description, Discovery and Integration (UDDI) [4] has received the most attention to date.

At the same time, recognition is growing of the need for richer semantic specifications of Web Services, so as to enable fuller, more flexible automation of service provision and use, support the construction of more powerful tools and methodologies, and promote the use of semantically well-founded reasoning about services. Because a rich representation language permits a more comprehensive specification of so many different aspects of services, they can provide a better foundation for a broad range of activities, across the Web service lifecycle. Furthermore, richer semantics can help to provide fuller automation of activities as verification, simulation, configuration, supply chain management, contracting, and negotiation of services [29].

To meet this need, researchers have been developing languages, architectures and related approaches for so called Semantic Web services [30]. The Ontology Web Language for Services (OWL-S) [28], which seeks to provide the building blocks for encoding rich semantic service descriptions in a way that builds naturally upon OWL [3], the Semantic Web language, supplies Web Service providers with a core set of markup language constructs for describing the properties and capabilities of their Web Services in unambiguous, computer-interpretable form. OWL-S markup of Web Services facilitates the automation of Web Service tasks, including automated Web Service discovery, execution, composition and interoperation.

WSDL-S [33] is another approach for annotating current Web Service standards with semantic descriptions. In WSDL-S, the expressivity of WSDL is enriched with semantics by employing concepts similar to those in OWL-S while being agnostic to the semantic representation language. The advantage of this approach to adding semantics to WSDL is multi-fold. First, users can, in an upwardly compatible way, describe both the semantics and operation level details in WSDL- a language that the developer community is familiar with. Second, by externalizing the semantic domain models, a language-agnostic approach to ontology representation is taken. This allows Web service developers to annotate their Web services with their choice of modelling language (such as OWL, or legacy models developed in UML or other knowledge representation languages). This is significant because the ability to reuse existing domain models expressed in modelling languages like UML can greatly alleviate the need to separately model semantics. Finally, it is relatively easy to update the existing tooling around WSDL specification to accommodate our incremental approach. Moreover, the externalization of the semantic domain models still allows for richer representations of domain concepts and relationships in languages such as OWL, thereby bringing together the best of both worlds. Use of expressive mapping representation and techniques can further enable this approach to deal with significant types of syntactic, structural, representational and semantic heterogeneity [1].

The Web Service Modeling Ontology (WSMO) [25] is a framework for Semantic Web Services which refines and extends the Web Service Modeling Framework (WSMF) [15] to a meta-ontology for Semantic Web services. WSMF defines a rich conceptual model for the development and the description of Web Services based on two main requirements: maximal decoupling and strong mediation. WSMO is accompanied by a formal language, the Web Service Modeling Language (WSML) that allows annotating Web Services according to the conceptual model. Also an execution environment (WSMX) [20] for the dynamic discovery, selection, mediation, invocation, and inter-operation of Semantic Web services based on the WSMO specification is included [13].

All three approaches, OWL-S, WSDL-S and WSMO, provide mechanism for semantically describing Web Services, with the major goal of allowing generic description of service functionality as well adding semantics to general service descriptions like provided/consumed messages or service bindings. This ambitious goal seems very useful for generic service descriptions; however its usage is limited in specific domains like in the ATM domain, since too specific features would complicate a generic approach too much. Therefore, we defined our own ontology-based architecture for describing the properties and features of the ATM services [34].

6.2.3 Service Matchmaking Approaches

Semantic matchmaking can be seen as major feature of semantic integration which supports designers and system integrators by providing sets of possible integration partners regarding both structural and semantic attributes. However, the relevant semantic concepts are hard to define unambiguously for general domains, thus the focus on a well-defined domain like ATM provides semantic clarity. Software components discovery and Web Service discovery can be classified into two categories: signature matching and semantic matching.

Purtilo and Atlee [43] propose a signature-matching approach by specifying the invocation parameters. Zaremski and Wing [52] describe exact and relaxed signature matching as a means for retrieving functions and modules from a software library. Wang and Stroulia [50] provide a structure-matching-based signature matching for Web Service discovery. Signature matching is an efficient means for software components retrieval, but two software components with similar signatures may have completely different behaviors.

Semantic matching addresses this problem by comparing software components based on formal descriptions of the semantics of their behaviors. Zaremski and Wing [53] extend their signature-matching work with a specification-matching scheme. Cho et al. [7] use a protocol to specify interoperability of objects. Semantic matching identifies suitable services more precisely than signature-matching methods, but the cost of formally defining provided and required services is considerable. Paolucci et al. [40] propose a DAML-S based approach for a declarative description of web services outside the representation capabilities of UDDI and WSDL. They provide an upper-level ontology of service profiles consisting of service actors, functional service attributes, and function service descriptions. Trastour et al. [46] define a set of requirements needed for service matchmaking based on Semantic Web techniques and evaluate a set of standard approaches (e.g., UDDI, ebXML) using these requirements. The potential complexity of the service descriptions, like attribute-value pairs or nested tree/graph style structures, requires a flexible and expressive metadata model. In order to support under-specified data structures like incomplete service advertisements, an approach needs to be able to express semi-structured data. Additionally, support for types and subsumption is needed to be able to work at different levels of generality. Finally, constraints need to be expressed to define and check the acceptable instances for service invocation.

Li and Horrocks [26] investigate how Semantic and Web Services technologies can be used to support service advertisement and discovery in e-Commerce. They describe the design and implementation of a service matchmaking prototype which uses a DAML-S based ontology and a Description Logic reasoner to compare ontology based service descriptions. By representing the semantics of service descriptions, the matchmaker enables to locate suitable web services automatically. The approach is evaluated using a realistic agent based e-commerce scenario. Although the initial classification of large numbers of service descriptions could be quite time consuming, subsequent matching of queries could be performed very efficiently.

Kolovski et al. [23] provide a mapping of WS-Policy to OWL. WS-Policy provides a general purpose model and syntax to describe the policies of a Web service. It specifies a base set of constructs that can be used and extended by other Web service specifications to describe a broad range of service requirements and capabilities. The main advantage of representing Web Service policies using OWL is that OWL is much more expressive than WS-Policy and thus provides a framework for exploring richer policy languages. Verma et al. [48] present an approach for matching the non-functional properties of Web Services represented using WS-Policy. Oldham et al. [39] present a framework for the matching of providers and consumers based on WS-Agreements. The WS-Agreement specification defines a language and protocol for capturing relationships with agreements between two parties.

Both WS-Policy and WS-Agreement define a generic framework for the representation of standard Web Service policies, however both frameworks seem too generic to be effectively used in a concrete scenario from a specialized domain like the ATM domain is. Therefore, we used the concept of describing Service policies using a knowledge representation language like OWL, but defined our own extendable policy representation language which is better suitable for the ATM domain [34].

6.3 Research Issues

Recent projects with industry partners from the ATM domain raised the need for semi-automated business process integration support in technology-driven integration environments. Recently, we developed a data-driven approach [16] that explicitly models the semantics of the problem space, i.e., business process integration requirements and network infrastructure capabilities [17]; the solution space, i.e., the connectors, and data transformations between software services. Finally, in this chapter we provide a process to bridge problem and solution spaces, i.e., identify feasible business process and software services pairs while fulfilling business requirements and optimizing the chosen integration solution according to multiple objectives. Figure 6.2 provides an overview on the integration layers, data flows between the integration layers, and the steps of the semantic service matchmaking process:

- SM1: For each business process, identify the suitable software services sets, which fulfil all business process service and data requirements. From these possible business process and software services sets, the system integrators choose the most promising sets, the so-called collaboration sets.
- SM2: The selected collaboration sets are then optimized regarding the original infrastructure requirements of both the business processs and the software services, as well as the available limited capabilities of the infrastructure's nodes and links. The outcome of SM2 is an optimized configuration of the integration solution, consisting of the selected collaboration sets as well as their grounding to the underlying integration network infrastructure.

Based on this, we derive the following research issues:

RI-1: Semantic Matchmaking of software service candidates for one business process (SM1). Provide machine-understandable descriptions for business process and software services requirements as well as software service and network capabilities to provide tool support for SM1 to make the search space reduction effective (low number of false negatives and false positives) and efficient (less human effort required) compared to the current human-based approach.

RI-2: Resource Feasibility Check and Optimization for all Collaborations (SM2). Provide a framework to enable a) checking the validity of a set of business processs and software services with the infra-structure capability constraints and b) ranking valid solutions by multiple optimization criteria like network cost and service delay.

6.4 ATM Scenario Description

This section describes the integration scenario from the ATM domain used throughout this chapter. The ATM use case (see Figure 6.3) represents information that is typically extracted from customers/participants in workshops on requirements and capabilities elicitation for information systems in the aviation domain. In safety-critical domains like ATM business process integration solutions have to pass certifications before deployment, which typical dynamic SOA solutions [6][31] cannot fulfill regarding the current rigid integration network in the ATM domain designed to guarantee integration requirements even in case of partial failure.

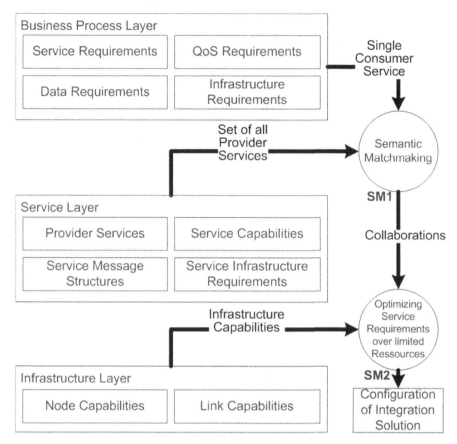

Fig. 6.2 Semantic Service Matchmaking Process Steps.

In the ATM domain semantic matchmaking is an effort for scarce human experts who have to cope with a huge search space and often miss better solutions due to their simple heuristic search strategies. Tool-supported semantic matchmaking provides designers and system integrators with a set of promising integration partner candidates and therefore strongly reduces the human matching effort by focusing on a much smaller space of feasible matchmaking candidates that can be rated according to relevant optimization criteria.

As shown in Figure 6.3, the integration network consists of business services connected to integration network nodes. Between these nodes, there may exist different kinds of network links using different transmission technologies (e.g., radio or wired transmission) as well as different middleware technologies for communication purposes. The capabilities of nodes and links, like throughput, availability, reliability, or security are explicitly modeled in order to be capable of selecting suitable communication paths for particular service requirements, e.g., the communication link

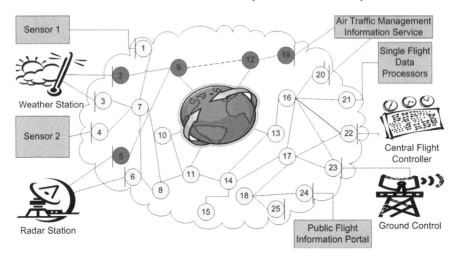

Fig. 6.3 A Typical ATM Domain Integration Network.

between the red ATMIS Node and the red Node 12 represents a reliable and secured communication path which may be requested by e.g., the ATMIS business service.

In the Air Traffic Management domain complex information systems need to cooperate to provide data analysis and planning services, which consist in the core of safety-critical Air Traffic Management services and also added-value services for related businesses. Air Traffic Management is a relevant and dynamic business segment with changing business processes that need to be reflected in the integration of the underlying information and technical systems.

A major integration challenge is to explicitly model the knowledge embedded in systems and Air Traffic Management experts to provide a machine-understandable knowledge model for integration requirements between a set of complex information systems. Complex information systems consist of a large number of heterogeneous subsystems. Each of these subsystems may have different data types as well as heterogeneous system architectures. In addition, complex information systems typically have significant quality-of-service demands, e.g., regarding security, reliability, timing, and availability. Many of today's Air Traffic Management complex information systems were developed independently for targeted business needs, but when the business needs changed, these systems needed to be integrated into other parts of the organization [19]. Most of the system knowledge is still represented implicitly, either known by experts or described in human-only-readable sources, resulting in very limited tool support for systems integration. The process of adapting the cooperation the business system is traditionally a human-intensive approach of experts from the Air Traffic Management and technology domains).

Making the implicit expert knowledge explicit (see Figure 6.4) and understandable for machines can greatly facilitate tool support for systems integrators and engineers by providing automation for technical integration steps and automatic validation of integration solution candidates. Consequently, we employ the EKB framework as a data-driven approach that explicitly models the semantics of the problem space, i.e., integration requirements and capabilities; the solution space, i.e., the connectors, and data transformations between heterogeneous legacy systems; and finally provide a process to bridge problem and solution spaces, i.e., find out whether there are feasible solutions and minimize the cost of integration.

6.5 Semantic Service Matchmaking Approach

This section describes the semantic service matchmaking approach as well as the multi-objective optimization of the chosen integration services candidates.

6.5.1 Identification of Possible Collaboration Candidate Sets

The identification of possible collaboration candidate sets is implemented as a heuristic algorithm. Step by step, the possible collaboration candidate sets are reduced by applying the rules described to the possible collaboration candidate sets. The heuristic rules that are applied during the source/sink matching are described in the following paragraphs.

Message mapping. During the description of the software service messages, each software service message segment was mapped to a domain concept, which has been specified in the common domain ontology. Therefore, for all segments of the message required by a certain business process, it is searched for messages of the software services that contain segments, which are mapped to the same domain concept, and if possible, to the same message format.

Service Policies. In addition, software services can define requirements (policies) regarding preferred or unwanted software service partners, as well as other non-functional requirements, e.g., QoS requirements regarding the underlying integration network. A policy is a restriction or a condition for a single collaboration or a set of collaborations, in order to allow the communication via the underlying integration network. In SWIS-based applications, there are two kinds of policies. On the one hand, there are policies which are valid for all collaborations. They specify global conditions that need to be fulfilled by all collaborations, e.g., a maximum time for the delivery of messages. On the other hand, there are policies which are required only for a specific subset of collaborations. These policies specify conditions that need to be fulfilled by the collaborations containing particular software services, e.g., the communication has to use only secure links, or only a specified set of other software services is allowed to participate in the collaboration. The software service policies that regard other software services are evaluated by checking whether the attributes and tags of every software service of the particular collabora-

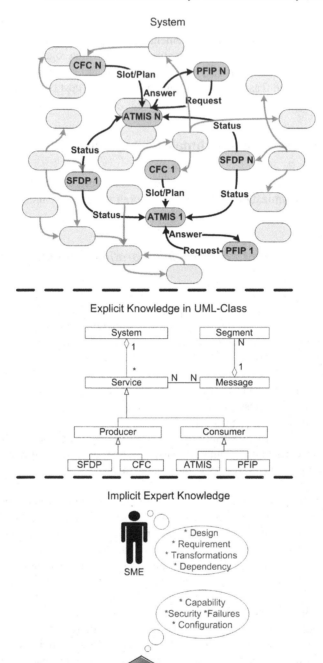

Fig. 6.4 Explicit and Implicit ATM Expert Knowledge [34].

tion candidate meet the service policies defined by the business process.

Format Translation. If a message segment is mapped to the same domain concept as the required message segment, but the formats of the two segments differ, check whether there is a converter defined for the two formats. A converter is used to convert the format of message segments from one basic data type to a different one. An explicit identifier is defined to allow the search for the converter at runtime (e.g., by using Java Reflection).

External Service Transformation. If the message segments differ in the domain concept they are mapped to, check if a service exists that consumes a segment mapped to the same domain concept as the segment of the message of the software service and provides a message with a segment mapped to the same domain concept of the segment of the message of the business process.

Route Deduction. As last rule it is checked whether there is an existing route between the nodes connecting the software services and the node connecting the business process.

If all the rules mentioned above are successfully applied to a set of one or more software services and a business process, then the particular set is accepted as collaboration candidate. If any of the rules cannot be met, the particular set is discarded as collaboration candidate.

6.5.2 Validity-Check and Optimization of Collaborations

Once all collaborations have been specified a Scenario is derived. A Scenario contains beside all collaborations a specification detailing how to configure the network infrastructure, so that the integration solution is optimized according to the given objectives. In the following the process steps needed to optimize the scenario is explained.

Preliminary Checks. The process step checks whether there is at least one single network route for each collaboration satisfying all global and collaboration specific policies. If this step cannot be completely satisfied the process raises an exception. The system integrator either updates or removes the collaborations which cannot be mapped to a network route, and restart the process step, or adapts the semantic infrastructure model, by adding additional nodes and links.

Route Derivation. Once it has been verified that each collaboration can be mapped to at least one route in the network, the process step derives every possible route for each collaboration. The only restrictions are that no node is allowed to appear twice within the same route and all policies have to be satisfied. The valid ones are retained; the ones violating the restrictions are removed. At the end of this process step, each collaboration will have either a single route or a set of valid routes to choose from.

Creating Scenarios. The processing step combines each route of each collaboration with each other. This means that a scenario consists of a set of collaborations where each collaboration represents exactly one route. The more scenarios are created, the higher the probability to find a scenario that is well suited for achieving the stated optimization objectives.

Evaluation. The process iterates through all scenarios and calculates their fitness according to the optimization objectives. The fitness of a scenario is the fitness of all its containing collaborations, and represents the real values (e.g. the time a message needs and the costs along the chosen route) of the objectives. The fitness represents the trade-off of the configuration, the routes of each collaboration predetermine. The set of fitness values is then analyzed according to the Pareto Front approach [12]. The Pareto Front contains either a single Scenario or a set of Scenarios. In the latter case there may be several "nearly equivalent" configurations as integration solutions. Thus, the system integrator has to decide which one to pick for practical deployment.

Multi-Objective Optimization. We have accomplished the process of optimizing collaborations by implementing a Java version of the mPOEMS approach into the SWIS framework. mPoems is an evolutionary algorithm using the concept of dominance for multi-objective optimization. The results and explanations of the approach can be found at [24].

6.6 Case Study

In this section, we evaluate the SWIS framework using a clear and comprehensible example to show the principles of our approach. In addition, we discuss the results with regard to the identified research issues.

An example for semantic service matchmaking in the SWIS framework is shown in Figure 6.5. There are three services of provided by legacy systems, two provider services (ATMIS and SFDP) and one consumer service (PFIP). The consumer service needs information that can be obtained from the provider services, i.e. FlightID, Departure, Destination and FlightStatus. This needed information is provided separately by the two provider services, so the system has to find the suitable information that match with the consumer service's needs. Additionally, the service AT-MIS_TransReqs defines a policy for the underlying integration network, stating that only secure network links may be used for the communication.

From the domain knowledge description, we know that Flight ID is a synonym for Flight Number, that Departure and Arrival are combinations of the airport code and country code of departure/arrival, and that the FlightStatus arrived or departed, can be derived by checking the occurrence of either TimeOfArrival or TimeOfDeparture.

Next, we calculate the network resources needed for sending messages from the SFDP Node to the PFIP Node with less capacity. From the integration network description, we can see several nodes connected by links. Each link contains information regarding source node and target node, support for secure transmissions and the transmission delay. The communication between ATMIS to PFIP needs to be done using secure connections only. There are two possible connections, either via Node Y or via Node Z. The system will choose connection via Node Y because it has less delay (6) than connection via Node Z (7).

6.6.1 Discussion

The example shows that even for small problems the solution space is typically large. However, large business process and software service integration networks consist of hundreds of integration nodes; and changes of software service properties and network capabilities make the correct and efficient identification of feasible business process and software service pairs a recurring complex and error-prone task. By providing only sets of feasible/promising service provider and consumer candidates, semantic matchmaking supports designers and system integrators by providing sets of possible integration partners regarding both structural and semantic attributes. However, the relevant semantic concepts are hard to define unambiguously for general domains, thus the focus on a well-defined domain like ATM provides semantic clarity.

We used the concept of describing Service policies using a knowledge representation language like OWL, but defined our own extendable policy representation language which is better suitable for the ATM domain. We do not use standardized Web Service description frameworks because, since the strengths of Web Service description frameworks lies in the generality of the approach, however their weakness is that it may become complicated to describe domain-specific issues. For specific domains, it may be useful to use the principles of web service descriptions but tailor them to the domain. Additionally, we defined our own ontology-based architecture for describing the properties and features of the ATM services.

We have developed a data-driven approach [34] that explicitly models the semantics of the problem space, i.e., business process integration requirements and network infrastructure capabilities [35]; the solution space, i.e., the connectors, and data transformations between software services. In this chapter, we described a process to bridge problem and solution spaces, i.e., identify feasible business process and software services pairs while fulfilling business requirements and optimizing the chosen integration solution according to multiple objectives. In order to evaluate the proposed process, we have derived two major research issues that will be discussed in the following paragraphs.

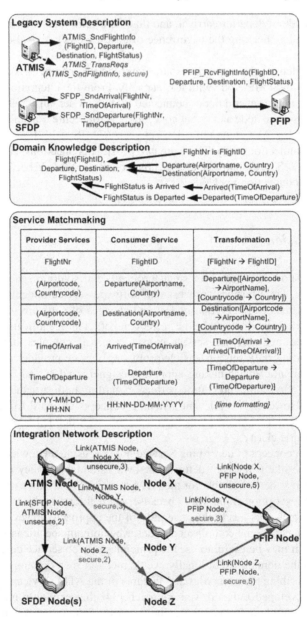

Fig. 6.5 Service Matchmaking Example.

Semantic Matchmaking of software service candidates for one business process. Current service matchmaking approaches focus on either technical or semantic integration issues [48], while business process support is, to our knowledge, missing. In the SWIS framework, we presented a combined service matchmaking approach that performs matching based on the data of the services and available service policies regarding other services. The SWIS framework's semantic service matchmaking enables an effective search space reduction and poses lower risk and effort compared to the current human-based approaches.

Resource Feasibility Check and Optimization for all Collaborations. The optimization process steps allow using existing resources efficiently. Out of all possible collaborations for a single business process which are creatable by means of the proposed semantic matchmaking approach, only those are desirable to be deployed in the integration solution which fulfills certain criteria. Those criteria are set up by the integration expert so that existing collaborations use the underlying integration network infrastructure with its limited resources as efficient as possible.

6.7 Conclusion

In this chapter we presented an approach for semi-automatic semantic matchmaking for software services, the "System-Wide Information Sharing" (SWIS) Business Process integration framework. The SWIS Business Process integration frameworks uses the machine-understandable SWIS models to describe business process and software service requirements as well as software service and network capabilities to provide sets of possible software services for each business process. Out of these possible sets, the system integrators choose the wanted sets. These wanted sets are then optimized with multiple objectives (e.g., costs, delay) while observing the capabilities of the underlying network infrastructure.

We evaluated the feasibility of the SWIS approach in an industry use case from the Air Traffic Management (ATM) domain. The example shows that even for small problems the solution space is typically large, and even bigger for large business process and software service integration networks consisting of hundreds of integration nodes. A tool-supported semantic matchmaking process like SWIS can provide system designers and integrators with a set of promising Software Service candidates and therefore strongly reduces the human matching effort by focusing on a much smaller space of matchmaking candidates.

Major contributions of this chapter are

- Large Business Process and Software Service integration networks consist of hundreds of integration nodes; and changes of Software Service properties and network capabilities make the correct and efficient identification of feasible Business Process and Software Service pairs a recurring complex and error-prone task. By providing only sets of feasible/promising service provider and consumer candidates, semantic matchmaking supports designers and system integrators by providing sets of possible integration partners regarding both structural and semantic attributes. However, the relevant semantic concepts are hard to define unambiguously for general domains, thus the focus on a well-defined domain like ATM provides semantic clarity.

- We used the concept of describing Service policies using a knowledge representation language like OWL, but defined our own extendable policy representation language which is better suitable for the ATM domain. We do not use standardized Web Service description frameworks because, since the strengths of Web Service description frameworks lies in the generality of the approach, however their weakness is that it may become complicated to describe domain-specific issues. For specific domains, it may be useful to use the principles of web service descriptions but tailor them to the domain. Additionally, we defined our own ontology-based architecture for describing the properties and features of the ATM services.

- Current service matchmaking approaches focus on either technical or semantic integration issues, while business process support is, to our knowledge, missing. In this chapter, we presented a combined service matchmaking approach that performs matching based on the data of the services and available service policies regarding other services. Semantic service matchmaking enables an effective search space reduction and poses lower risk and effort compared to the current human-based approaches.

- The optimization process steps allow using existing resources efficiently. Out of all possible collaborations for a single Business Process which are creatable by means of the proposed semantic matchmaking approach, only those are desirable to be deployed in the integration solution which fulfills certain criteria. Those criteria are set up by the integration expert so that existing collaborations use the underlying integration network infrastructure with its limited resources as efficient as possible

Further Work. Further work will include a detailed description of the semantic design to translate between matched services and an evaluation measuring the effectiveness and efficiency of deriving the semantic transformation with tool-support compared to a manual approach.

Acknowledgements The authors would like to acknowledge all project members of the SWIS (System-Wide Information Sharing) project performed from 2006-2008 at Vienna University of Technology together with Frequentis AG and Austro Control GmbH. This work has been supported by the Christian Doppler Forschungsgesellschaft and the BMWFJ, Austria. In addition, this work has been partially funded by the Vienna University of Technology, in the Complex Systems Design & Engineering Lab.

References

1. Akkiraju, R., Farrell, J., Miller, J., Nagarajan, M., Schmidt, M.T., Sheth, A., Verma, K.: Web service semantics-wsdl-s. W3C Member Submission **7** (2005)
2. Balasubramanian, K., Gokhale, A., Karsai, G., Sztipanovits, J., Neema, S.: Developing applications using model-driven design environments. COMPUTER pp. 33–40 (2006)
3. Bechhofer, S., van Harmelen, F., Hendler, J., Horrocks, I., McGuinness, D.L., Patel-Schneider, P.F., Stein, L.A.: Owl web ontology language reference. W3C Recommendation **10** (2004)
4. Bellwood, T., Clement, L., Ehnebuske, D., Hately, A., Hondo, M., Husband, Y.L., Januszewski, K., Lee, S., McKee, B., Munter, J.: Uddi version 3.0. Published specification, Oasis (2002)
5. Bergamaschi, S., Castano, S., Vincini, M.: Semantic integration of semistructured and structured data sources. SIGMOD Rec. **28**(1), 54–59 (1999). 309897
6. Chappel, D.A.: Enterprise Service Bus. O'Reilly Media, Sebastopol, CA (2004)
7. Cho, I.H., McGregor, J.D., Krause, L.: A protocol based approach to specifying interoperability between objects. In: 26th International Conference on Technology of Object-Oriented Languages (TOOLS 26), pp. 84–96 (1998)
8. Christensen, E., Curbera, F., Meredith, G., Weerawarana, S.: Web services description language (wsdl) 1.1 (2001)
9. Cruz, I.R., Huiyong, X., Feihong, H.: An ontology-based framework for xml semantic integration. In: International Database Engineering and Applications Symposium (IDEAS '04), pp. 217–226. IEEE (2004)
10. Doan, A., Halevy, A.: Semantic integration research in the database community: A brief survey. AI Magazine **26**(1), 83–94 (2005)
11. Doan, A., Noy, N.F., Halevy, A.Y.: Introduction to the special issue on semantic integration. SIGMOD Rec. **33**(4), 11–13 (2004). 1041412
12. Ehrgott, M.: Multicriteria Optimization. Springer (2005)
13. Feier, C., Roman, D., Polleres, A., Domingue, J., Stollberg, M., Fensel, D.: Towards intelligent web services: The web service modeling ontology (wsmo). In: International Conference on Intelligent Computing (ICIC) (2005). International Conference on Intelligent Computing (ICIC)
14. Fensel, D.: Ontologies: A Silver Bullet for Knowledge Management and Electronic Commerce. Springer (2003)
15. Fensel, D., Bussler, C.: The web service modeling framework wsmf. Electronic Commerce Research and Applications **1**(2), 113–137 (2002)
16. Gail, E.H., David, L., Jeromy, C., re, Fred, N., John, C., Martin, N.: Application servers: one size fits all ... not? In: Companion of the 18th annual ACM SIGPLAN conference on Object-oriented programming, systems, languages, and applications. ACM, Anaheim, CA, USA (2003). 949414 284-285
17. Gangemi, A., Guarino, N., Masolo, C., Oltramari, A.: Sweetening wordnet with dolce. AI Magazine **24**(4), 13–24 (2003)
18. Goh, C.H.: Representing and reasoning about semantic conflicts in heterogeneous information systems. Ph.D. thesis, MIT (1996)
19. Halevy, A.: Why your data won't mix. Queue **3**(8), 50–58 (2005). 1103836
20. Haller, A., Cimpian, E., Mocan, A., Oren, E., Bussler, C.: Wsmx-a semantic service-oriented architecture. In: International Conference on Web Services (ICWS 2005), pp. 321–328. IEEE (2005). Web Services, 2005. ICWS 2005. Proceedings. 2005 IEEE International Conference on
21. Hohpe, G., Woolf, B.: Enterprise Integration Patterns: Designing, Building, and Deploying Messaging Solutions. Addison-Wesley Professional (2004)
22. Juric, M.B.: Business Process Execution Language for Web Services BPEL and BPEL4WS 2nd Edition. Packt Publishing (2006)
23. Kolovski, V., Parsia, B., Katz, Y., Hendler, J.: Representing web service policies in owl-dl. In: 4th International Semantic Web Conference (ISWC 2005), pp. 461–475. Springer (2005)

24. Kubalk, J., Mordinyi, R., Biffl, S.: Multiobjective prototype optimization with evolved improvement steps. In: Evolutionary Computation in Combinatorial Optimization (2008)
25. Lausen, H., Polleres, A., Roman, D.: Web service modeling ontology (wsmo). W3C Member Submission 3 (2005)
26. Li, L., Horrocks, I.: A software framework for matchmaking based on semantic web technology. International Journal of Electronic Commerce 8(4), 39–60 (2004)
27. Martello, S., Toth, P.: Knapsack problems: algorithms and computer implementations. John Wiley & Sons (1990)
28. Martin, D., Ankolekar, A., Burstein, M., Denker, G., Elenius, D., Hobb, J., Kagal, L., Lassila, O., McDermott, D., McGuinness, D., McIlraith, S., Paolucci, M., Parsia, B., Payne, T., Sabou, M., Schlenoff, C., Sirin, E., Solanki, M., Srinivasan, N., Sycara, K., Washington, R.: Owl-s 1.1 release (2004)
29. Martin, D., Paolucci, M., McIlraith, S., Burstein, M., McDermott, D., McGuinness, D., Parsia, B., Payne, T., Sabou, M., Solanki, M.: Bringing semantics to web services: The owl-s approach. In: First International Workshop on Semantic Web Services and Web Process Composition, pp. 26–42. Springer (2005). Proceedings of the First International Workshop on Semantic Web Services and Web Process Composition (SWSWPC 2004)
30. McIlraith, S.A., Son, T.C., Zeng, H.: Semantic web services. IEEE Intelligent Systems 16(2), 46–53 (2001)
31. Mike, P.P., Willem-Jan, H.: Service oriented architectures: approaches, technologies and research issues. The VLDB Journal 16(3), 389–415 (2007). 1265298
32. Miller, J., Mukerji, J.: Model driven architecture (mda). Object Management Group, Draft Specification ormsc/2001-07-01, July 9 (2001)
33. Miller, J., Verma, K., Rajasekaran, P., Sheth, A., Aggarwal, R., Sivashanmugam, K.: Wsdl-s: Adding semantics to wsdl-white paper (2004)
34. Moser, T., Mordinyi, R., Mikula, A., Biffl, S.: Efficient system integration using semantic requirements and capability models: An approach for integrating heterogeneous business services. In: 11th International Conference on Enterprise Information Systems (ICEIS 2009), pp. 56–63. Milan, Italy (2009)
35. Moser, T., Mordinyi, R., Mikula, A., Biffl, S.: Making expert knowledge explicit to facilitate tool support for integrating complex information systems in the atm domain. In: International Conference on Complex, Intelligent and Software Intensive Systems (CISIS 2009), pp. 90–97. Fukuoka, Japan (2009)
36. Niles, I., Pease, A.: Towards a standard upper ontology. In: 2nd International Conference on Formal Ontology in Information Systems, pp. 2–9. ACM (2001). Proceedings of the international conference on Formal Ontology in Information Systems-Volume 2001
37. Noy, N.F.: Semantic integration: a survey of ontology-based approaches. SIGMOD Rec. 33(4), 65–70 (2004). 1041421
38. Noy, N.F., Doan, A.H., Halevy, A.Y.: Semantic integration. AI Magazine 26(1), 7–10 (2005)
39. Oldham, N., Verma, K., Sheth, A., Hakimpour, F.: Semantic ws-agreement partner selection. In: 15th International World Wide Web Conference, pp. 697–706. ACM, Edinburgh, Scotland (2006). 1135879 697-706
40. Paolucci, M., Kawamura, T., Payne, T.R., Sycara, K.: Semantic matching of web services capabilities. In: First International Semantic Web Conference, pp. 333–347. Springer (2002)
41. Piyush, M., Michael, P.: Benchmarking message-oriented middleware: Tibco versus sonicmq: Research articles. Concurr. Comput. : Pract. Exper. 17(12), 1507–1526 (2005). 1085000
42. Pollock, J.: Integrations dirty little secret: Its a matter of semantics. Whitepaper, Modulant: The Interoperability Company (2002)
43. Purtilo, J.M., Atlee, J.M.: Module reuse by interface adaptation. Software - Practice and Experience 21(6), 539–556 (1991)
44. Rosenthal, A., Seligman, L., Renner, S.: From semantic integration to semantics management: case studies and a way forward. SIGMOD Rec. 33(4), 44–50 (2004). 1041418
45. Satoh, F., Nakamura, Y., Mukhi, N.K., Tatsubori, M., Ono, K.: Methodology and tools for end-to-end soa security configurations. In: Services - Part I, 2008. IEEE Congress on, pp. 307–314 (2008)

46. Trastour, D., Bartolini, C., Gonzalez-Castillo, J.: A semantic web approach to service description for matchmaking of services. HP LABORATORIES TECHNICAL REPORT (2001)
47. Uschold, M., Gruninger, M.: Ontologies and semantics for seamless connectivity. SIGMOD Rec. **33**(4), 58–64 (2004). 1041420
48. Verma, K., Akkiraju, R., Goodwin, R.: Semantic matching of web service policies. In: 2nd International Workshop on Semantic and Dynamic Web Process (SDWP 2005) (2005). SDWP Workshop
49. Wache, H., Vgele, T., Visser, U., Stuckenschmidt, H., Schuster, G., Neumann, H., Hbner, S.: Ontology-based integration of information-a survey of existing approaches. In: Workshop on Ontologies and Information Sharing (IJCAI-01), vol. 2001, pp. 108–117. Seattle, USA (2001)
50. Wang, Y., Stroulia, E.: Flexible interface matching for web-service discovery. In: Fourth International Conference on Web Information Systems Engineering, (WISE 2003), pp. 147–156 (2003)
51. Xiaoying, B., Jihui, X., Bin, C., Sinan, X.: Dresr: Dynamic routing in enterprise service bus. In: e-Business Engineering, 2007. ICEBE 2007. IEEE International Conference on, pp. 528–531 (2007)
52. Zaremski, A.M., Wing, J.M.: Signature matching: A tool for using software libraries. ACM Transactions on Software Engineering and Methodology (4), 146–170 (1995)
53. Zaremski, A.M., Wing, J.M.: Specification matching of software components. ACM Trans. Softw. Eng. Methodology (TOSEM) **6**(4), 333–369 (1997). 261641

Chapter 7
Developing Knowledge Representation in Emergency Medical Assistance by Using Semantic Web Techniques

Heloise Manica, Cristiano C. Rocha, José Leomar Todesco, and M. A. R. Dantas

Abstract In this research, a knowledge-based architecture for a mobile emergency medical assistance system is presented. It is based on the France SAMU model and adopts the ontology and mobile computing approaches. The contribution is characterized for providing routines and medical protocol specifications for specialists through the use of their natural language, collecting elements from this language to develop an ontology domain, and using a semantic cache for an enhanced utilization of mobile devices. A prototype of the proposal was implemented in order to support specialists during a day-to-day basis considering knowledge engineering aided by mobile computing techniques. These differentiated characteristics have proved to be successfully at early experiments utilizing the implemented prototype.

7.1 Introduction

The Semantic Web, which is a development of the World Wide Web with metadata-annotated information, contributes to produce information faster and can be shared

Heloise Manica
Post-Graduate Program in Knowledge Engineering and Management (EGC), Federal University of Santa Catarina, Florianópolis, SC, Brazil e-mail: `heloise@egc.ufsc.br`

Cristiano C. Rocha
Computer Science Graduation Program (PPGCC), Federal University of Santa Catarina, Florianópolis, SC, Brazil e-mail: `crocha@inf.ufsc.br`

José Leomar Todesco
Post-Graduate Program in Knowledge Engineering and Management (EGC), Federal University of Santa Catarina, Florianópolis, SC, Brazil e-mail: `tite@stela.org.br`

M. A. R. Dantas
Computer Science Graduation Program (PPGCC) and Post-Graduate Program in Knowledge Engineering and Management (EGC), Federal University of Santa Catarina, Florianópolis, SC, Brazil e-mail: `mario@inf.ufsc.br`

W. Du and F. Ensan (eds.), *Canadian Semantic Web: Technologies and Applications*, DOI 10.1007/978-1-4419-7335-1_7, © Springer Science+Business Media, LLC 2010

through Web Services. Elements of the Semantic Web are expressed in formal specifications, including the Resource Description Framework (RDF), RDF Schema (RDFS), and Web Ontology Language (OWL). In this research, we use the OWL in order to provide a formal description of concepts, terms, and relationships within a medical emergency domain.

The growth of published biomedical literature has resulted in an increasing number of independent and heterogeneous data sources. As observed in [15], the biomedical language contains many synonymous terms, abbreviations and acronyms that can refer to the same concept. The terminological diversity is producing a high level of inefficiency, especially when researchers are searching for specific issues. Thus, the task of building a common controlled vocabulary can be considered as a challenge. Such a vocabulary could be developed for different purposes, for instance: automatic search in free-text records, literature indexing and retrieval, electronic patient records, and statistical reports. A formal ontology can be seen as a controlled vocabulary expressed through an ontology representation language.

The knowledge represented in health domain ontology is important to develop a *clinical decision support system* (CDSS). The work in [10] defines a CDSS as a computer based system that helps health-care professionals to make clinical decisions. Despite the advantages, CDSSs are not widely used in practice, especially in the emergency management domain [9].

In this chapter, we present an approach to circumvent the problem of knowledge communication and representation in the emergency assistance scenario. The proposed approach is based on mobile devices to provide information anytime and anywhere at the point of care. The model contributes to the ontology development and maintenance in the emergency domain. In the context of ontology maintenance, the proposed approach enhances the controlled vocabulary in emergency domain. A Semantic Cache (SC) model was adopted to deal with mobile computing limitations, such as battery autonomy and wireless connection interferences. Moreover, in order to demonstrate the proposed model, it was designed and implemented a prototype that executes on mobile devices.

The chapter is structured as follows. Ontology and characteristics of mobile devices are introduced in section 2. Section 3 illustrates the proposed approach and describes the prototype implementation. In Section 4 it is shown an experimental environment and some results of the proposal. Finally, in Section 5 we present our conclusions and directions for future work.

7.2 Ontology and Mobile Devices Background

The first step in the design of a knowledge base is the decision related to how elements will be represented. The domain ontology defines classes of concepts and its relationships. It can be used, for example, as a source of a controlled terminology to describe biomedical entities in terms of their functions. Associating research data with ontology terms can provide efficient data search by querying terms at different levels within the ontology [18].

According to [21], there is not a common definition for ontology and artifacts called ontologies. It ranges from very lightweight ones, as a list of terms to heavyweight ontologies, such as rigorously formalized logical theories [21]. The lightweight and heavyweight ontology approaches are often used differently. Lightweight ontologies consist of a set of concepts and hierarchical relationships among the concepts and are often used to support data standardization. On the other hand, a heavyweight ontology is used for interoperability purposes and uses axioms to explicitly represent subtleties and has inference capabilities. In this work, a lightweight ontology provides a vocabulary for use in indexing documents as well as for its searching and retrieving.

The development of the ontology is seen as a collaborative activity among people with different expertise [23]. The person who provides the knowledge in a given domain is referred to as expert. Therefore, the ontology implementation may be guided by a knowledge engineer. As [8] notes, different approaches for ontology development have been proposed. A common element in these approaches is the enumeration of important terms in the domain. Part of the work described in this chapter includes the identification of important terms in the emergency assistance domain. Recent technological advances in mobile computing makes it feasible to consider the development of mobile CDSS to be employed at the point of care. Mobile devices are well known to offer limited computing capabilities in comparison to desktop systems. They have battery and local storage constraints, data input and display restrictions and limited computational performance to execute complex applications [14].

The mobile user must contend with operating the mobile devices with its limited resources. Moreover, care must be taken in the development of the application to ensure that the end user can easily find critical information. This is true in emergency situations where the emergency personnel are often interacting with other people or patients, so they cannot have all their attention focused on the device. In addition, wireless environments offer low-quality communication when compared to wired networks. Specifically, frequent network disconnections and local noise complicate the provision of information to mobile users.

The mobile and network challenges described above are addressed in our research by considering the use of a semantic cache model. This model, suggested in [5], can enhance query processing and reduce network traffic flow in a mobile environment. Data caching plays a key role in data management since its use can improve the system performance and availability in case of disconnections. Furthermore, it can save battery power in a client-server communication model and mobile users are still able to work using the cached data when the network is unreachable, as it is shown in our experimental tests.

7.3 Proposed Approach

In this section, we describe our approach using an ontology-based architecture applied to a mobile emergency service. The major idea is to provide an ubiquitous tool to the emergency staff, then this tool can increase the level of available knowledge about the procedures. As a result, the tool can help the emergency staff to increase their probability of success in any intervention. For less experienced personnel, the system may also be used to access knowledge to assure that appropriate protocols are being followed.

The proposed approach, shown in Fig. 7.1, enhances the captured knowledge and maintains the ontology updated with new instances in a semi-automatic way. The user is an expert who submits a query by selecting a keyword and some filters from his PCS (*Personal Communication System*).

The first action of the system consists to verify if a full (or partial) answer for this query exists inside the local module, i.e. inside the semantic cache. In the case that it is necessary to contact the server (partial answer), the system forwards the query.

Inside the local server, the indexing module correlates keywords from the query with several files (reports, clinical guidelines, and clinical procedures, for example) by using the appropriate local ontology emergency vocabulary. When the user initiates a search utilizing a term which can not be found in the local ontology, the local server initiates a search inside the DeCS system [6]. DeCS is a controlled vocabu-

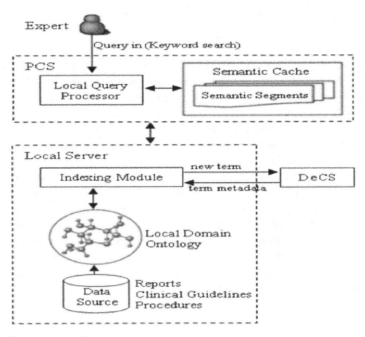

Fig. 7.1 The proposed architecture

lary developed from the MeSH (Medical Subject Headings U.S. National Library of Medicine).

After acquiring data from the new vocabulary, the indexing module feeds the local ontology. If the vocabulary does not exist within the DeCS, the unknown term will be stored in a temporary area to be subsequently reviewed by experts to determine if this term will be included within the ontology. Consequently, the present proposal adopts a strategy, which utilizes a semi-automatic approach to feed the domain ontology. If the term occurs inside the DeCS, it is immediately inserted in the local domain ontology. In the case that the term does not exist in the DeCS, it is considered later by an expert.

Nowadays, the DeCS cannot be considered as a sufficient element of captured vocabulary for the urgency and emergency domain. The main reason is due to the emergency terms are distributed over different categories. Therefore, it represents a challenge for a searching. An example that helps to illustrate this point is a query for the topic "emergency burning". A third degree burning is considered an emergency. However, if this occurrence is an accident of six months age and the patient is being treated, it is not considered as an emergency burning. Therefore, new relevant documents are returned for the query.

In addition, if there is enough time available to the user, it can refine the query and match the desirable results. Nevertheless, it is not the case in urgent or emergency situation. Other well-known challenge is the utilization of specific terms related to a particular language and slang characteristics by a set of specialists.

7.3.1 Ontology Development

This study aims to contribute to the knowledge formalization in UE (Urgency and Emergency) area through the utilization of the ontology paradigm. The proposed ontology considers the Brazilian SAMU mobile health care system (the characteristics of the SAMU can be found in [7]). Emergency experts from the Santa Catarina State [17] were involved with the modeling process supported by the Protégé tool [13], which is an open source ontology editor and knowledge-based framework.

Emergency medical services (EMS) have been created to offer first aid, primary medical treatment, basic life support, stabilization, and rapid transfer to the closest appropriate hospital and advanced life support [20]. A major characteristic of the SAMU system is the analysis of emergency calls (medical regulation) by a physician at the communication center. Medical regulation may result in medical advice to the caller, and if necessary an ambulance is sent to the scene of medical emergencies.

The health professional (it includes physicians, nurses, nursing assistants, and rescuers) respond to a wide range of emergencies including trauma, medical, pediatric, surgical, gynecology, obstetrics, and mental health. Thus, mobile medical urgency and emergency calls represent a challenge to professionals involved with these tasks because it requires knowledge from different areas with specific skills. The use of computational systems to help professionals is not expected to introduce any modification in clinic and well-established procedures [2]. In other words, physicians cannot be obliged to leave a patient to query a remote computational system.

Recent technological advances in mobile computing makes it feasible to consider the development of searching applications to be used at the point of care. When an emergency assistance unit is on the way to help a patient, a mobile device can be used to provide helpful knowledge regarding the patient healthcare. In a typical scenario, emergency personnel could review a clinical procedure for a complex situation by using a portable device.

In this context, the development of the UE ontology contributes with knowledge representation and sharing by providing a set of a consistent vocabulary necessary for clear communication and information retrieval at the point of care. In addition of a common vocabulary for experts, the ontology defines a machine-interpretable vocabulary in UE area.

7.3.1.1 Ontology Modeling

In the development of a terminological system, e.g. in a specialized medical area, such as UE, the analysis and design phases are followed by the implementation in some programming language or environment [1]. There is a growing number of methodologies that specifically address the issue of the development and maintenance of ontologies [8]. The Protégé tool [13] was used as an ontology-developing environment. Protégé is an open source ontology engineering environment that supports the implementation of knowledge-based systems. This platform can be used to the development of a medical terminological system, which can be considered as a lightweight ontology.

The ontology development process was based on ontology development 101, proposed in [8]. According to Noy and Mcguinness [11], in summary, developing an ontology includes: defining classes; arranging the classes in a taxonomic hierarchy; defining properties; describing the allowed values for these properties; and determining the values for these properties. The design and implementation are described in the following sub-sections.

7.3.2 Determining the Ontology Domain

The design of the ontology started with the domain definition. The proposed ontology considers the Brazilian SAMU mobile health care system [16, 17]. The proposed lightweight ontology will cover the medical vocabulary that is used for indexing, cataloging, and searching for documents used by the support Brazilian UE personnel. Since the lightweight ontology is used as a common vocabulary for UE domain, we do not focus on inference capabilities.

Emergency experts from the Santa Catarina State [17] were involved with the modeling process. Several meetings and visits to the SAMU environment were performed in order to verify if all the concepts and development direction were appropriated. The main competency questions that the ontology should be able to answer were:

- "Which documents have the x keyword?";
- "Which documents are related to y syndromes (or gestures)?";
- "Which procedures can be suitable to z type of urgencies?"; and
- "What are the new terms recently identified?".

In Portuguese there are no major ontologies in UE domain, then we started developing the ontology from the scratch. Therefore, we considered the controlled vocabulary DeCS [6] and extended its content with new terms identified from urgency and emergency domain.

7.3.3 Enumerating Important Terms, Classes and the Class Hierarchy

The NEU (Core for Emergency and Urgency) is a formalized structure to implement training, qualification, and continuing education of human resources. The NEU from Santa Catarina State maintains a website with several documents that are used to support the UE activities. Initially, it was considered a comprehensive list of emergency related terms without a special attention about theirs relationships or any properties that the concepts may have. The first set of classes was created from this list of general concepts previously identified. Then, classes were organized into a hi-

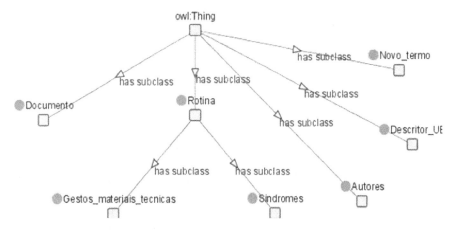

Fig. 7.2 Some classes, instances and relationships among them

erarchical taxonomy. Fig. 7.2 shows the main classes identified with a human expert help.

Considering documents available at the webpage [1], it was possible to define the main concepts related to the SAMU-SC documents. Each document stores data related to emergency calls (e.g. protocols, manuals, exams). As a result, characteristics related to the documents are unified in a class called Documento (Document). On the other hand, the class Autor (Author) specifies its authors.

The *Descritor_UE* (Descriptor_UE) class is compounded by a set of terms related to the UE domain used to routines indexing. Descriptors from this class follow the DeCS standard. In the class *Novo_termo* (New_term) there is a set of terms that were not analyzed by experts. All new terms are captured by the system through this class. In other words, all accepted terms exist inside the class Descritor, where the class Novo_termo terms candidates to be adopted are stored. This procedure is executed manually by experts.

The *Rotina* (Routine) class describes protocols for urgency and emergency calls. This class has two subclasses, *Gestos_materiais_tecnicas* (Gestures_ materials_techniques) and *Sindromes* (Syndromes). As mentioned before, each one has specific characteristics related to the protocol by following the SAMU-SC procedure. Considering characteristics and relationships captured by this class, it is possible to obtain a more appropriated class of documents related to a specific emergency call.

7.3.4 Defining Properties and Restrictions of Classes

After establishing all classes, the next step consisted to define properties related to these classes. The calls' protocols are organized in two groups: 1) large syndromes; and 2) gestures, materials and techniques.

Authors from SAMU-SC documents are obliged to follow a template. Observing this template, it was possible to identify properties from each class. In this step, we also defined different restrictions, such as value type, allowed values, the cardinality, and other features that the property can have.

7.3.5 Creating Instances and New Terms Extraction

In the last step we introduced some instances of classes in the hierarchy. Adopting the Protégé tool it was possible to introduce instances to check whether competences could be answered. Figure 7.3 shows the following competency questions answered by the ontology in Protégé query interface: "Which documents are related to electrocardiography interpretation?". This query returns five documents, as illustrated in the search results chart of Protégé queries interface (Fig. 7.3). Since the proposed ontology is expected to be used by emergency assistance personnel from Santa Catarina State, in Brazil, the content is in Portuguese.

The process of defining and instantiating a knowledge base is referred to as knowledge markup or ontology population [4]. Domain entities are represented as instances of concepts in ontologies. According to [22], domain ontology captures knowledge in a static way, as it is a snapshot of knowledge concerning a specific domain from a particular point of view in a specific time-frame. Thus, domain ontology might contain an incomplete or out-of-date knowledge regarding its instances.

The maintenance of its captured knowledge is crucial to the performance of the application that uses it. Maintaining ontological knowledge through population and enrichment is a time-consuming, error prone and labor-intensive task when performed manually [22]. In our effort to enhance the knowledge captured and ontology maintenance, we propose an application for mobile devices. This application allows a user to query through the proposed ontology for relevant documents (e.g., a medical procedures or clinical guidelines). The expert enters the keyword and the available filters to enhance his query. Used terms are usually associated to emotions and the environment context where the context is being conducted. As a result, we propose the extraction and analysis of these terms, in addition to the context, as a new input to update and introduce new ontology instances.

When the expert initiates a search utilizing a term which cannot be found in the local ontology, the system initiates a search inside the DeCS [6]. After acquiring the data from the new vocabulary, the system feeds the UE ontology. If the vocabulary does not exist within the DeCS, the unknown term will be stored in a temporary area to be subsequently reviewed by experts to determine if this term should be included within the ontology. Finally the candidate instances and the proposed lexical synonyms are validated by a domain expert.

Consequently, the present proposal adopts a strategy which utilizes a semi-automatic approach to feed the proposed UE ontology. In summary, if the term exists inside the DeCS, it is immediately inserted in the local domain ontology. Otherwise, it is considered later by an expert.

Fig. 7.3 An example from Protégé query interface

7.3.5.1 New Terms Instantiation

In our effort to improve the domain ontology we developed a query interface that is shown in Fig. 7.4. This interface allows a user to query into the ontology for relevant documents (e.g., medical procedures or clinical guidelines). The specialist enters the keyword and the available filters to enhance his/her query. In the Brazilian SAMU routines (or protocols) are classified as gestures or syndromes. The filter specifies the desirable knowledge, for example, indications of which type of material will be necessary, and some tips about risk and accidents.

Three scenario examples were conceived in order to evaluate the prototype. The first scenario considers a key term present into the domain ontology; the second exploits the case where a term exists into the DeCS and not into the domain ontology; in the final test the term does not exist into of the domain ontology or DeCS. The following considerations are relevant to the domain ontology: i) files named as *ecg_indicacoes* and *ecg_materiais* have information related to the utilization and related materials of an electrocardiogram; ii) the ECG is a synonymous for electrocardiography; iii) specialists know that the term EKG is a synonymous for both ECG and electrocardiography.

In the example 1, the user executes a query (Q1) which results in a search of available materials for occurrences of ?electrocardiography? as a keyword. This is

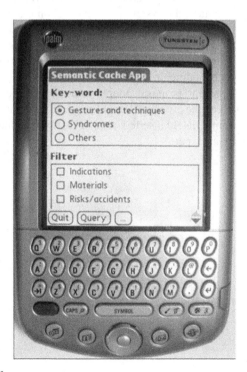

Fig. 7.4 Query interface

the simplest case because the term exists into the domain ontology, therefore the query is executed without any problem.

Example 2 is characterized by a similar query from example 1, however now the user seeks for the term "EKG". This term is synonymous for "electrocardiography", and the system does not have this knowledge. Because the term does not exist into the domain ontology, the system initiates a search into the DeCS, where the term "EKG" is found to be synonymous with "electrocardiography", as shown in Fig. 7.5. As a result, the system automatically feeds the domain ontology with this new synonymous term.

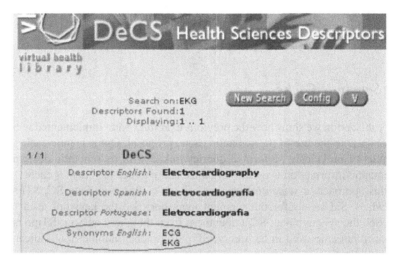

Fig. 7.5 Searching into the DeCS with the term "EKG"

In the example 3, the user enters a query (Q2) and searching for material and indications of a keyword "electrode". Since this term does not exist into the domain ontology or the DeCS (Fig. 7.6), it is inserted as a possible new term into a specific class called *Novo_termo* (New_term). The procedure of inserting this term into the domain ontology will be executed manually latter upon a specialist's agreement that this term is adequate.

As study examples shown, while specialists are executing their queries, used keyword vocabulary is employed in order to enhance the ontology development. Reliability is an advantage of this approach because only those elements that were verified by a specialist or DeCS will be inserted in the ontology. In addition, another advantage is that the constant insertion of new terms turns the ontology updated. The action of populating and updating the ontology when it is done manually is a time-consuming mechanism for specialists.

When a query generates new data for the mobile user, his PCS will also receive a semantic description, which will be used for cache management purposes. The following sub-section describes how this operation is realized.

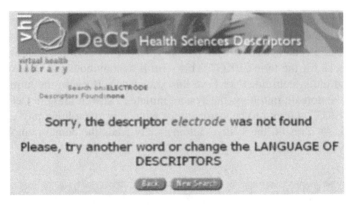

Fig. 7.6 Searching into the DeCS with the term "electrode"

7.3.6 Semantic Cache

In this sub-section we show how the previous examples were implemented with special emphasis to the use of the semantic cache proposal. Our semantic cache keeps the results of previously performed queries linked with its semantic descriptions. The semantic information is used to organize and manage the client?s cache.

In this approach, a *semantic segment* is a tuple (Sid, Scc, Sco, SC, STipo, SF, SFq), where Sid stands for the segment identifier; Scc the keyword used by the query, Sco the synonymous; SC a document from the query answer; STipo and SF both are filters employed in the query; SFq a frequency number that indicates the segment utilization.

An answer from any query can be a result from three computational cases: the answer can be only found at a specific server; the answer is found completely into the SC; and part of the answer exists into the SC. These are essentially the scenarios addressed in the three previous examples. The following revisits them in the context of the SC.

When executing Q1 (from example 1), the system verifies that the cache is empty, thus it sends a complete query to the server, which replies by sending the *ecg_indicacoes* and *ecg_materiais* files. Consequently, each file is stored as a new semantic segment.

Suppose a user executing the query Q1 again, but using the keyword "ECG". In that case, the system verifies that the answer is inside the cache because the domain ontology indicates that this term is synonymous of the term "electrocardiography". Therefore, the query is completely answered with the existing content in the SC without a required communication with a server. The system updates the frequency of the documents? utilization. In this study, we use the LFU (Least Frequently Used) policy to the data cache replacement.

Finally, suppose a user executing a query Q1, but now a filter *riscos/acidentes* (risks/accidents) is added. The answer for this query is composed of two parts. The first part, *ecg_indicacoes* and *ecg_materiais*, exists inside the cache. The second part *ecg_riscos* exists inside a server. As a result, only the second part is requested from the server. When the results of this query comes from the server, they are stored in the cache together with the semantic description. Then, the frequency of the use of *ecg_indicacoes* and *ecg_materiais* is updated.

7.4 Experimental Environment and Results

The experimental environment consisted of a server connected to a wired network and the PCS network. The prototype was implemented using the Java language on the server-side and J2ME in the client (PCS). The mobile devices used in our experiments were two Palm Tungsten C, with 200MHz processor, 64 MB memory, 802.11b wireless network interface card and Palm OS 5.2.1 as an operating system.

The domain ontology was expressed using the Ontology Web Language (OWL) [12], the language recommended by the World Wide Web Consortium (W3C). OWL provides a powerful constraint language for precisely defining how concepts in ontology should be interpreted by machines. The SparQL language [19] and the Jena API (Application Programing Interface) [7] were utilized for automatic updating the domain ontology.

A traditional object cache application was designed and implemented in order to draw a comparison with the proposed environment. In this implementation, the object cache model only reuses the cache data when the query is the same as another in cache.

In the following we present some empirical results adopting the query battery consumption and cache hit rate as metrics for performance measurements. These metrics are especially important for emergency services because the intensive use of the devices and help with the available information.

A set of fifteen different queries was conceived aiming to allow an automatic process of test and provide a comparison between the applications. A first experiment verifies the battery consumption. This measurement was performed through the BatteryGraph [3] software package, measuring the two applications before starting and after finishing its execution. Results from this experiment are shown in Fig. 7.7.

The second experiment was characterized by a mechanism that informs the cache successful rate. In other words, it was measured the number of cache hit ratio. By considering all queries it was observed the cache hit ratio as illustrated in Fig. 7.8.

7.5 Conclusions and Future Work

In this chapter we described the use of ontology technique and semantic cache for a mobile emergency medical assistance system. The proposed architecture was interesting to identify new terms that were used during an emergency heath-care query.

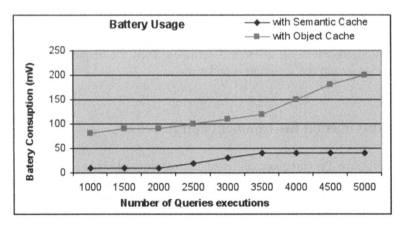

Fig. 7.7 Battery usage

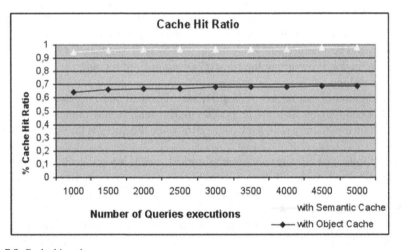

Fig. 7.8 Cache hit ratio

This vocabulary is required to the ontology populating and to keep the ontological knowledge up-to-date.

By using Semantic Web techniques, the information is given explicit meaning, making it easier to process and share information available on the Web. The ontology expressed in OWL provides a powerful constraint language for precisely defining how concepts in ontology should be interpreted by machines. The indexing and retrieving mechanism proposed in this work were limited to Brazilian SAMU. However, the ideas can easily adapted for other emergency services.

Simulation results show that the semantic cache approach achieves a significant performance gain over the object caching in mobile environments. Moreover, the semantic cache is suitable for environments where permanent connection between clients and the server cannot be guaranteed, in addition to those cases where crucial functionalities are required without the support of a server.

In the future, the proposed lightweight ontology can be used to provide a structure for organizing context descriptions to account for the subtleties of concepts in a heavyweight ontology development.

References

References may be *cited* in the text either by number (preferred) or by author/year.[1] The reference list should ideally be *sorted* in alphabetical order – even if reference numbers are used for the their citation in the text. If there are several works by the same author, the following order should be used:

1. all works by the author alone, ordered chronologically by year of publication
2. all works by the author with a coauthor, ordered alphabetically by coauthor
3. all works by the author with several coauthors, ordered chronologically by year of publication.

The *styling* of references[2] depends on the subject of your book:

- The *two* recommended styles for references in books on *mathematical, physical, statistical and computer sciences* are depicted in [1, 2, 3, 4, 5] and [6, 7, 8, 9, 10].
- Examples of the most commonly used reference style in books on *Psychology, Social Sciences* are [11, 12, 13, 14, 15].
- Examples for references in books on *Humanities, Linguistics, Philosophy* are [16, 17, 18, 19, 20].
- Examples of the basic Springer style used in publications on a wide range of subjects such as *Computer Science, Economics, Engineering, Geosciences, Life Sciences, Medicine, Biomedicine* are [21, 22, 24, 23, 25].

1. Broy, M.: Software engineering — from auxiliary to key technologies. In: Broy, M., Dener, E. (eds.) Software Pioneers, pp. 10-13. Springer, Heidelberg (2002)
2. Dod, J.: Effective substances. In: The Dictionary of Substances and Their Effects. Royal Society of Chemistry (1999) Available via DIALOG.
   http://www.rsc.org/dose/titleofsubordinatedocument.
   Cited15Jan1999
3. Geddes, K.O., Czapor, S.R., Labahn, G.: Algorithms for Computer Algebra. Kluwer, Boston (1992)
4. Hamburger, C.: Quasimonotonicity, regularity and duality for nonlinear systems of partial differential equations. Ann. Mat. Pura. Appl. **169**, 321–354 (1995)
5. Slifka, M.K., Whitton, J.L.: Clinical implications of dysregulated cytokine production. J. Mol. Med. (2000) doi: 10.1007/s001090000086

---

[1] Make sure that all references from the list are cited in the text. Those not cited should be moved to a separate *Further Reading* section or chapter.

[2] Always use the standard abbreviation of a journal's name according to the ISSN *List of Title Word Abbreviations*, see http://www.issn.org/en/node/344

6. J. Dod, in *The Dictionary of Substances and Their Effects*, Royal Society of Chemistry. (Available via DIALOG, 1999), `http://www.rsc.org/dose/titleofsubordinatedocument.Cited15Jan1999`

7. H. Ibach, H. Lüth, *Solid-State Physics*, 2nd edn. (Springer, New York, 1996), pp. 45-56

8. S. Preuss, A. Demchuk Jr., M. Stuke, Appl. Phys. A **61**

9. M.K. Slifka, J.L. Whitton, J. Mol. Med., doi: 10.1007/s001090000086

10. S.E. Smith, in *Neuromuscular Junction*, ed. by E. Zaimis. Handbook of Experimental Pharmacology, vol 42 (Springer, Heidelberg, 1976), p. 593

11. Calfee, R. C., & Valencia, R. R. (1991). *APA guide to preparing manuscripts for journal publication*. Washington, DC: American Psychological Association.

12. Dod, J. (1999). Effective substances. In: The dictionary of substances and their effects. Royal Society of Chemistry. Available via DIALOG. `http://www.rsc.org/dose/Effectivesubstances`. Cited 15 Jan 1999.

13. Harris, M., Karper, E., Stacks, G., Hoffman, D., DeNiro, R., Cruz, P., et al. (2001). Writing labs and the Hollywood connection. *J Film* Writing, 44(3), 213–245.

14. O'Neil, J. M., & Egan, J. (1992). Men's and women's gender role journeys: Metaphor for healing, transition, and transformation. In B. R. Wainrig (Ed.), *Gender issues across the life cycle* (pp. 107–123). New York: Springer.

15. Kreger, M., Brindis, C.D., Manuel, D.M., Sassoubre, L. (2007). Lessons learned in systems change initiatives: benchmarks and indicators. *American Journal of Community Psychology*, doi: 10.1007/s10464-007-9108-14.

16. Alber John, Daniel C. O'Connell, and Sabine Kowal. 2002. Personal perspective in TV interviews. *Pragmatics* 12:257–271

17. Cameron, Deborah. 1997. Theoretical debates in feminist linguistics: Questions of sex and gender. In *Gender and discourse*, ed. Ruth Wodak, 99–119. London: Sage Publications.

18. Cameron, Deborah. 1985. *Feminism and linguistic theory*. New York: St. Martin's Press.

19. Dod, Jake. 1999. Effective substances. In: The dictionary of substances and their effects. Royal Society of Chemistry. Available via DIALOG. http://www.rsc.org/dose/title of subordinate document. Cited 15 Jan 1999

20. Suleiman, Camelia, Daniel C. OConnell, and Sabine Kowal. 2002. 'If you and I, if we, in this later day, lose that sacred fire...': Perspective in political interviews. *Journal of Psycholinguistic Research*. doi: 10.1023/A:1015592129296.

21. Brown B, Aaron M (2001) The politics of nature. In: Smith J (ed) The rise of modern genomics, 3rd edn. Wiley, New York

22. Dod J (1999) Effective Substances. In: The dictionary of substances and their effects. Royal Society of Chemistry. Available via DIALOG. `http://www.rsc.org/dose/titleofsubordinatedocument. Cited15Jan1999`

23. Slifka MK, Whitton JL (2000) Clinical implications of dysregulated cytokine production. J Mol Med, doi: 10.1007/s001090000086

24. Smith J, Jones M Jr, Houghton L et al (1999) Future of health insurance. N Engl J Med 965:325–329

25. South J, Blass B (2001) The future of modern genomics. Blackwell, London

Chapter 8
Semantically Enriching the Search System of a Music Digital Library

Paloma de Juan and Carlos . Iglesias

Abstract Traditional search systems are usually based on keywords, a very simple and convenient mechanism to express a need for information. This is the most popular way of searching the Web, although it is not always an easy task to accurately summarize a natural language query in a few keywords. Working with keywords means losing the context, which is the only thing that can help us deal with ambiguity. This is the biggest problem of keyword-based systems. Semantic Web technologies seem a perfect solution to this problem, since they make it possible to represent the semantics of a given domain. In this chapter, we present three projects, Harmos, Semusici and Cantiga, whose aim is to provide access to a music digital library. We will describe two search systems, a traditional one and a semantic one, developed in the context of these projects and compare them in terms of usability and effectiveness.

8.1 Introduction

For some years now, we have been living in a world where the Web has been dominated by plain textual contents. These have been reachable thanks to search engines and directories, which have been designed to work in a keyword environment. The main problem of a keyword-based system is ambiguity. Unfortunately, the meaning of a keyword can only be determined by its surroundings (if available). The concept of "context" can not be applied in this situation.

Paloma de Juan

Departamento de Ingeniera, de Sistemas Telemticos, Universidad Politcnica de Madrid, e-mail: paloko@dit.upm.es

Carlos . Iglesias
Germinus XXI (Grupo Gesfor), e-mail: cif@germinus.com

W. Du and F. Ensan (eds.), *Canadian Semantic Web: Technologies and Applications*, DOI 10.1007/978-1-4419-7335-1_8, © Springer Science+Business Media, LLC 2010

The same happens when we look for multimedia resources, which are becoming more and more important lately. A picture (or a video or audio file) can not usually be reduced to a set of words[1]. In order for users to share this kind of contents, they must provide some keywords to make them reachable by other users. In this way, a conventional system can give access to both textual and multimedia resources. There are hundreds of relationships between the semantic descriptors used to tag the multimedia resources. However, this information is not taken into account when a search is processed.

The type of queries a keyword-based system can accept are quite limited and semantically poor. A keyword in a text field can mean anything. We have no information about its nature: it could be the name of a city, an address, the title of a book, a date, a person's name or even an identifier. If we named that text field, we could partially restrict the meaning of the keyword, e.g. the keyword is a date. But what is the semantics of this date? In the context of the projects this chapter presents, it could be the date a master class was recorded, the date a composition was composed, the birth date of a composer... We need to move to a new search paradigm that allows us to ask more semantically complex questions, e.g. "I want to find compositions by Nordic composers."

Changing the search paradigm or, let us say, the system interface, would not be enough to provide better results. We could find a way to let the user express very accurately what she is looking for but we will need to change the structure that supports the knowledge of the system if we really want to exploit the semantic relationships that link all the concepts involved. An ontology may help us define rules that would enrich the knowledge base with more information than what is explicitly stated.

In this chapter, we will present the changes we have introduced in a traditional system in order to improve its searchability both in terms of usability (changing the interface) and effectiveness (changing the structure that supports the knowledge base). We will also discuss how we have progressively improve our system in the context of three projects we have been or are involved in: Harmos, Semusici and Cantiga.

In Section II, we will present our previous and current work in the field, describing the three projects we have just introduced. In Section III, we will describe MagisterMusicae, the system built for Harmos. In Section IV, we will explain how we have improved this system in the context of Semusici and Cantiga. In Section V, we will describe Cantiga Search System. An evaluation of the improvements of this system over the one introduced in Section III will be conducted in Section VI. Finally, we will review some related projects and present our conclusions and future work in Sections VII and VIII, respectively.

---

[1] It is possible to automatically extract features from multimedia resources and use them as tags, but this is a complex process.

8.2 Research Context

8.2.1 Previous Work

The work presented in this article comes from the experience in several projects related to music digital libraries with the common aim of providing Internet access to music resources hold by different institutions. The collection we have been working with contains more than 700 audiovisual hours of recorded master classes, property of Fundacin Albniz [1]. These resources have been tagged according to a set of tags that define a vocabulary of pedagogical concepts, which we will talk about later.

The first of this series of music related projects we have been involved in was European eContent Harmos project. Harmos produced a collection of audiovisual contents belonging to the music heritage, where education was the principal focus and the project's main objective. The resulting system is available at http://www.magistermusicae.com. We will describe this system in the next section. The aim of the second project, Semusici, was to improve Harmos system by applying Semantic Web technologies. The main output of this project was Semusici ontology.

8.2.2 Cantiga Project

The goal of the last of this series of projects, Cantiga, is to investigate how Web 2.0 technologies can be applied to the cataloging and search of music resources. In this project, we are trying to develop a platform that will help users annotate and find contents of digital libraries from different music institutions. This platform is also intended to provide a framework to help these institutions communicate (both internally and externally) and interact, allowing them to create workflows. These workflows should help automating such tasks as translation, quality control and other administrative procedures. The system will also support federated search across all the libraries available.

In order to decrease the high cost of manual cataloging, the system uses advanced tools to semi-automatically extract features from the multimedia resources. This will help users annotate these resources, which will make it easier to retrieve them. We are also using Semusici ontology to classify the resources. Using a formal structure to model the domain will make searching faster and will increase the precision and recall of the system. The reason is that users will be able to produce more accurate queries and will get a whole set of semantically related results.

8.3 MagisterMusicae Search System

MagisterMusicae, the system developed in the context of Harmos, is a simple search system based on facets. This is a search paradigm in which keywords are placed in slots[2], the so-called *facets*, that have a certain semantics. The main interface consists on a series of drop down menus (as shown in Fig. 8.1) that allow the user to search a master class given the instrument it is oriented to, the teacher giving the lecture and the composer who composed the piece of music being played in the class. To simplify the process of searching, a teacher can only be selected in case an instrument has already been chosen. Also, a teacher has to be selected before chosing a composer.

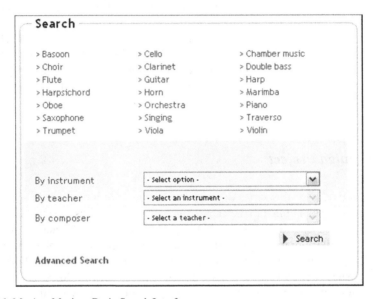

Fig. 8.1 MagisterMusicae Basic Search Interface

The advanced search interface (Fig. 8.2) allows the user to select a series of keywords belonging to seven different categories: Instruments, Teachers, Students, Concepts, Composers, Works and Movements. This makes it possible to look for a master class without knowing anything about the instrument it is addressed to. There is much more information about the master classes available in the knowledge base (dates, places, languages...) that can not be used to build a query in this system. Including a tab for every single category would probably make the system less attractive to the users.

Neither of the two search systems allow the user to type any term of her choice, as they both provide a guided search service. Internally, MagisterMusicae uses a

---

[2] In this case, the user is asked to select values instead of filling text fields.

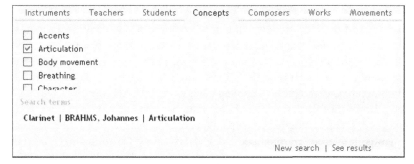

Fig. 8.2 MagisterMusicae Advanced Search Interface

relational database to store the information (no ontology is used). The selected keywords are used to build a simple SQL query which is expected to deliver a list of master classes fulfilling all the requirements the user has posed.

8.4 Improving Searchability

The system we have just described has certain limitations, which will be discussed in the next section. The following subsections will present our work in improving the way users access the contents of the Fundacin Albniz master classes collection. We have been particularly concerned about the effectiveness of the system in terms of number of results delivered when the knowledge base has no explicit information about some fact. This is a key point in Semantic Web technologies, since the structures they propose have the ability to make explicit knowledge that is implicit in a given domain [2].

8.4.1 Applying Semantic Web Technologies

As we have already said, Semusici intended to improve the results of Harmos by introducing Semantic Web technologies. An ontology was built in order to support all the information contained in Harmos database. As we will see later in this section, most of the knowledge is hidden behind the relationships between the concepts involved. An ontology, by definition, represents a formal model of the common interpretation of the entities and relationships of a given domain (or, as Gruber said, "an explicit specification of a conceptualization" [3]). Therefore, it has great powerful retrieval and inferential capabilities. Another reason why we chose this structure is that it makes it possible to easily import information from external sources in order to enrich the knowledge base.

The knowledge base we have been working on has two distinct parts. The first one captures all the information that can be useful to answer any query that is not directly related to the pedagogical aspects of a master class. For instance, "Show me all the recordings related to composers born in the 18th century." This part of the knowledge base contains all the information about the context of a master class, mainly biographical and bibliographical data.

The other part of the knowledge base is the concepts taxonomy. This taxonomy contains over 350 pedagogical concepts that are used as tags to describe the recordings. It was built from Harmos pedagogical taxonomy [4] following a bottom-up strategy in order to redistribute the concepts in a way their relationships could be exploited[3]. This taxonomy aims to cover the whole spectrum of music practice and teaching, focusing on pedagogical aspects, such as technique (general or specific of an instrument), mechanics, musicology, musical elements (rhythm, melody, harmony, form...), etc.

Semusici ontology consists of more than 150 classes and almost 40 properties. These are the main parts and some of the most important classes:

8.4.1.1 The Domain Ontology

The first thing Semusici ontology has to express is all the information that is available in the knowledge base but is not related to the pedagogical concepts. In every master class, a piece of music is performed in order to let the teacher give a lecture about a certain matter related to the composition itself, the instruments used in that composition, the composer's style, the period or era in which the composition was created...

Therefore, we introduced concepts such as Composition (a piece of music), Teacher (a person who gives a master class), Instrument (a device that can be used to produce music), Composer (someone who composes music as a profession), Era (a period of time defined by a series of events)... We identified some other concepts that characterize a composition, such as Genre (an expressive style of music), Style (a way of expressing something that is characteristic of a particular composer or period) or Form (a perceptual structure). We created a parent class to represent those who are involved in a master class or have composed a piece of music. This is Person (a human being), parent of both Composer and Participant (someone who takes part in a master class). This last one is at the same time parent of Performer (someone who plays an instrument or sings for an audience), Student (a person who attends a master class in order to learn) and Teacher.

We also included the concept Place (a location) to help us locate the master classes, as well as indicate where a person was born or dead. We created a number of relations between all these concepts. We identified most of these properties by posing a series of competency questions, which helped us find keywords and define

---

[3] The original distribution had very little semantic information and the elements in each level were not always equally specific.

the terminology of the ontology. These were the questions the ontology must be able to answer in order to meet the initial specification. The domain ontology is displayed in Fig. 8.3.

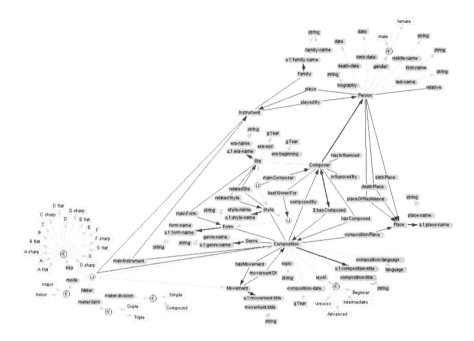

Fig. 8.3 The Domain Ontology

8.4.1.2 The Instrument Taxonomy

The Instrument taxonomy is part of the domain ontology. Instruments have been classified according to the family they belong to. Every instrument is an instance of a class representing its family (`StringInstrument`, `WindInstrument`, `PercussionInstrument`...). These families conform a taxonomy (Fig. 8.4), which has been modelled using SKOS.

The Simple Knowledge Organization System (SKOS) [5] is a Semantic Web language for representing controlled structures vocabularies, including thesauri, classification schemes, subject heading systems and taxonomies. SKOS provides a framework for publishing a thesaurus or classification scheme, and for publishing a subject index over a collection of items (e.g. books), in the Semantic Web. By publishing in the Semantic Web, applications may harvest and merge these data, allowing them for example to implement a combined retrieval service across multiple collections (e.g. libraries) [6].

A key feature of controlled structured vocabularies is that they are intended for use within information retrieval applications, i.e. they are used to describe items in a collection in a controlled way, allowing semantically precise and unambiguous retrieval. SKOS is an application of the Resource Description Framework (RDF). Because RDF is a formal language that has well defined logical properties, any controlled structured vocabulary represented using SKOS is machine-understandable, i.e. a computer application can read it, "make sense" of it and use it to provide functionalities such as rich visual search.

We found SKOS suited our need for a language for representing the Instrument taxonomy. It provided us with all the semantic relations we needed to turn the classification we have just presented into a semantic structure. These include relations such as "narrower" or "broader", which helped us build the instruments tree, among other properties, such as "related" and "partOf" [7], which would be interesting in case of expanding the tree.

SKOS does not only provide a set of semantic relations. It also contains a series of lexical labels which can help us name the concepts in our structure. The main feature of these lexical labels is that they allow to make a distinction between "preferred labels" and "alternate labels". This can help us specify a series of synonymys or alternative spellings to improve the search. We can use the "prefLabel" (which must be unique for each concept and language) to render the tree but both this and every "altLabel" will be considered for the search. This can be a very important issue if used in combination with a lexical database like WordNet.

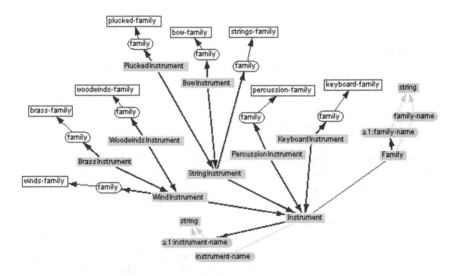

Fig. 8.4 The Instrument Taxonomy as Part of the Domain Ontology

8.4.1.3 The Resources Ontology

The ontology should also be able to represent the different resources that will be retrieved through the search system. This system is supposed to allow users look for master classes. These master classes are modelled through the class `Class`. We associate valuable information to the instances of this class through properties such as `title`, `place`, `date`, `language`, `synopsis`, `targeAudience`, etc. We also connect these instances to the corresponding `Teacher` and `Student` individuals, as shown in Fig. 8.5.

Each class is associated to a physical resource. These resources are mostly videos, but they can also be audio files or even documents. Therefore we created a class `Multimedia` representing them all and a single child class for each type of media: `Video`, `Audio`, `Document`. All these classes contain information particular for each kind of resource. Whereas a class is an abstract concept, representing a event happening in a certain place at a certain time, a `Multimedia` instance is univocally associated to a specific recording of one of those events and it exists in the form of a file.

As we have seen, each class is assigned a series of concepts, which identify the pedagogical content of the lesson. These concepts are represented by the class `Concept`. We will now study this class and the hierarchy we have created to semantically organize the pedagogical concepts.

8.4.1.4 The Concept Taxonomy

The `Concept` class is meant to represent all the pedagogical concepts that can be associated to a master class. Every instance of this class is assigned a concept name. This name is the term annotators use to tag the digital recordings. Each concept belongs to a category according to the class it is instance of. We modelled the taxonomy of categories using SKOS, just like we did with the Instrument taxonomy. Elements representing each of the subclasses of `Concept` have been introduced as instances of `skos:Concept` and associated with the corresponding concepts through the property `category`.

We followed a bottom-up strategy in order to find the most natural way of classifying the elements of the original taxonomy and created the hierarchy below `Concept`. Starting from the most specific tags, we gathered all the concepts having basic semantic features in common in order to make it easy to define relations between different classes. We paid special attention to maintaining a consistent level of specificity among the instances of each class. The highest level of the hierarchy is divided into nine disjoint classes: `Composing`, `Ensembles`, `InstrumentFamilies`, `Mechanics`, `MusicalElements`, `Musical-Expression`, `Musician`, `Musicology` and `Technique` (Figure 8.6).

We also created some properties, such as `relatedTo`, `partOf` and `element Of`, whose aim was linking semantically related concepts. Some of these semantic relations were established between concepts that stood under disjoint classes, in

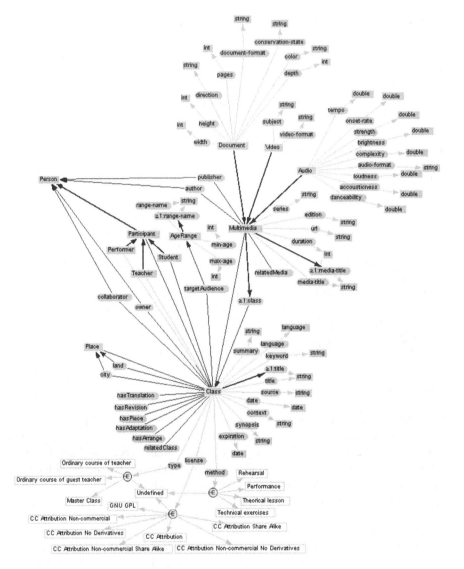

Fig. 8.5 The Resources Ontology

order to help the system make future recommendations. The first one was defined as a symmetric property and was meant to connect concepts that could be interesting to the same users. For instance, if a user searches for a master class about hammers, he will probably be interested in lessons about keyboards too.

Both `partOf` and `elementOf` are transitive properties. This means that if a first concept is part/element of a second one and this is part/element of a third one, we can state that the first concept is also part/element of the last one. The difference between these properties is that if a concept A is part of a concept B, every instance of B has A (e.g. the frog is part of the bow because every bow has a part called frog). However, if concept A is element of concept B, that means only some instances of B have A (e.g. the reed is an element of the embouchure because there is at least one wind instrument that has no reed in its embouchure). With this difference in mind, we can state that if concept A is part of concept B and this concept is related to a concept C, A is related to C. This is not true if A is element of B though.

We have also included restrictions to enforce the definition of the classes to make it easy to preserve the consistency of the ontology if extended. For example, every instance of `BowParts` must be `partOf` the pedagogical concept `bow` (`partOf ∃ bow`) and every individual represented by the class `SpecificTechnique` must be `relatedTo` *some* instance of `InstrumentFamilies` (`relatedTo ∃ bow`).

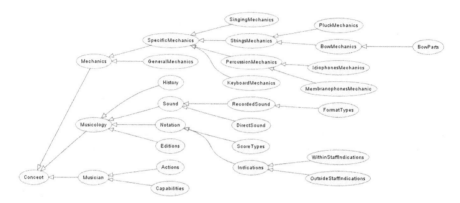

Fig. 8.6 A Fragment of the Concept Taxonomy

8.4.2 Linking the Ontology with External Data Sources

What really makes ontologies valuable, aside from the fact they contain much more information than what is explicitly stated, is their capacity of being linked to other resources of the same nature. An ontology represents a common understanding of a given domain, so once a model has been established (and accepted by the users), it should turn into a reference for any application based on that domain. Formalizing this model in OWL (or any other W3C standard) so that it can be understood and managed by both humans and machines and publishing it is the first step of building a huge net of knowledge. This net would provide support to very precise and complex queries.

Most search engines pay special attention to the connectivity of the Web sites (in terms of the quantity and quality of the links a page contains and receives). An ontology should be evaluated the same way, because its worth is determined by its contribution to the net of knowledge. That is why we decided to include links to external data sources. Our aim was to populate our ontology with information that is not usually provided by the annotators, but is related to the contents of the master classes. There are many sites that offer a wide variety of RDF data sources, like Geonames [8], MusicBrainz [9], CIA Factbook [10]... The most remarkable one is DBpedia [11].

DBpedia is a community effort to extract structured information from Wikipedia and to make this information available on the Web. DBpedia allows users to ask expressive queries against Wikipedia and to interlink other datasets on the Web with DBpedia data. DBpedia knowledge base consists of 274 million pieces of information (RDF triples). This knowledge base has several advantages over existing knowledge bases: it covers many domains, it represents real community agreement, it automatically evolve as Wikipedia changes and it is truly multilingual.

8.4.2.1 Geographical Enrichment

We decided we wanted to provide a way to allow the system perform geographical entailments. We chose the CIA Factbook as our source. The CIA Factbook is an annual publication of the Central Intelligence Agency of the United States with information about the countries of the world. The Factbook provides a summary of the demographics, geography, communications, government, economy, and military of 266 countries, dependencies and other areas in the world.

We linked our geographical resources (instances of Place) with the corresponding entries in the CIA Factbook. This means we can now relate composers, compositions and master classes in terms of their location. We could even geolocate them and draw a map with all the items associated to a place, in order to help users find information in a more visual way. Moreover, this newly incorporated knowledge can help us find resources in an area of any size, even if the only information we have is the city associated to those resources.

8.4.2.2 Lexical Enrichment

We have already talked about the possibility of including lexical information in order to semantically expand both the results of certain queries and the terms that could be identified as concepts belonging to the ontology. One could be interested in *compositions* of a certain *era* (these are the terms we have chosen to represent the corresponding concepts), but express it as "I would like to find *pieces* of the *period*...". Both terms are referring to the concepts we introduced before, which have been modelled in the ontology. The problem is the words we have chosen are not contained within Semusici terminology and therefore will not be identified and linked to those concepts.

A solution would be to assign different names (using the corresponding property) to the instances. This would help us find master classes on the falsetto technique using the concept name "head voice" instead of "falsetto" (which is the tag used by the annotators). Classes can not be assigned names, but we can use labels instead. SKOS instances can be assigned different labels and distinguish between the main label and alternative terms used to represent the same concept.

This is very useful if we want to include synonyms, but we may also be interested in other lexical relationships, such as hyponymy or hypernymy. For example, there is no tag such as "polka", but we have a concept called "dance forms" that would get us some results instead of an empty set. Using different labels means associating a single concept to a series terms. Therefore it would not be right to use this mechanism to assign hyponyms and hypernyms to concepts. Besides, labelling is a costly method. If we found a new term once the ontology has been built, we would need to add new statements to include this term.

For all these reasons, we decided to use WordNet, a large lexical database of English. Nouns, verbs, adjectives and adverbs are grouped into sets of cognitive synonyms (synsets), each expressing a distinct concept. Synsets are interlinked by means of conceptual-semantic and lexical relations. This results in a network of meaningfully related words [12]. By linking Semusici ontology to WordNet we keep a connection to an updated source of terms. We just have to include the necessary *owl:sameAs* statements to establish a link between our concepts and the corresponding Wordnet synsets.

8.4.3 Alternative Search Paradigms

The purpose of the Semantic Web is to improve the way users access the vast amount of information that is available through the Internet. The systems providing this access have made users change their natural way of expressing their need for information, that is using natural language. At this moment, the use of keyword-based queries is so extended that it seems hard to conceive any other mechanism of searching the Web. For most people, it is very simple and fast to summarize what is in their heads in a few words (which is actually very little information about what they are looking for).

The main problem of keyword-based systems is ambiguity. The correct meaning of a word can not be determined without considering its context. Unfortunately, in a traditional keyword-based system there is no such context. The key to solve this is adding semantics both to the query and the resources users are looking for. Of course this would mean to restructure the whole Web, which is impossible. But applying this to restricted domains can really improve the search.

There are many ways users can express their need for information without losing the context. A popular paradigm of search is faceted search. As we have already seen (as it is the case of MagisterMusicae), we build the context of the query by navigating through different categories, which are usually arranged in a taxonomy.

In order to fully keep the context of the query, users should express it in natural language. Unfortunately, it is very difficult for a system to correctly process a natural language query. We would then need a solution combining both the advantages of semantics and keywords. The nearest solution to a natural language processing (NLP) system would be a template-based one.

In a template-based system, we associate a template to a keyword (or a set of keywords). This makes it possible to produce more complex queries. For instance, we could specify that the date in the example we proposed in the Introduction is "the date when the composer of the composition that is referred to in the master class I am looking for was born." The only thing the user has to do is select the template that best suits the semantics of the keyword she wants to search for.

The number of templates should be limited to a few ones in order not to overwhelm the users with too many alternatives. Otherwise, they may feel they are choosing an option among the available ones. Instead, we want to provide them with an intuitive way to build the request they have in mind. Users may be able to quickly choose the proper context to what they know about what they are looking for.

8.5 Cantiga Semantic Search System

The prototype built in the context of Cantiga is a result of all the improvements presented in the last section. Its core is an extended version of Semusici ontology and its interface is based on templates. We analyzed the current state of the knowledge base and discarded those queries that would not retrieve any content. This dramatically decreased the number of possible templates. However, the underlying ontology allows a much more diverse set of queries, based on properties of compositions and composers that have not yet been used. This will make it possible to include a whole lot of new queries when the knowledge base grows.

We have adapted the traditional one-level model of templates into a hierarchical one. Instead of using a single level of templates, we decided to group the queries according to common components of meaning, in order to let the user combine these pieces and build a whole template. Our intention is to give her the impression of being progressively restricting the meaning of the piece of information she wants to search for. Besides, we do not want to overwhelm her by offering her too many options at a time, as we have already said.

We built a tree with the fragments of templates. This tree has up to 5 levels of depth. Each branch defines a restriction on the meaning of the piece of information the user is looking for. A total of 35 templates were defined, each of them represented by a path that goes from the parent node to each leaf node of the tree.

The parent node of this tree is *"Which classes,"* since the user is assumed to be looking for certain master classes. The first level contains fragments of queries about the parameters of a master class. For example, we find the piece *"were held in X?,"* which means that the value "X" introduced by the user is not only a place, but "the place where the master classes took place." In the case of *"are addressed to X?,"* "X" is "the audience for whom the classes are meant."

Whenever we found a parameter representing a complex concept, (for example a Composition), a new level was added to the tree. Following this example, we created a second level whose parent node is *"refer to a composition."* This level contains new fragments of queries concerning the properties of a composition, e.g. *"of the form X,"* *"composed by,"* etc. We proceeded the same way until every path reached a leaf node, i.e. one that contained a field to be filled by the user.

This way, the user would build a template selecting the path that best restricts the meaning of the term she intends to look up, e.g. *"Which classes refer to a composition composed by someone born in X?"* The interface of this system can be seen in Fig. 8.7.

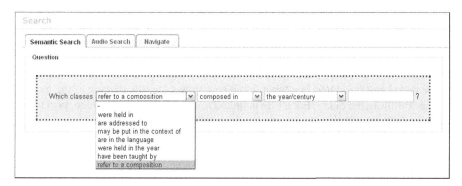

Fig. 8.7 Cantiga Semantic Search System

8.5.1 Details on the implementation

Cantiga Search System was integrated in a semantic portal, whose aim was to provide the user with an easy and intuitive way to access the contents of the Fundacin Albniz master classes collection, which we have already presented. After choosing the templates, we proceeded to translate each query into a query language. This language had to be compatible with that of the knowledge base. Also, it had to be supported by Sesame [13], the repository storing the ontology. We chose SeRQL, developed by Aduna for this repository. This language not only shares the main features of other common query languages, like RQL, but also includes new search and visualization capabilities.

The interconnection between the portal, built using portlets technology, and Sesame was carried out throught the latter's API. Sesame API is a Storage And

Inference Layer or SAIL, which is intended to abstract from the storage format used (i.e. whether the data is stored in an RDBMS, in memory, or in files, for example), and provides reasoning support. SAIL implementations can also be stacked on top of each other, to provide functionality such as caching or concurrent access handling.

On top of the SAIL, we find Sesame's functional modules, such as the SeRQL, RQL and RDQL query engines, the admin module, and RDF export. Access to these functional modules is available through Sesame's Access APIs, consisting of two seperate parts: the Repository API and the Graph API. The Repository API provides high-level access to Sesame repositories, such as querying, storing of RDF files, extracting RDF, etc. The Graph API provides more fine-grained support for RDF manipulation, such as adding and removing individual statements, and creation of small RDF models directly from code. The two APIs complement each other in functionality, and are in practice often used together.

We wrote a JSP file to access the repository from the portal. Establishing a connection between the repository and the portal was very simple, because both of them were running in the same Java Virtual Machine. Sesame API provides a series of methods to access the repository both locally and remotely, and ours was the simplest case of all. The value the user introduces to complete the query is sent through a form to the server, where it is collected by a Java bean. This value is used to build a SeRQL query, which is run in Sesame. The retrieved values are sent back to the portal and presented in a table. Each row shows the title of each of the master classes fulfilling the query. Each title is linked to the corresponding video, providing the user with an easy way to access the physical resource.

8.6 Evaluation

Cantiga seach interface proved to be much more easy-to-use and intuitive than MagisterMusicae's. First, in MagisterMusicae the user was expected to select an instrument before continue searching, which is pretty convenient in case one is a performer or a music student. However, this is a huge drawback if you are just interested in master classes taught by a certain teacher or referring to a certain piece of music, no matter what instrument they are focused on.

This system also has an advanced search interface, which is more flexible than the main one as the selection of parameters is not expected to be done in any particular order. Still, neither of MagisterMusicae interfaces allows the user to provide any keyword of her own. She will need to find the piece of information she already knows among hundreds of options in order to select the proper value.

Cantiga search interface, on the other hand, provides a simple way to build a query that is really expressed in natural language. As opposed to MagisterMusicae's case, the user will not be selecting search parameters but the context of a keyword she will be able to provide. In the worst case, the user will have to make five selections (which is the number of levels of the template tree) in order to complete a whole template. However, the feeling she will get is the feeling of building a sentence and not just adding conditions to a query. In short, Cantiga template system provides a natural way that feels closer to the way human beings express restrictions.

One thing that has not been considered in Cantiga is conjunctive queries. While MagisterMusicae advanced search allows the user to look for a master class establishing more than one condition, Cantiga search system is only able to take one piece of information provided by the user at a time. This could be arranged by letting the user choose not just one template, but any number of them (one for each known detail about the master class she is looking for). For example, *"Which classes refer to a composition composed by someone born in X and composed for an instrument of the Y family?"*

Speaking about the coverage, we tested both systems in order to check if they met the users' needs. We took 73 sample queries that were collected[4] during the specification phase of the ontology building process as a test set. We had previously used those queries as competency questions [14] in order to select the concepts the ontology was expected to formalize. This set included all kinds of questions, from rather simple ones (e.g. "I want to find classes taught by Argentinian teachers") to very complex biographical ones (e.g. "Find all the classes referring to composers who used to work on commission").

It turned out only 8 of the 73 test queries were supported by MagisterMusicae search system, whereas the 35 template set of Cantiga search system covered 18 of those queries. Even if we increased the number of facets, only 13 more queries could be processed by MagisterMusicae search system. This limitation is due to the lack of flexibility of the facet search paradigm, in terms of semantics. It is impossible to express a complex relationship in a system based on facets. For instances, we could never build a query such as "Which classes have been taught by a teacher whose first name is the same as Liszt's?" or "Find all the classes referring to works composed by the author of 'Tosca.' "

The combination of a semantic layer and a template-based interface is what makes Cantiga search system much more powerful. That is why up to 30 more of the test queries could be included as templates in this system. In fact, the reason why there are yet 25 more questions that could not be processed by this system is that they deal with rare concepts we decided not to include in the ontology.

Perhaps the greatest value of Cantiga search system lies in its expandability. Adding a new query to this system can be done by just adding the corresponding template, whereas adding a new query to MagisterMusicae's involves not only including a new facet, but also showing every possible search value the user could introduce. And this would only be possible assuming the semantics of the query can be expressed using facets.

Finally, there is still another important reason why Cantiga search system performs better than MagisterMusicae. Let us say a user wants to look for master classes about strings technique. The knowledge base may have no record of any class related to the concept "strings technique," yet the system would be able to retrieve some results concerning "violin technique" or "double bass technique." The

---

[4] A survey was carried out among musicians and music students and lovers in order to find out what kind of queries they would like to be able to ask.

reason for this is that the ontology contains information that links these concepts. The mere fact of placing them in a hierarchy represents some implicit knowledge that can be used in situations such as this (i.e. a parent-child is inferred).

The interconnection with an external datasource such as the CIA Factbook also allows to search using all kind of geographical data. For instance, the system would provide an answer to "Which master classes have taken place in a European country?," although such information is not present in our knowledge base. We could even find "master classes referring to a composer born in any country bordering Austria."

8.7 Related Work

In the past few years, there has been interesting research on the field of semantic search. In [15], the possibilities of using a view-based search paradigm to create intelligent search interfaces on the Semantic Web are explored. This thesis also presents a survey on semantic search related projects. Five research directions are identified: augmenting traditional keyword search with semantic techniques, basic concept location, complex constraint queries, problem solving and connecting path discovery. Our system belongs to the third group. According to this analysis, the main concern of this group is developing user interfaces that make creating complex query patterns as intuitive as possible. Other examples following this direction would be [16], [17] and [18].

There are some other approaches to template-based semantic search. In [19], a non-hierarchical template system is presented. This system uses templates of queries expressed in natural language with variable parts for substitution purposes. These queries correspond to real-life questions and problems, just like in our case. The system was built into the JeromeDL [20] system, a semantic digital library engine that uses Semantic Web and Social Networking technologies to improve browsing and searching for resources.

This template-based system intends to provide access to publications, such as articles, books, etc., using only five templates. We have to consider that the domain it covers is much more limited than the one covered by Cantiga. The semantics of these templates is rather simple. Therefore, in this case it would not be necessary to split up the templates. Still, a flat structure such as this would not be acceptable if the number of templates increased. Another difference with our system is that their system works with conjunctive queries, as one of the templates presents two slots to be filled by the user.

A more complex solution to semantic search is proposed in [21]. They present an approach for translating keyword queries to DL conjunctive queries using background knowledge available in ontologies, i.e. formally interpretating keyword queries. As we too did before, they discuss whether users really want to express themselves using natural language or maybe they find working with queries satisfying enough.

Finally, we can find some interesting web portals related to semantic search in the specific domain of music resources. The most important one is mSpace [22]. This service provides access to musical contents using bibliographical information associated to those contents, their classification and the relation between the corresponding categories. There are also some other interesting works on applying Semantic Web technologies to digital libraries, like [23] or [24].

8.8 Conclusions and Future Work

In this chapter, we presented our work in the field of semantic search through three projects whose purpose was to provide access to a music digital library. We have compared two different systems developed in the context of these projects in terms of usability and effectiveness. The semantic search system proved to be more flexible and powerful than the traditional one, thanks to the use of an ontology and a template-based interface.

We have proposed a solution to semantic search that combines both the advantages of semantics and keywords. Our hierarchical template-based prototype does not support user-generated natural language queries, but it includes a set of real-life questions that can be extended as needed. We will keep on researching new ways of searching that do not entail the drawbacks of a NLP system, but allow a more flexible and intuitive way of expressing the semantics of a query.

Finally, we have enriched our ontology by linking it to the CIA Factbook. We are currently working on linking it to other DBpedia datasets in order to improve the coverage of the system.

Acknowledgments

The research presented in this chapter has been partially supported by the Spanish Ministry of Industry, Tourism and Trade under the National Plan of R&D, in the context of Semusici (FIT-350200-2006-70 and FIT-350200-2007-44) and Cantiga (FIT-350201-2007-8) projects.

References

1. Fundacin Albniz, http://www.fundacionalbeniz.com
2. Uschold, M., Grninger, M.: Ontologies: Principles, Methods, and Applications. In: Knowledge Engineering Review, vol. 11, no. 2, pp. 93–155 (1996)
3. Gruber, T. R.: Towards Principles for the Design of Ontologies Used for Knowledge Sharing. In: Formal Ontology in Conceptual Analysis and Knowledge Representation (1993)

4. Iglesias, C.., Snchez, M., Guibert, ., Guibert, M.J., Gmez, E.: A Multilingual Web based Educational System for Professional Musicians. Current Developments in Assisted Education (2006)
5. SKOS Simple Knowledge Organization System, http://www.w3.org/2004/02/skos
6. Miles, A., Prez-Agera, J.R.: SKOS: Simple Knowledge Organisation for the Web (2005)
7. SKOS Extensions Vocabulary Specification, http://www.w3.org/2004/02/skos/extensions/spec
8. GeoNames, http://www.geonames.org
9. Swartz, A.: MusicBrainz: A Semantic Web Service. IEEE Intelligent Systems, vol. 17(1), pp. 76–77 (2002)
10. CIA - The World Factbook, https://www.cia.gov/library/publications/the-world-factbook
11. DBpedia, http://dbpedia.org
12. WordNet: A lexical database for the English language, http://wordnet.princeton.edu
13. Sesame, http://www.openrdf.org
14. Grninger, M., Fox, M. S.: Methodology for the Design and Evaluation of Ontologies. In: Workshop on Basic Ontological Issues in Knowledge Sharing (IJCAI'95) (2005)
15. Mkel, E., Frfattare, T.: View-based Search Interfaces for the Semantic, Tech. Rep. (2006)
16. Athanasis, N., Christophides, V., Kotzinos, D.: Generating on the fly queries for the semantic web: The ics-forth graphical RQL interface (GRQL), pp. 486–501 (2004)
17. Catarci, T., Dongilli, P., Mascio, T. D., Franconi, E., Santucci, G., Tessaris, S.: An Ontology Based Visual Tool for Query Formulation Support. In: Proc. of the 16th European Conference onArtificial Intelligence (ECAI'04), pp. 308–312 (2004)
18. Zhang, L., Yu, Y., Yang, Y., Zhou, J., Lin, C.: An Enhanced Model for Searching in Semantic Portals. In: Proc. of the 14th international conference on World Wide Web (WWW'05), ACM Press, pp. 453–462 (2005)
19. Kruk, S. R., Samp, K., O'Nuallain, C., Davis, B., Grzonkowski, B. M. S.: Search Interface Based on Natural Language Query Templates. In: Proc. of the poster session of IADIS International Conference WWW/Internet (2006)
20. Kruk, S. R., Woroniecki, T., Gzella, A., Dabrowski, M.: JeromeDL - a Semantic Digital Library. In: Semantic Web Challenge, ser. CEUR Workshop Proceedings, vol. 295 (2007)
21. Tran, T., Cimiano, P., Rudolph, S., Studer R.: Ontology-Based Interpretation of Keywords for Semantic Search. In: ISWC/ASWC, ser. Lecture Notes in Computer Science, vol. 4825, Springer pp. 523–536 (2007)
22. mSpace, http://mspace.fm
23. Hollink, L., Isaac, A., Malais, V., Schreiber. G.: Semantic Web Opportunities for Digital Libraries. In: Proc. of 32nd Library Systems Seminar of the European Library Automation Group (ELAG), Wageningen, The Netherlands (2008)
24. Kruk, S.R., Woroniecki, T., Gzella, A., Dabrowski, M., McDaniel, B.: The anatomy of a Social Semantic Digital Library. In: Proc. of International Semantic Web Conference (ISWC), Athens, GA, USA (2006)

Chapter 9
Application of an Intelligent System Framework and the Semantic Web for the CO_2 Capture Process

Chuansan Luo, Qing Zhou, and Christine W. Chan

Abstract This chapter describes how an implemented domain ontology provides the semantic foundation of an intelligent system framework in the domain of carbon dioxide capture process. The developed ontology has been implemented in the Knowledge Modeling System (KMS), which stores knowledge in the XML format. The intelligent system can process this XML schema to support construction of different solution application for the domain. As a sample application, an expert system for monitoring and control of the CO_2 capture process operating at the International Test Centre for carbon Dioxide Capture (ITC) located on the campus of University of Regina in Saskatchewan, Canada is presented.

9.1 Introduction

The carbon dioxide (CO_2) capture process operated by the International Test Centre for CO_2 (ITC) at the University of Regina, Saskatchewan, Canada is a complicated process which involves over one hundred parameters and manipula-tion of a number of valves and pumps. The objective of our work is to develop an ontology for this problem domain and use it as the basis of web-based applications. The Knowledge Modeling System (KMS) has been adopted for document-ing the ontology of the CO_2 capture domain and provides the semantic basis of an intelligent system (IS) framework [5]. The implemented ontology is in the Extensible Markup language (XML) format. The intelligent system hosts a web service which consists of various web methods, it supports sharing of the semantic knowledge among solution applications built for the CO_2 capture domain. A sample solution application is a web-based expert system that is presented in this chapter. It shows how the CO_2 ontology provides the basis for an automated software system, which makes use of the implemented ontology for supporting daily operation of the process.

Energy Informatics Laboratory, Faculty of Engineering University of Regina, Regina, Saskatchewan, Canada, e-mail: `Christine.chan@uregina.ca`

W. Du and F. Ensan (eds.), *Canadian Semantic Web: Technologies and Applications*, DOI 10.1007/978-1-4419-7335-1_9, © Springer Science+Business Media, LLC 2010

This chapter is organized as follows. Section 2 presents some background on the CO_2 capture process at the ITC and some related knowledge about semantic web and ontology. Section 3 presents ontology design and management; section 4 introduces the intelligent system framework and its applications; section 5 presents a web-based expert system and section 6 gives the conclusion and future work.

9.2 Backgroundt

9.2.1 Application Problem Domain

The CO_2 capture process at ITC can be summarized as follows. Prior to CO_2 removal, the flue gas is cooled down by the gas scrubber. Then the flue gas is pumped to the bottom of the absorber column and counter-currently contacts with the amine solvent, which is supplied by the lean amine storage tank. The amine solvent selectively absorbs CO_2 from the gas. The off gas, free from CO_2, is discharged from the top of the absorber and vented into the atmosphere. The rich amine solvent is heated by the lean/rich amine heat exchanger, and then fed to the stripper. A reboiler located at the bottom of the stripper provides the heat to the stripper. Under high temperature, the CO_2 is extracted from the rich amine solvent in the stripper column, and thus the lean amine solvent is regenerated. The CO_2 is condensed and purified by the post treatment. The lean amine solvent is filtered in the reclaimer, passed through the heat exchanger, and sent back to the lean amine storage tank for further CO_2 absorption [12].

9.2.2 Ontology and Semantic Web

Ontology is an explicit specification of a conceptualization, and it can be seen as the study of the organization and classification of knowledge. Ontology can be used as the basis of knowledge acquisition tools for collecting domain knowledge or for generating intelligent expert systems [4]. Ontology modeling can facilitate the knowledge analysis and representation processes [6]. With the growth of the semantic web in the past decade, ontological engineering has been greatly emphasized. The development of the semantic web is important for management of the vast amount of information available on the web, and an ontology enables automated processes or agents to more effectively share information. The conceptual structures defined in a domain ontology provide the basis for machine-processable data on the semantic web. Ontologies serve as metadata schemas, which provide a controlled vocabulary of concepts with explicit machine-processable semantics. By defining shared and common domain theories, ontologies support semantic as well as syntactic exchanges, thereby helping people and machines to communicate concisely. Hence, the semantic webs success significantly relies on the construction of domain-specific ontologies [7]. Fundamental to the semantic infrastructure are ontologies, knowledge bases, and agents along with inference, proof, and sophisticated semantic querying capabilities [10].

9.3 Knowledge Modeling and Ontology Construction

9.3.1 Ontology Design

The process of constructing the CO_2 domain ontology was conducted after the knowledge acquisition process, which consists of the three phases of knowledge elicitation, knowledge analysis and knowledge representation. The primary knowledge source was the expertise of the experienced operators. The Inferential Modeling Technique (IMT) was applied during the knowledge acquisition phase. The IMT provided the knowledge engineer with a template to identify the possible knowledge types in a domain. Details about the IMT approach of knowledge acquisition can be found in [2]. According to the IMT, the knowledge elements in the CO_2 capture process include the following: (1) classes of objects contained in the plant, such as plant components and reactants, (2) attributes that describe a class, such as the temperature or flow rate of a reactant, (3) values of attributes that specify the desirable operating range, and (4) tasks that specify the control operations to remedy the abnormal performance of a certain component. The knowledge elements clarified using the IMT formed the basis for building an ontology of the domain. The CO_2 ontology structure consists of three major categories under the root of plant. The three sub-categories are class, attribute, and task (see Fig. 9.1). Class consists of the plant components and reactants. The plant component is divided into the reaction instruments, pumps and valves. The pumps and valves are further classified into subclasses based on their control mechanism and function. The reactant includes water, solvent, and gas which circulate in the plant. The attribute involves the levels of the reaction instruments, the flow rate, temperature and pressure of the reactants. Each attribute consists of values to de-scribe its normal operating range. The tasks in the domain include various control tasks, applied to the attributes of inlet gas, off gas, CO_2, solvent, water and reaction instruments.

The class, attribute, value and task are interdependent and their relationships are illustrated in Figure 9.2. In the real plant, each reaction instrument, valve, pump, and attribute has tags as their identifiers, and the tags are shown in Figure 9.2. The sample ontology class given in Figure 9.2 is reaction instrument, in which one instance is the reclaimer. Two sample attributes of the reclaimer are: reclaimer pressure (PT-670) and level control (LC-670). For example, the reclaimer pressure has a desirable range of values from 12.0kPa to 22.8kPa. If the pressure exceeds the high limit of 22.8kPa, the remedial task is to open the reclaimer back pressure valve (PCV-670).

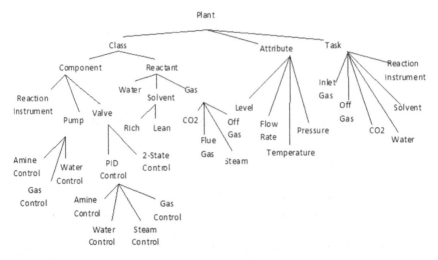

Fig. 9.1 Ontology Design of the CO_2 Capture Domain

If the pressure drops below its low limit of 12.0kPa, the remedial task is to close the reclaimer back pressure valve (PCV-670).

Ontology Class	Object	Attribute	Value	Task
Reaction Instrument	Reclaimer	Reclaimer Pressure (PT-670)	High: 22.8 kPa	Open reclaimer back pressure valve (PCV-670)
			Low: 12.0 kPa	Close reclaimer back pressure valve (PCV-670)
		Reclaimer Level Control (LC-670)		

Fig. 9.2 A Sample class and its relevant attributes and task

Fig. 9.3 Representation of classes, attributes and values in KMS

9.3.2 Ontology Management

The ontology was designed and documented in the Knowledge Modeling System (KMS), which provides automatic support in implementing and documenting industrial ontologies. The KMS enables the user to specify the knowledge elements specified in the IMT. It consists of two primary modules: the class module and the task module. The classes, sub-classes, attributes and values are stored in the class module. The interface of the class module is shown in Fig. 9.3 The class tree including the classes and subclasses is listed in the upper left panel of the screen. The highlighted object is reclaimer under the class of reaction instrument, and its related class attributes are shown in the lower right panel. The attribute of re-claimer pressure (PT-670) is highlighted, and its values are shown in the lower left panel.

Fig. 9.4 shows the interface of task module. The rules are grouped into different task categories are shown in the left panel. The entire set of the rules are listed in the right panel. The behaviour control panel is the rule editor, which is shown in the center panel of the screen. The condition and action parts of the rule are written separately at the right panel of the rule editor. When the rule is specified, it is transferred to the right panel of the rule editor and converted to XML format, and stored in the KMS.

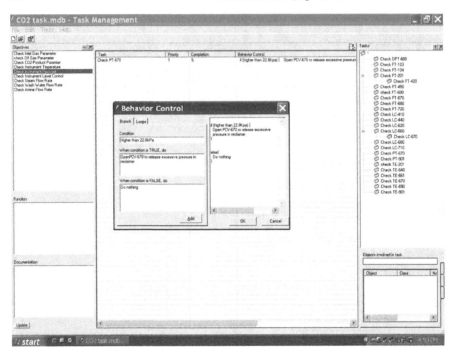

Fig. 9.4 Representation of tasks in KMS

9.4 Intelligent System Framework

The objective of the architectural framework, called the Data Management and Analysis Framework for CO_2 capture (CO_2DMAF), is to support data filtering and data rendering, and provides various application program interfaces (API) for development of software modules in the domain of CO_2 capture. The CO_2DMAF has been developed at the Energy Informatics Lab of University of Regina. This chapter focuses on how the CO_2DMAF makes use of the semantic knowledge in the ontology for constructing solution application in the CO_2 capture domain.

The Knowledge Modeling System (KMS) exports the domain ontology consisting of the classes, sub-classes, attributes, values and tasks of the CO_2 capture domain in an XML format. This ontology provides the semantic foundation for the intelligent system framework. The framework can read the semantic metadata and separate the semantic information into two sub sets. One is called the set of static knowledge, which consists of the definitions and properties of the classes, sub-classes, attributes, and their hierarchic relationships, as shown in Fig. 9.5 A sample relationship among classes in the CO_2 capture domain is that of the inheritance or is a relationship. For example: valves controlling amine solution (FCV-680) is a subset or child class of the valve controlling amine solution class, which is also a child class of the valve class. Similarly, as shown in Figure 9.5, the class of reboiler is a child class of the absorber-based CO_2 capture unit class. This inheritance relationship indicates that the re-boiler has some attributes that are inherited from the absorber-base CO_2 capture unit, such as temperature, pressure and flow rate. Based on this hierarchy, a set of custom-tailored C# classes are defined manually, which becomes the library of the data structure classes available in the framework. Then the framework is able to use these prototypes to instantiate the identical components stored in the ontologies and the ontologies become executable through the framework.

```
– <Recorder>
    <name>Reboiler</name>
    <ontologyname/>
    <role>concrete</role>
    <superclass>Absorber-Based CO2 Capture Unit</superclass>
    <constraint/>
  – <documentation>
      Instrument Tag: H-660. It provides the stripper with the steam to strip out the CO2 from the
      rich amine solution.Its heat medium is the steam from the boiler system. It also temporarily
      stores the lean amine solution from the stripper then returns it to the lean/rich heat exchanger.
    </documentation>
  </Recorder>
```

Fig. 9.5 Sample representation of the class knowledge

The other subset of semantic information in the ontology is called task knowledge, which includes all constrain values of attributes and corresponding instructions. It is able to identify the attributes state and to give the appropriate instructions. The task knowledge is the basis for building the expert system for monitoring and control of the CO_2 capture process, which will be discussed later.

Both knowledge sets are explicitly and formally represented and stored in an XML file. The XML schema is the sharable semantic knowledge that is machine processable. A web service is designed to support interoperable machine to machine interaction. This resides within the intelligent system framework and en-ables distributed data sharing and processing over the network among various solution applications operating on different platforms. In this project, a web service called Ontology_CO_2_ITC was developed; it is shown in Fig. 9.6. It includes various web methods, also called web application programming interfaces (APIs), which can be accessed by remote computers that require the CO_2 domain knowledge. The GetAtttibutes, GetClass, GetRulesByAttrName and GetSubClasses are four sample web methods. For example, the method of GetRuleByAttrName accepts a single attribute name and the framework searches the task knowledge XML schema and returns the XML schema block describing the attribute and containing the threshold values and related rules for that particular attribute. This is shown in Figure 9.6. The rules and threshold values contained in the semantic knowledge block can be utilized by any solution applications.

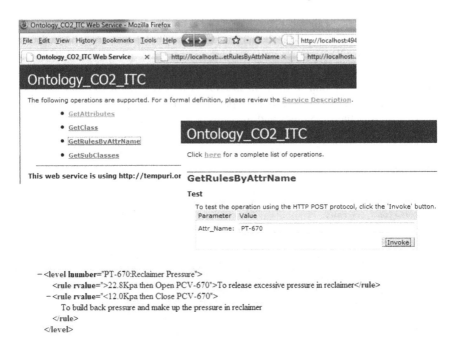

- <level lnumber="PT-670:Reclaimer Pressure">
   <rule rvalue=">22.8Kpa then Open PCV-670">To release excessive pressure in reclaimer</rule>
- <rule rvalue="<12.0Kpa then Close PCV-670">
    To build back pressure and make up the pressure in reclaimer
   </rule>

Fig. 9.6 Web service sharing the knowledge base in XML schema

9.5 Application of the Semantic Knowledge A Web-based Expert System

The web-based expert system is a solution application developed based on the semantic knowledge from the implemented ontology. The ontology consists of classes of plant components which correspond to those in the hierarchical structure of Fig. 9.1. The classes are listed in the top left panel of the screen shown in Fig 9.7. One class is selected in the panel, which is the Absorber-based CO_2 capture unit. The sub-classes that belong to the selected main class are extracted from the subset of class knowledge in the XML schema and listed in the middle left window. When a sub-class is selected, the expert system searches the class knowledge in the XML schema again, and retrieves all the attribute tags that be-long to the selected sub-class. These are shown in the bottom left panel. At the same time, the detailed profile of the sub-class is retrieved and listed beside the window. The three objects of main class, sub-class and attribute are related in the ontological hierarchy, which enables the user to easily identify the classes or at-tributes of interest. When the user selects a particular attribute; the system uses the attribute as the index to identify the task knowledge in the XML schema, and retrieves the corresponding threshold values and task rules. For example, in Fig. 9.7, when the attribute of reclaimer pressure (PT-670) is selected in the bottom left panel of the screen, the sample task rules related to PT-670 are retrieved and listed in the top right panel of the screen. It is noted the rule for normal state is not listed in Fig. 9.7, because the knowledge base only contains the rules for abnormal value ranges. The rules associated with PT-670 include:

1. if PT-670 > 22.8kPa :

   i It is too high;
   ii Should open reclaimer back pressure control valve (PCV-670) to release excessive pressure in reclaimer.

2. if 12.0Kpa < PT-670 < 22.8kPa:

   i Normal

3. If PT-670 < 12.0kPa:

   i It is too low
   ii Should Close reclaimer back pressure control valve (PCV-670) to build back pressure and make up the pressure in reclaimer.

According to the time range selected by the user, the framework retrieves the data records of the selected attribute from the database and lists them in the bottom right panel. The expert system evaluates the data records based on the rules retrieved for the attribute of PT-670 and gives the attribute state (i.e. Low, High or Normal) and corresponding remedial advice in the fourth and fifth columns of the data record table shown in the bottom right panel of Fig. 9.7. The attribute state and remedial advice instruct the operator of the CO_2 capture process in controlling the daily operation. In Fig. 9.7, it can be seen that the value of the reclaimer pressure (PT-670) is around 0.487 kPa at 12:00 AM on 1st, Feb. 2008, which is lower than 12.0Kpa, so the system advises the operator to close the reclaimer back pressure control valve in order to build back pressure and make up the pressure in the reclaimer. The automated system can provide decision support to the operators and enhance reliability of the CO_2 capture process by providing most of the information necessary for monitoring and troubleshooting the system. Since the system is accessible on the Internet, the operator can monitor the critical process parameters of the CO_2 capture process and maintain the desired production rate and normal operation of the plant anywhere in the world.

9.6 Conclusion and Future Work

This chapter presents an intelligent system framework that interacts with an ontology developed for the CO_2 capture domain. A web-based expert system for monitoring and troubleshooting the CO_2 capture process operation has been developed to demonstrate utilization of the semantic knowledge in the ontology. Before using the knowledge in the ontology, the intelligent system framework has to separate the

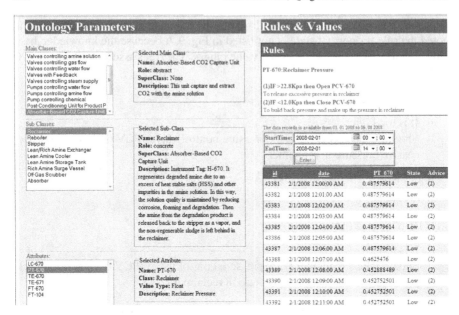

Fig. 9.7 Web-based CO_2 capture monitoring expert system

implemented ontology into the two sets of class knowledge and task knowledge. This separation ensures that (1) the static knowledge is formally rep-resented and (2) the formalized domain knowledge can support a more efficient search through ontology for retrieval of the task knowledge. This is necessary be-cause the knowledge had been implemented in the Knowledge Modeling System, which represented the domain knowledge formally, but left the task knowledge in the non-formalized representation of pseudo code. An item on the future research agenda is how the task knowledge in the XML schema can be further formalized to facilitate machine processing. To facilitate knowledge sharing, the data and rules stored in the XML format need to be converted to the standard representation of RDF and OWL.

Since the CO_2 capture pilot plant is still in its test phase, the configuration and procedures of the domain change periodically. When that happens, the code of the intelligent system framework would no longer be consistent with the model of the new configuration. As we known, it takes time and cost for software engineers to keep maintaining the software system in order to ensure the consistency between the code and the updated model. The ontology driven software engineering (ODASE) [8] development process could be adopted to dynamically implement the model objects based on the ontologies. [1, 9] provide some approaches on how to map OWL ontologies into an object-oriented language as well. Then, the model can evolve independent of the implementation, which means only the ontology needs to be updated and implementation will follow.

Acknowledgments

We gratefully acknowledge the generous support of the Canada Research Chair Program (CRC) and the Natural Sciences and Engineering Research Council of Canada (NSERC).

References

1. Aditya KalyanpurDaniel Jimenez Pastor, Steve Battle, and Julian Padget.: Automatic mapping of OWL ontologies into Java. In 16th International Conference on Software Engineering and Knowledge Engineering (SEKE), Banff, Canada (2004)
2. Chan, C.W.: A knowledge modeling system. IEEE Canadian Conference on Electrical and Computer Engineering (CCECE 04). Niagara Falls Ontario (2004)
3. Chan, C.W.: A Knowledge Modeling Technique for Construction of Knowledge and Databases, invited book chapter, Chapter 34 in Volume 4 of Leondes, C., Ed., Knowledge-Based Systems Techniques and Applications, 4 volumes, Academic Press, USA, p. 1109-1140, (2000)
4. Chan, C.W.: Cognitive Modeling and Representation of Knowledge in Ontological Engineering. Brain and Mind, Vol. 4. 1389-1987, (2003)
5. Chan, C.W.: Towards Ontology Construction for An Industrial Domain. Proceedings of the Third IEEE International Conference on Cognitive Informatics. 158 167, (2004)
6. Chen, L.L., Chan, C.W.: Ontology Construction from Knowledge Acquisition. Proceedings of Pacific Knowledge Acquisition Workshop (2005)
7. Maedche, A., Saab, S.: Ontology Learning for the Semantic Web. IEEE Intelligent Systems, Vol. 16.72-79 (2007)
8. Michel Vanden Bossche, Peter Ross, Ian MacLarty, Bert Van Nuffelen, Nikolay Pelov, On tology Driven Software Engineering for Real Life Applications, 3rd International Workshop on Semantic Web Enabled Software Engineering (SWESE 2007) Innsbruck, Austria (2007)
9. Neil M. Goldman. Ontology-oriented programming: Static typing for the inconsistent programmer. In 2nd International Semantic Web Conference (ISWC 2003), Sanibel Island, FL (2003)
10. Uschold, M.: Where are the semantics in the semantics web. AI Magazine, Vol. 24(3). 25-36 (2003)
11. Ouksel, A., Sheth, A.: A Brief Introduction to the Research Area and the Special Section. Special Section on Semantic Interoperability in Global Information Systems, SIGMOD Record. Vol 28(1). (1999)
12. Zhou, Q.: A Monitoring and diagnostic Expert System for Carbon Dioxide Capture. Expert System with Applications, Vol. 36. (2009)

Chapter 10
Information Pre-Processing using Domain Meta-Ontology and Rule Learning System

Girish R. Ranganathan and Yevgen Biletskiy

Abstract Around the globe, extraordinary amounts of documents are being created by Enterprises and by users outside these Enterprises. The documents created in the Enterprises constitute the main focus of the present chapter. These documents are used to perform numerous amounts of machine processing. While using these documents for machine processing, lack of semantics of the information in these documents may cause misinterpretation of the information, thereby inhibiting the productiveness of computer assisted analytical work. Hence, it would be profitable to the Enterprises if they use well defined domain ontologies which will serve as rich source(s) of semantics for the information in the documents. These domain ontologies can be created manually, semi-automatically or fully automatically. The focus of this chapter is to propose an intermediate solution which will enable relatively easy creation of these domain ontologies. The process of extracting and capturing domain ontologies from these voluminous documents requires extensive involvement of domain experts and application of methods of ontology learning that are substantially labor intensive; therefore, some intermediate solutions which would assist in capturing domain ontologies must be developed. This chapter proposes a solution in this direction which involves building a meta-ontology that will serve as an intermediate information source for the main domain ontology. This chapter proposes a solution in this direction which involves building a meta-ontology as a rapid approach in conceptualizing a domain of interest from huge amount of source documents. This meta-ontology can be populated by ontological concepts, attributes and relations from documents, and then refined in order to form better domain ontology either through automatic ontology learning methods or some other relevant ontology building approach.

University of New Brunswick, Fredericton, New Brunswick, Canada
e-mail: girish.ranganathan@unb.ca · e-mail: biletski@unb.ca

W. Du and F. Ensan (eds.), *Canadian Semantic Web: Technologies and Applications*,
DOI 10.1007/978-1-4419-7335-1_10, © Springer Science+Business Media, LLC 2010

10.1 Introduction

Information processing and management has evolved into an interdisciplinary research field, which includes the modeling of real-world information in machine-
readable formats. These models represent human knowledge in a way that allows a computer to simulate human cognitive processes with the goal of creating
knowledge-based computer applications which involve reasoning, decision making,
problem solving, and other tasks such as analysis and synthesis of knowledge. Ontologies play an extremely significant role in knowledge-based applications, primarily because they facilitate automatic semantic interpretation and interoperability of
data from various information sources. Defined by Gruber as an explicit specification of conceptualization [1], an ontology can serve as an effective and powerful
tool to capture, store, and work with domain knowledge in knowledge-based information systems. The definition of ontology has many variants, which can be generalized to define ontology, in the field of computer science, as a machine-readable,
structured representation of information [2]. A tremendous amount of research has
been conducted in the past decade regarding domain ontologies and their management. Generally, domain ontologies are intended to specify the conceptualization
of a particular real-world domain. Domain ontologies in particular, usually describe
a set of concepts and activities related to domains such as finance, commerce or
industry involved in the production and/or delivery of goods and services, etc. Various domain ontologies have been proposed during the last few years, for instance:
Enterprise Ontology [3], ontology for enterprise modeling [4], TOVE Ontology
Project for enterprise modeling [5], Resource Event Agent Ontology [6] and its
OWL-formalization [7], and many others. Ontologies are popular not only in business domains but in many other domains related to e-Activities i.e. e-Business, e-
Learning, Semantic Web, etc., and information processing (information retrieval,
extraction, delivery, etc.). The success of knowledge-based applications mainly depends on how well the applications domain ontology, intended to specify the conceptualization of a particular real-world domain, is designed. In most organizations,
domain knowledge is stored across countless semi-structured and unstructured documents (i.e. MS Word, Excel, PDF, etc.), which are user friendly, but are without
any type of ontology or semantics in the background. As a result, knowledge engineers (KEs) are tasked with the design, development and population of well designed ontologies using the information from these user friendly documents. This
is a time- and resource-consuming process that requires extensive involvement of
domain experts and advanced ontology learning methods. If the knowledge in the
source documents is first pre-processed and converted to/organized into a consol-
idated, intermediate, ontology-based format, even if that intermediate format does
not properly specify the domain knowledge, the job of the KE becomes immensely
simplified. Although there are many methodologies for building ontologies [2], the
generic approach - Skeletal Methodology, proposed by Uschold and King [8], is one
of the most widely used methodologies to build ontologies. The Skeletal Methodology provides very general guidelines for developing ontologies through four stages:
identification of purpose, building the ontology, evaluation, and documentation. The

phase of building ontology itself consists of sub-stages of ontology capture, ontology coding, and integration of ontologies. The idea presented in this work involves a deviation from the Skeletal Methodology, specifically during the process of building (domain) ontologies. The proposed (domain) ontology engineering methodology includes the additional phase of Information Preprocessing prior to the building ontology phase. Pre-processing includes: defining a set of objects participating in the subsequent phases of building the ontology; identifying sets of attributes characterizing objects; identifying data sources (source documents); and defining domains. As a result, the original information is transformed into structured ontological instance data, which is machine interpretable and compatible with existing ontology learning methods. Pre-processing source documents content in this way greatly simplifies the subsequent process of producing (using ontology learning methods) a true, semantically rich domain ontology, which includes all necessary ontological components [2]: concepts, attributes, taxonomies, non-taxonomical relations, functional relations, constraints, axioms, and instances, which can be used by applications to improve their performance. Thus, this chapter proposes to pre-process domain knowledge from various source documents using a general, domain-independent, background meta-ontology. The idea behind this work is to ease or accelerate the process of ontology learning when creating domain ontology(ies) from documents. Pre-processing domain knowledge can aide several steps in the ontology learning process, especially concept formation, concept hierarchy(ies) induction, and ontology population [9]. The other ontology learning steps, such as relation identification and relation hierarchy induction may or may not benefit from the creation of this meta-ontology depending on the nature of the information being captured and stored because the relations used in the presented meta-ontology were manually created. But these manually created relations might serve as a starting point to extract relations and relation hierarchy (ies) from source documents. For creating the domain meta-ontology from the source documents, ontology capture methods [9, 10] can be used which form a part of the ontology building process. Ontology capture deals with the extraction of information necessary for the creation of ontology like the concepts which constitute the ontology, the relationships between them and more. The meta-ontology can have a fixed structure, which means it can be manually created but can be manually or semi-automatically populated, because this structure is simple and this is an initial structure. This meta-ontology has to be populated with instances which can be classes, relationships, attributes, instances of classes and may be constraints. Ontology is normally captured from sources which contain information about the domain of interest. There are two general methods of ontology capture: Manual capture and, in general, information extraction based capture. In the present chapter, the focus is only on populating the created meta-ontology using information extraction methods. Information extraction methods [11, 12] deal with semi-automatic or automatic information extraction of necessary information from structured or semi-structured or even unstructured documents that are normally human readable and relevant to the domain of interest. Some useful methods of Information Extraction are described in [13, 14, 15]. The extracted information can be stored in an appropriate format which can be used for further processing. The most popular information extraction methods are based on a smaller subset of information extraction called Machine Learning. Information extraction also includes Rule induction which is the focus of this chapter. Rule induction [11, 15, 16, 17] is an area of information extraction in which formal rules are extracted from sets of observations. In the context of this chapter, the set of observations are created by the annotation system. The rules extracted may represent a full scientific model of the data, or merely represent local patterns in the data. In the context of this chapter, rule induction is used to learn extraction rules. Rules can be induced from a large variety of documents with or without structural information like free form text, XML and many more. In the example presented below, rules are induced from source documents in the Microsoft Excel format. The chapter has the following structure: section 2 presents the structure of the domain meta-ontology; section 3 describes the approach to populating the proposed domain meta-ontology; and section 4 describes details of customizing and populating the meta-ontology for an example source document.

10.2 The domain meta-ontology

The goal of the presented work is to create a general domain meta-ontology as well as to deploy an extendable ontology population tool capable of populating this background meta-ontology with instances extracted from structured and semi-structured domain related source documents. The resulting populated meta-ontology can then be used (possibly using ontology learning methods as well as ontology re-engineering techniques like OntoClean [18] and/or METHONTOLOGY [19] to create a semantically rich domain ontology. The meta-ontology need not necessarily have a fixed structure. The knowledge engineer can create a meta-ontology suitable for the domain of his interest. Some examples of possibly simple meta-ontologies are shown in Fig. 10.1, Fig. 10.2 and Fig. 10.3. These meta-ontologies are proposed to model the information from domain source documents (solid line   subclassOf relations, broken line   non-taxonomical relations):

- Enterprise   an upper-level concept conceptualizing the entire enterprise information system (or whole domain) such as Enterprise itself. In order to keep the name of the upper-level concept open to modifications, the default name Enterprise is used;
- Document   conceptualizes source documents of any type used in the domain;
- Domain   conceptualizes domains;
- Class   conceptualizes particular concepts in the domain;
- Attribute   conceptualizes data type properties (or characterizations) of concepts.
- Taxonomical Relations   conceptualizes hierarchical object type properties (or characterizations) of concepts.
- Non-taxonomical Relations   conceptualizes data type properties (or characterizations) of concepts other then hierarchical relations.

- t_relationbelongsto   represents the taxonomic relations between instances of Classes;
- relationsbelongsto represents the non-taxonomic relations between instances of Classes;
- attributebelongsto represents the relations between instances of Classes and instances of Attributes;
- entityHasAttributes   represents the relations between instances of Classes and instances of Attributes;
- entityBelongsToDomain   represents the relations between instances of Classes and instances of Domain;
- entitySourceDocument represents the relations between instances of Classes and instances of Document.

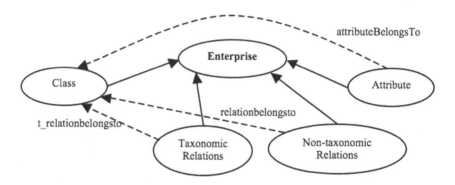

Fig. 10.1 Domain meta-ontology: variant 1

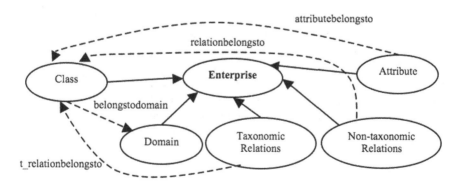

Fig. 10.2 Domain meta-ontology: variant 2

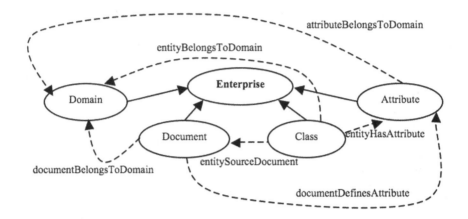

Fig. 10.3 Domain meta-ontology: variant 3

In summary, a Class or Entity is a concept or term defined in a Document that is important in a particular Domain and an Attribute describes an aspect of a corresponding Class. For example, a Database Mapping Document in the Insurance Domain could contain a Sale Class, which would have a corresponding Active Attribute, which is set to either true or false depending on the status of a sale. Additionally, both Classes and Attributes have facets (not shown in figures 10.1 to 10.3), which are essentially string literals describing them (i.e. datatype properties). For example, a Class could have a name facet and a code facet or an Attribute could have default value or sample value facets. The meta-ontologies shown in Fig. 10.1, Fig. 10.2 and Fig.10.3 also include non-taxonomical relations; for example: Similar inter-concept relationships (i.e. object-type properties) can be found between all concepts in the meta-ontology. The structure of the meta-ontology is independent of the domain knowledge. Hence, the instance data can be extracted from the source documents using semi-automatic or fully automatic information extraction techniques, effectively pre-processing the information and storing it in a general, platform-independent, ontological format. The following sections of this chapter describe the details of the domain meta-ontology and the rule learning system for meta-ontology population with instances from human-structured documents in excel format. As it is mentioned in the introduction, the Domain Meta-Ontology can be built manually. For semi-automatic population of Domain meta-ontology the Rule Learning system is proposed. This system uses the Annotation system to create annotations for the Rule Learning system.

10.3 The system for semi-automatic population of domain meta-ontology

The meta-ontology can be populated with information from sources using a semi-automatic Rule Learning System. To populate the meta-ontology a Rule Learning system [16] is used. The Rule Learning System adopts an implementation of RIPPER: Repeated Incremental Pruning to Produce Error Reduction, a set of fast rule induction algorithms [17]. For building the Rule Learning System itself, the Java API of the RAPIDMINER tool, which includes the implementation of RIPPER as a part, has been used. The RAPIDMINER used to be called YALE (Yet Another Learning Environment) [20]. The RAPIDMINER tool, which is developed using Java programming language, offers an environment for performing machine learning and data mining experiments with the most successful algorithms. The operators are described in XML format, which allows creating operators manually or using the tools graphical user interface. The Rule Learning System presented in this chapter primarily uses the RuleLearner operator of the RAPIDMINER tool to perform the rule induction. An Annotation system is used to create the training data for the Rule Learning System from the source data. The Annotation system is developed to work with MS Excel files. It allows the information in the Excel files to be annotated. The annotation information is stored in XML files with a predefined schema.

The Rule Learning system [16] is invoked after the Annotation system produces the XML files containing the annotation information. The XML files with annotation information are parsed to create the training data set for the Rule Learning system. The parsed data is mapped back to the source documents to extract appropriate structural information, which will be useful for extracting rules with a relatively high accuracy. The parsed data and the extracted structural information (training data set) are organized in a specific format enabling the Rule Learning System to learn the model efficiently. The Rule Learning system learns the model from the training data set and creates rules according to the learnt model. The created rules have to be converted to the appropriate Business Rules Management System (BRMS) format such as OpenL tablets [21], because the rules cannot be used by the information extractor directly; the converted rules are given to the information extractor appropriately, to perform extraction of ontology instances (facts) from the parsed source documents. The extracted ontology instances, along with the background ontology, serve as inputs for the reasoning engine, enabling the users to issue effective queries to get meaningful results. As proof of concept, an OWL (Web Ontology Language [22]) model of one of the above meta-ontologies (Fig. 10.3) has been created using Protg [23], the ontology editor used in the present work. When the background meta-ontology is initially created, there are no instance or property values, just concepts and properties, which allow the knowledge engineer to specify precisely what information they wish to capture, independent of the information extracted from the source documents. OWL is used for many reasons, specifically because it is portable, widely used, supports declaration of properties at the object level (i.e. properties are part of the background ontology, not extracted with the instances), and stores validation information in the ontology as OWL constraints, which simplifies any subsequent validation processes.

10.4 Details of the Rule Learning System flow

Attr. / ID	Headline/Value	Containing Section	Page Number	Published In	Keywords	Text	Urgent
INS_054	Reporter_Joe						
Name	Joe Schmo						
Salary	120000						
Service	CNN						
						Sojourner Truth, will soon come down on the barren surface of Mars. It will open up like an egg, releasing a remote control probe to conduct a geological survey of the red planet. The mission marks the first landing on Mars in 20 years. And along with the orbiting Mars Global Surveyor, which arrives two months later, it ushers in a bold new era of Mars exploration. In Destination Mars,	
					Space Science	CNN Interactive provides a multimedia	
AR_03	Destination Mars	Science	2	08/22/97	Mars rover	rich sneak preview of	No

Fig. 10.4 Example data in Excel table format

The annotation information is given to the Rule Learning System in XML files. The XML files contain details from the source documents like the column number or row number, or cells column and row numbers along with the annotation information like the ontology name, class name, instance and property names and the cell content etc. This information is stored in predefined XML tags. The XML tag structure is used to parse the information stored in between the tags. The parsed information is initially stored in the memory and then organized into a tabular Excel format (learning test data) making it easy for the knowledge engineer to edit and troubleshoot (Fig. 10.4). The learning test data now contains the annotation information in tabular format. The information in the learning test data is used to collect more information from the source document to expand the learning test data. The row and column number information is used to collect some contextual information around the source cell (for instance: the next column content and column name, previous column content and column name, etc.) and appended to the learning test data.

Then, the information in the learning test data is re-organized to keep the attributes to be learnt (in particular: the ontology name, class name, instance name, property name, attribute name etc.) to the right end. For now, there are four attributes to be learnt but this is not fixed. The re-organized learning test data is then used to learn the rules. The rule learning is performed incrementally in four stages (depending on the number of attributes to be learnt). In the first stage, the remaining attributes are hidden facilitating the learning of the first attribute. In the second stage of the learning, the first unknown attribute column is included. In the third stage of the learning, the first and second unknown attribute columns are included. In the fourth stage, the first, second and third unknown attributes columns are included. In each stage, rules for learning the appropriate unknown attributes are created. This type of learning can be called Incremental Rule Learning. In the presented example there are four unknown attributes. The way the attributes are selected is crucial. The attribute columns are ordered based on the diversity of the data in the column from least diverse to the most diverse. This is because when there is less diverse data the accuracy of the created rules using this less diverse data is low. On the other hand, the set of rules created using a high diverse data is much more accurate than the set of rules created using less diverse data. Hence, it is important to give higher priority to the set of rules created using more diverse data. The learning is performed by the Rule Learner operator of the RAPIDMINER tool. The result of the Incremental Rule Learning process is a set of rules in human readable format represented using a bunch of if-then-else statements. The set of rules output by the RAPIDMINER tool is then processed to convert them into appropriate syntax to be used by the information extraction system. In the presented example, the rules created by the RAPIDMINER tool are converted to java syntax to be used by a suitable BRMS Then the new rules are stored in the appropriate rules file to be used by the BRMS as follows:

```
if(Prev_Column_Value == "AR_03")
Class = "Article";
if(Prev_Column_Value == "Destination Mars")
Class = "Article";
if(Prev_Column_Title == "Attr. / ID")
Class = "Reporter";
if(Prev_Column_Value == "Science")
        Class = "Article";
if(Prev_Column_Value == "08/22/97")
        Class = "Article";
if(Prev_Column_Value == "Space
Science
Mars rover")
        Class = "Article";
if(Prev_Column_Value == "Sojourner,
named for Sojourner Truth,")
Class = "Article";
if(Prev_Column_Title == "N/A")
```

```
        Class = "Reporter";
else Class = "Article";
if(Class == "Article")
        Instance_Name = "instance_00044";
else Instance_Name = "instance_00045";
if(Prev_Column_Title == "Attr. / ID" and
Prev_Column_Value == "INS_054")
        Assigned_Property = "N/A";
if(Prev_Column_Value == "AR_03" and
Prev_Column_Title == "Attr. / ID")
        Assigned_Property = "N/A";
if(Prev_Column_Value == "Name")
        Assigned_Property = "Name";
if(Prev_Column_Value == "Salary")
        Assigned_Property = "Salary";
if(Prev_Column_Value == "Service")
        Assigned_Property = "Service";
if(Prev_Column_Title == "N/A")
        Assigned_Property = "is_author_of";
if(Prev_Column_Value == "Destination Mars")
        Assigned_Property = "Containing_Section";
if(Prev_Column_Value == "Science")
        Assigned_Property = "Page_Number";
if(Prev_Column_Value == "N/A")
        Assigned_Property = "Published_In";
if(Prev_Column_Value == "08/22/97")
        Assigned_Property = "Keywords";
if(Prev_Column_Value == "Space
Science
Mars rover")
        Assigned_Property = "Text";
else Assigned_Property = "Urgent";
```

As a result of this information extraction, the meta-ontology gets populated. This meta-ontology can be then used as an intermediate information source for constructing the necessary domain ontology.

References

1. T.R. Gruber, A translation approach to portable ontologies, Knowledge Acquisition 5(2) (1993) 199-220.
2. A. Gomez-Perez, O. Corcho, and M. Fernandez-Lopez, Ontological Engineering: with examples from the areas of Knowledge Management, e-Commerce and the Semantic Web (Advanced Information and Knowledge Processing), Springer-Verlag, 2004.

3. M. Uschold, M. King, S. Moralee, and Y. Zorgios, The Enterprise Ontology, The Knowledge Engineering Review, Special Issue on Putting Ontologies to Use, pp. 31-89, 1998.
4. M. S. Fox, M. Barbuceanu, and M. Gruninger, An organization ontology for enterprise modeling: Preliminary concepts for linking structure and behavior, Computers in Industry, vol. 29, no. 1-2, pp. 123-134, 1996.
5. M. S. Fox and M. Gruninger, Enterprise Modeling, AI Magazine, vol. 19, pp. 109121, 1998.
6. F. Gailly, and G. Poels, Towards Ontology-Driven Information Systems: Redesign and Formalization of the REA Ontology, Lecture Notes in Computer Science, vol. 4439, 2007, pp. 245-259.
7. G. L. Geerts and W.E. McCarthy, An Ontological Analysis of the Economic Primitives of the Extended-REA Enterprise Information Architecture, International Journal of Accounting Information Systems, vol. 3, pp. 116, 2002. [
8. M. Uschold and M. King, Towards a methodology for building ontologies, The IJCAI-95 Workshop on Basic Ontological Issues in Knowledge Sharing, 1995.
9. P. Cimiano, Ontology Learning and Population from Text: Algorithms, Evaluation and Applications, Springer-Verlag, New York, 2006.
10. S. Maedche and S. Staab, Ontology Learning for the Semantic Web, IEEE Intelligent Systems archive, vol. 16 , no. 2, pp. 7279, 2001.
11. I. H. Witten and E. Frank, Data Mining: Practical Machine Learning Tools and Techniques (Second Edition), Morgan Kaufmann Series in Data Management Systems, 2005.
12. E. Alpaydin, Introduction to Machine Learning, The MIT Press, 2004.
13. K. M. Sim and P. T. Wong, Towards agency and ontology for web-based information retrieval, IEEE Trans Syst., Man, Cybern. C, Appl. Rev., vol. 34, no. 3, pp. 257269, Aug. 2004.
14. D. Zhang and L. Zhou, Discovering golden nuggets: Data mining in financial application, IEEE Trans. Syst., Man, Cybern. C, Appl. Rev., vol. 34, no. 4, pp. 513522, Nov. 2004.
15. D. Gregg and S. Walczak, Adaptive web information extraction, Commun. ACM, vol. 49, no. 5, pp. 7884, May 2006G. Holmes, A. Donkin, H. Witten, Weka: A machine learning workbench, Second Australia and New Zealand Conference on Intelligent Information Systems, Brisbane, Australia (1994) 357-361.
16. G. R. Ranganathan, Y. Biletskiy. An annotation based Rule Learning System for ontology population from business documents, Canadian Semantic Web Working Symposium, Kelowna, Canada, pp. 78-88, 2009.
17. W. W. Cohen, Fast Effective Rule Induction (RIPPER), In Proc. Twelfth International Conference on Machine Learning, pp. 115-123, 1995.
18. C. Welty, N. Guarino, Supporting Ontological Analysis of Taxonomic Relationships, Data and Knowledge Engineering 39(1) (2001) 51-74.
19. M. Fernndez-Lpez, A. Gmez-Prez N Juristo, METHONTOLOGY: From Ontological Art Towards Ontological Engineering, Spring Symposium on Ontological Engineering of AAAI, Stanford University, California, 1997, pp 3340
20. M. Ingo, W. Michael, R. Klinkenberg, M. Scholz, T. Euler, YALE: Rapid Prototyping for Complex Data Mining Tasks, in Proceedings of the 12th ACM SIGKDD International Conference on Knowledge Discovery and Data Mining (KDD-06) (2006) 935-940.
21. OpenL Tablets (2006), Available (February 28, 2010): http://openl-tablets.sourceforge.net/
22. OWL (2004): Web Ontology Language, Available (February 28, 2010): http://www.w3.org/2004/OWL
23. Protg (2000), Available (February 28, 2010): http://protege.stanford.edu/